T·H·E
GHOSTLY
REGISTER

Arthur Myers

DORSET PRESS

NEW YORK

Copyright © 1986 Arthur Myers
All rights reserved.

This edition published by Dorset Press
a division of Marboro Books Corporation,
by arrangement with Contemporary Books, Inc.
1990 Dorset Press

ISBN 0-88029-472-8

Printed in the United States of America

M 9 8 7 6 5 4 3 2 1

Contents

Author's Note

The original intent of this book was to provide, along with interesting reading, a sort of guidebook to haunted houses, places the reader could take the family for a spooky afternoon's browse. But as any author knows, between the beginning and the end of writing a book, there are likely to be a few policy changes.

In perusing this collection of accounts of 64 haunted places, the reader will note there are slightly over a dozen that can't be visited. Either the names or addresses are not given, at the request of the sources, or if they are given, it is noted that the residents don't want visitors.

The reason the author and publisher decided to include these no-can-show places is simply because they seemed too interesting to leave out. For example, the ghost in Massachusetts who pushed a young mother and her baby down the stairs; the haunted radio station in Virginia; the angry bootlegger in the Pennsylvania milltown; the widow in Georgia whose dead husband keeps giving her dreadful haircuts— we decided that these and others were just too good to toss out. So here they are, for your entertainment and edification. And of course, there still are some fifty places to which you *can* go.

—Arthur Myers

Introduction

When I began writing this book, I wasn't at all sure I believed in ghosts. However, I do believe in checking things out. And the six months I spent researching and writing this book have been possibly the most enjoyable in a long journalistic career of checking things out.

By the time I was finished, I had interviewed more than 200 people, and I believed in ghosts as much as I believe in anything. None of my interviewees seemed demonstrably off their rockers, although they told me of sighting apparitions, hearing mysterious sounds, including voices, smelling mysterious smells, seeing objects move by themselves, being touched by unseen hands. Could these people, living in all parts of the country, be part of a conspiracy to deceive the rest of us? Are they liars, and, if so, why? Few have anything to gain by such conduct. Are they simply overimaginative? They sounded as sane as you or me—or, at least, me. None of them sounded

1

as though the butter was slipping off their noodles.

So, after being immersed in hauntings for half a year, I feel reasonably secure about putting my name on this book, reasonably certain I am not an unwitting instrument of misinformation. These things certainly seem to happen. A lot of things seem to go bump in the night, and quite a few by day, too.

The next question is: What are they? What is causing these phenomena? Those who profess to know usually divide hauntings into two categories. A New Jersey psychic, Jean Quinn, put it this way:

"I view hauntings in two different ways. Sometimes a repeated haunting is like a movie that replays itself on a certain vibration. Other times I'm aware of a real spirit."

She was interviewed in connection with a restaurant outside Philadelphia that has quite a variety of quirks and twitches. Most of the apparitions there, Quinn feels, are of the TV screen variety—people who had once been alive in the place and left the imprint of their energies. They aren't there, but their images are. But others, she felt, were the actual spirits of people who had been there and who are still attached to the place, aware of our physical plane and sometimes reacting with living people.

The real spirits seem much more interesting. Such phenomena certainly indicate that we maintain our personalities, for a time at least, after death. And most of us are egotistical enough to be fond of our current personalities and want to hang on to them for a while.

Students of the spiritual take the view that when we die each of us drops our physical body but retains other bodies, similar but vibrating at different frequencies. The natural course for one who leaves this physical plane is to move on to higher spiritual realms, but many people hang around for a variety of reasons—fear, ignorance, love, greed, attachment to a place or person. They are the real ghosts, and to me they seem much more fun than any energy carryover. These real spirits will sometimes interact with living people, but the energy carryover goes strictly about its own business, oblivious of our time and space and probably of anything else.

There are also, it is said, other energies that human beings can become aware of, represented in this book by an elemental and a thought form in Utica, New York; a troll in Somerville, Massachusetts; and a dragon in Texas. Who knows?

While doing this book, I was struck by the number of people who, when they heard I was researching haunted houses, were eager to tell me about their own experiences. It does seem that mankind is opening up its awareness to other aspects of reality. People talk about these things much more openly than in the past. To be psychic today is not so suspect; in some of our more sophisticated circles, it tends to be rather chic.

The general public's attitude toward the parapsychological seems to be changing, too. In my newspaper days, a good many years ago, when Halloween came it was time for stories making fun of ghosts. While I was preparing this book, many people sent me current newspaper stories from all over the country in which the Halloween stories were serious accounts of hauntings. That's the way newspapers from *The New York Times* to the *Honolulu Advertiser* and points in between handle Halloween these days. It's a commentary on the public's changing awareness. Many of these newspaper stories led to chapters in this book.

One surprise to me was how easy it is to find

hauntings, in any part of the country. "Hauntings are not rare," one psychic told me. "People don't realize how frequent they are." Another person, whom I had never realized was psychic, said, "All houses that have been lived in are haunted. You simply have to learn how to pick up their vibes."

But enough philosophizing! Let's get down to specifics. Turn the pages, and you'll meet spooks, and rumors of such, from Alaska to Florida, from California to Maine. Good people, bad people, disappointed lovers, murderers, murderees, little old ladies, and wild, wild women. Not to mention a cat, a dog, and a rat. So read on, and don't forget to look under your bed tonight!

The Ones That Got Away

In the course of gathering material for a book like this, a writer experiences many frustrations. Many a good story, for one reason or another, just couldn't be put in the book, at least as a fully written case. But they still make intriguing conversation pieces, and here are a few of them.

When I began the book I remembered a story that a friend of mine told me some years ago, not long after she had moved into a house in a suburb of New York City.

"I woke up in the middle of the night," she said, "and looked out into the living room. There I saw the dark outline of a man. There was a bright red light at his side, and I realized he was holding a lighted cigarette. I managed to quaver, 'Who's there?' And a man's voice replied, in a very disgusted tone, 'Jesus Christ!' Then the form disappeared." My friend felt the ghost's reply was meant as an epithet, not as information. In any case, she wouldn't let me use her name; she's a psychotherapist and is afraid that her neighbors will decide she's crazier than her patients.

I tried to make this book as factual as possible,

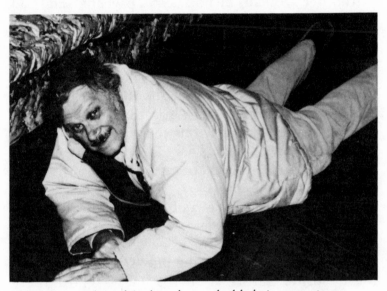

The author in rehearsal for his role as a dead body in an amateur production of the play, The Real Inspector Hound. *Arthur Myers has been a newspaperman and a magazine writer and editor. This is his ninth book. He lives in a suburb of Boston, Massachusetts.*

with names, places, interviews, and pictures. Sometimes people would tell me stories about houses that they'd lived in, but which are now owned by other people, who are not eager to see their houses written up in a book of this sort. I was in an amateur play recently—playing a dead body, appropriately enough—and one of the makeup women, when she heard I was writing a book on haunted places, told me this one. A number of years ago she and her husband lived in a house in Pennsylvania where a woman had committed suicide. The dead woman still seemed to frequent the place, with the usual array of parapsychological tricks—footsteps, cold spots, opening doors—but she had a fetching habit that was all her own. She constantly rearranged the flowers of my friend the makeup lady.

Another woman, in northern New England, told me an intriguing story of the ghost of a man who had loved chocolate. The odor of chocolate pervaded the house when this ghost walked. There were other interesting aspects to this story, too, but when I suggested putting it in my book, the woman, who had been very forthcoming in conversation, balked. "I don't think it would be fair to the ghost," she said. This was a new one, and I asked her what she meant. "Well," she said, "it's kind of an invasion of privacy— the privacy of the ghost."

One great story got away because the people who owned the house had let a television station do a program on its ghosts in hope of raising the sale value and found out that the publicity had done just the opposite. Suffice it to say that a ghost there appeared to be a woman of the 18th century whose husband—according to a medium—had brought home his mistress. The wife committed suicide, and her spirit remained trapped—self-trapped—on the astral plane in the house all through the lives of the errant husband and mistress and to this day. An eminent parapsychologist who investigated the case asked the ghost, through the medium, why she did not free herself and move on to higher planes. She replied that she wouldn't because her husband was there. As the parapsychologist put it, "She wouldn't go to heaven because her husband was there."

At one point, I was told by a folklorist about a ghost in an Elks Club who, among other things, would open a can of beer and somehow dispose of the contents if the can were left all night on the bar. "It's been scaring the hell out of everybody," my informant said. The Elks thought they knew who the thirsty ghost was—the victim of a murder on the site of the building. My enthusiasm cooled, however, when the folklorist told me that he had planned to put the story into one of his own books but a relative of the murder victim had in no uncertain terms threatened to sue.

While I was writing this book, the TV series "Spenser for Hire" was being shot in Boston, where I live, and every would-be actor in town applied to play extra parts. I was cast in one sequence as a Red Sox fan; my role was to sit quietly in the bleachers and get rained on while the action went on at the other end of Fenway Park. A young man playing a hot dog vendor, as bored as I was, struck up a conversation and asked me why I was wearing a cap that said, "I Believe in Elves." "To get into the spirit of my work," I said, mentioning that I was writing a book about ghosts. When he heard this, he told me that when he was about twelve an apparition of his great-aunt walked by his bedroom door, which mystified him since she lived a few hundred miles away. The next day his family got word of the death of the lady.

Mary Slaughter, a young woman in Oregon with a lively sense of humor about ghosts, told me three choice anecdotes. One involved a ghost who would constantly be heard urinating in the toilet. Another was a ghost who didn't approve of card playing, who would scatter the cards on the card table. The third was a ghost who would borrow books for varying periods of time. They would just disappear. "One book on roses was gone for two years till it suddenly reappeared," Mary says. "It was yellowed."

A woman in the South contacted me to tell me of buying a house and one day looking out a window and seeing the apparition of a woman walking her dog. She often would hear the woman's voice, calling the dog, whose name was Henry. She and her mother-in-law sometimes felt something furry rubbing against their legs—and they hoped it was just Henry. However, when I told her I would have to contact the present owners of the house to get permission to write about the place, there was a dead silence. When she sold the house, she had neglected to tell the new owners about the ghosts. Another good story up in smoke!

Some amusing incidents have more to do with live people than ghosts, such as the pleasant young woman psychic who was hiding out. She had had an excellent professional position in a large city and did her psychic work on the side. She made the mistake, however, of allowing herself to be interviewed on television about her psychic activities. From then on, she got constant wild calls at her home and at her office. She could feel her colleagues glancing at her sidewise. She quit, moved to another part of the country, and got into a different line of work. She's now a psychic in the closet. "Trouble is," she says, "when people hear you're a psychic, they think you've got a handle on God or something."

It seems that people are opening up more about psychic experiences, but it wasn't always so. A wife of a physician wrote me that she and her husband and two children had lived in a haunted house in California about fifteen years before and had been so perturbed that there was almost a curtain of silence lowered on the subject, until much later, when they no longer lived there. Their small son who had told them something was shaking his bed. "We ignored him," the woman wrote. The daughter told of seeing a man and boy walking around the grounds almost every night. The woman herself saw a sea captain and a little girl. But as little was said as possible, and it wasn't until some years later that the husband and wife would talk about the place and she found out that he too had had experiences while they lived there. Let's hope this book will open up many people to what seems to be a deeper reality.

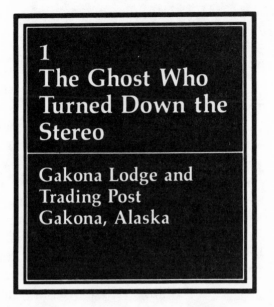

1

The Ghost Who Turned Down the Stereo

Gakona Lodge and
Trading Post
Gakona, Alaska

Location: To get to Gakona, start at Anchorage, a major Alaskan city on the coast, and go northeast on Route 1 about 200 miles.

Description of place: The place includes about a dozen log structures, the earliest of which were built in 1900, which makes them antiquities in Alaska. The largest building, the main lodge, has an attic, rooms on the second floor, and a lobby, grocery store, and liquor store on the first floor. A bar in another building is called the Trappers Den, and there is a dining room in still another building. The place is owned by Jerry Strang, his wife, Barbara, and his brother, John.

Gakona is a settlement of about seventy people, some two hundred miles northeast of Anchorage, on a route called the Tok Cutoff. "It's not a town," says Barbara Strang—the Strangs originally came from upstate New York. "We have a post office and a two-room schoolhouse and us, the lodge and trading post. The people work construction; they're school-teachers; they work for the electric company and at the post office. There's some gold mining."

Ghostly manifestations: Jerry Strang says, "I never did believe in ghosts till we spent our first winter here." But he does now.

Barbara says: "The thing that made me believe in ghosts was that one night we were sitting in our living room, off the lobby of the lodge. We were closed. The front door opened and closed, and we heard heavy footsteps, like someone in logging boots, go across the lobby. We were waiting for someone to come in the door of our living room, but no one did. We got up and looked around, and there weren't any footsteps in the snow, and there wasn't anybody in the building. That was a ghost, we figured.

"The ghost would do weird things, like locking the doors of the rooms upstairs from the inside. I've been upstairs cleaning, and I've heard sounds like somebody jumping on a bed. I'd open the room, and there wouldn't be anybody there.

"One time when John was staying in the lodge he had a room upstairs, and another guy was in a room

Gakona Lodge

downstairs. They each heard voices at night, and they thought it was the other one. The next day they found that neither had been talking with anybody.

"One time a lady thought her room was on fire. She saw something like smoke coming from between the floor and the walls, but there was no smell. She said it just went away after a little while.

"Sometimes all the doors upstairs—we have nine rooms—will open and then slam.

"Sometimes we smell pipe tobacco. No one smokes a pipe who lives here now. So we've come to the conclusion that the ghost smokes a pipe."

But Barbara's favorite incident involves the ghost's proclivities as a music critic. "One time I was in the kitchen doing dishes," she says, "and I had a Joan Baez tape on the stereo out front, and it stopped playing. I went out there, and the tape was still running, but every knob on the stereo had been turned. The volume was on the right side, so it looked like he had started on the left side and turned all the knobs, like balance and treble and so on, until he got to the volume. I was alone, and I got someone to come over and help me finish the dishes."

(It makes the serious parapsychologist ponder as to whether the ghost disliked Joan Baez or just loud music—or, perhaps, the sentiments in the songs. Barbara says it was an old tape with a song called "Sailing" and one about *Time* magazine, among others.)

History: "The place was built in 1900 by a guy named Doyle," says Jerry Strang. "It was originally a freight station and then became an inn, called Doyle's Ranch." Doyle sold it in 1920 to a man named Sundt, who made additions in the 1920s and more in the 1940s. The Strangs have also made additions. They note that no ghostly manifestations seem to have occurred in the newer parts of the complex. Sundt died in the 1940s. His widow, Henra, sold the place to the Strangs in 1974. She now lives in Anchorage and says she never heard anything unusual around the place while she lived there.

Identity of ghost: Truly an enigma. Barbara says: "We have a couple of guesses. One of the guys who built some of these old buildings, we found pictures of him smoking a pipe, so maybe that's the ghost. And there's a rumor that one of the owners committed suicide, but we don't know anything about that."

Personality of ghost: Says Barbara: "It's a friendly ghost, never hurt anybody, but. . . ."

Witnesses: Barbara, Jerry, and John Strang; visitors, including a lady named Sadie.

Best time to witness: Things happen day and night, but there is a tendency toward more activity during the hours of darkness. That means the manifestations step up in the wintertime, because at that latitude it is mostly dark in the winter and almost completely light in the summer.

Still haunted? Seems to be.

Investigations: No formal psychic investigations have been done, but Barbara says a woman guest from Anchorage whom she knows only as Sadie and who says she is a psychic claims that she could feel the ghost's presence and that one time he touched her.

Data submitted by: Barbara and Jerry Strang, Henra Sundt, Debbie McKinney of the staff of the *Anchorage Daily News.*

**2
The Ghostly
Bartender**

Mangy Moose Saloon
Tonsina, Alaska

Location: To get to Tonsina, start at Anchorage. Go
northeast on Route 1 about 180 miles to Glennallen,
then turn south on Route 4 and go about 50 miles.

Description of place: The Tonsina Lodge, a three-
story wooden building, is situated on the Richardson
Highway, the oldest road in Alaska, about two
hundred miles east of Anchorage. It's a weathered
old hulk, sagging at the seams, that hasn't been used
in the past four years, except for storage. Most of
the worldly action takes place across the road in the
Mangy Moose Saloon, one-time storage building
that was made into a cafe several years ago. The
present owner of the two places, Robert Sorenson,
says previous owners established the bar so that the
drunks and rowdies would move over there from the
lodge. "They built it," Sorenson says, "so those guys
could shoot up that place instead of the lodge." Now
it's a restaurant and bar, and in the summer it offers
rooms for rent. The restaurant offers international

15

cuisine, featuring sourdough hotcakes, hamburgers, and Mexican food. Bullet holes can still be seen in the cafe, a legacy from rowdier days. Tonsina is not exactly a bustling town. Debbie McKinney, an *Anchorage Daily News* reporter who did a series of articles on Alaskan bush roadhouses, says, "Tonsina is the tavern, and that's about it. There are some interest-

The Tonsina Lodge

ing old characters out in the bushes who wander in every now and then." And in the summer it's a stop for the tourist buses. Hard by the Mangy Moose is an airstrip that locals call Rotten Robert's International Airport, after a previous owner.

Ghostly manifestations: About five years ago, a waitress, Lorraine Coleman, says she saw a ghost behind the bar of the Mangy Moose. It was about three in the morning, and she was closing up the place. She was alone, listening to the jukebox. She says, "I turned around and saw this image of a man behind the bar, a man with a mustache. He smiled at me, and I walked out, real quick-like." She says the image was very clear, but she knew immediately it was a ghost, partly because she was alone and the doors were locked. "He was tall, dark, and thin," she says. "He had no hat, longish hair, a white shirt, a little black tie, and a mustache." She says she hasn't seen him since but has had feelings of a presence in the bar, which she suspects might be attributable to her one memorable sighting.

Jan Sorenson, wife of Robert, has had a number of experiences. Once she was in the walk-in freezer in the old lodge. She had her arms full of groceries, and the door was shut. As she turned toward the door to leave, it opened by itself. She walked through it and said, "Thank you," and it swung shut after her. "Several of the girls have had experiences like that," she says.

Jan's two dogs seem to have had some sort of experience a few years ago when they were puppies. "I was going to do some cleaning up on the second floor," she says, "and I tried to take my puppies up. They got to the top of the stairs and started yelping and ran back down again. To this day they refuse to go back into the lodge."

Susie Best, now a waitress at the Mangy Moose, had a number of experiences when she was a maid at the lodge. Often, she says, she would find the door to Room 18, which seems to be the chief habitat of the ghost, bolted from the inside. "There's an indent on the bed where he sits all the time," Susie says of Room 18. She'd see the indentation and smooth it out. "I'd go on to the other rooms," she says, "and then I'd come back, because I double-check all the rooms, and the indentation would be back in the bed."

In 1981, she recalls, four members of a road crew checked in and were given Room 18. One of them had slept there before and decided instead to sleep in

The Mangy Moose Saloon

their truck. The other three took the room, says Susie, but in the middle of the night changed their minds and came down to sleep in the truck. The ghost was harassing them, Susie says, although she's not sure how.

History: In the early 1920s, the lodge was hauled over the road in sections from Fort Liscomb in Valdez, about a hundred miles to the southeast. It had been a bachelor officers' quarters. It replaced an older log roadhouse that had burned down. At one time it was owned by a man called Happy Henry, who painted it pink and turned it into a casino and bordello. For several years, up through the 1950s, it was owned by Bill Ogden. It was then acquired by Bob and Margaret Fraser, who owned it for 22 years, until the Sorensons bought it in 1982. Margaret Fraser, incidentally, still lives in Tonsina, and thinks all the talk about ghosts in the lodge comes from the groaning of the building as it settles.

Identity of ghost: No one seems to know, but

there is a vague legend to the effect that it is a man named Bill Ogden, who owned the place for several years up through the 1950s, mainly because he is the only person known to have died there.

Another theory is that there was a suicide there. In 1985, Susie Best received an anonymous letter with a poem calculated to make Robert Service turn over in his grave. She wonders if the ghost might have written it, since if he can open freezer doors he ought to be able to write poetry. Here is the poem:

The Ghost of Tonsina Lodge

He escaped from a place
that was lower than hell
through the swamps and the hate
of a Louisiana jail.

Under the Big Dipper
among the ice and trees
he found a place called home
where his soul ran free.

He stayed to himself
cutting a state from the land
working through the Roaring '20s
as a railroad man.

In the Tonsina Lodge
as night settled in
two Canadian Mounties
closed in on him.

In final desperation
at the point of a gun
he committed his soul
to the land he loved.

Forever in Room 18
in the Alaska night
you can see the reflection of his soul
off the Northern Lights.

Personality of ghost: Says Bob Sorenson: "He's usually quite polite. It isn't every ghost that opens doors for people."

Susie Best says: "He seems like a very tormented person."

Witnesses: Lorraine Coleman, Susie Best, Jan Sorenson, Jan Sorenson's two dogs, four road workers, various others.

Best time to witness: The manifestations seem to occur both day and night.

Still haunted? No reason to think it's not.

Investigations: Susie Best says, "We haven't had a psychic in, but we've thought about it."

Data submitted by: Bob and Jan Sorenson, Lorraine Coleman, Susie Best, Judy Williams, Margaret Fraser, Debbie McKinney, Elaine Blickle. Much information from article in September 2, 1985, issue of the *Anchorage Daily News,* by Debbie McKinney. Tip from Roy Gravem.

3

The Ghost Who Tidied Things Up

A Former Army Officers' Quarters Nogales, Arizona

Location: The exact location of this house is not known. Gordon St. Thomas is deceased. But from the indications in his account, an enterprising searcher might be able to trace down this distinctive-looking building that overlooks Nogales to the east.

Description of place: A long, low, one-story house atop a hill overlooking Nogales. On the south side, looking toward Mexico, was a long dining room. In the center of the house was a living room, and on the north side were three bedrooms.

Ghostly manifestations: In 1942, Gordon St. Thomas, a U.S. Immigration officer, was transferred to Nogales. He found a former bachelor officers' building, rented it, and he and his wife, Sarah, and two small children moved in. From the beginning they had the feeling that a presence was there, that when they walked into a room someone had just left it. Before long, St. Thomas became aware that unusual things were really happening. He'd toss his hat on a chair and find it hanging on a hook a few minutes later. He'd leave a book open on the dining room table and a few minutes later find it replaced in a nearby bookcase. The unseen presence had a thing about cigarettes. If St. Thomas left a pack lying around, he'd find it in the wastebasket. These things happened when the rest of the family was not around. The ghost could be helpful, though. St. Thomas says once he left the gas on full tilt under the coffeepot when he went to shave. Several minutes later, he remembered, and dashed for the kitchen. He found the gas turned down and the coffee perking gently.

St. Thomas's most striking memory of the unseen tenant stems from one night when he came home from his work about midnight and went into a back bedroom to sleep to avoid waking his wife. He was drifting off to sleep when he felt someone grab his foot and shake it vigorously. He turned on the light, but no one was there. Then he saw a poisonous scorpion on the ceiling directly over the bed. St. Thomas says that as the temperature drops at night a scorpion senses heat emanating from a body and goes to it, seeking warmth. He feels the ghost may have saved his life. In return, he says, he tried being a little neater around the house.

History: The house, built during the nineteenth century, was considered somewhat of a landmark in the area. It was the bachelor officers' quarters of an army post that dated back to the skirmishes with the Indian leader Geronimo.

Identity of ghost: St. Thomas suspected it was someone connected with the former Army post, accustomed to military neatness.

Personality of ghost: Neat and fussy, but concerned about the welfare of the living inhabitants.

Witnesses: St. Thomas and his family.

Best time to witness: The presence seemed to be around both day and night.

Still haunted? Not known.

Investigations: None during the St. Thomases' sojourn in the house.

Data submitted by: Gordon St. Thomas, suggested by an article in *Fate* magazine, April 1983 issue.

4

The Best Haunted House in Town

The Allen House
Monticello, Arkansas

Location: The Allen House is located at 705 North Main St., Monticello.

Description of place: "It's the most striking-looking house in Monticello," says Dr. Stacy Clanton, who lived there when he and his wife were students at the University of Arkansas and who now teaches English at Louisiana State University. "A faculty member who took us by it when we were looking for a place to live called the architecture 'bastard Gothic,' and it's sort of Victorian as well. The house has seventeen columns on the outside. The house is very unusual in its architecture. None of the rooms are square. There were always elaborations and corners. In our bedroom there were curved windows, the only time I've ever seen curved windows. I dare say that house looked haunted the day it was built."

Ghostly manifestations: Aside from its appearance, the house seems to have gained its reputation for being haunted after one of the daughters of the Allen family, LaDell, comitted suicide in the house by cyanide of mercury in the 1940s. In the 1950s the Allen family moved out and the place was divided into apartments. Monticello is the seat of a branch of the University of Arkansas, and many of the tenants, although not all, have been students at the university.

The Allen House

The best witness this reporter could find was Stacy Clanton, who lived there with his wife in 1968–69. "The house seemed haunted," Clanton says. "You would think it was under any circumstances. One of our favorite stories is that we were sitting in our living room one evening, and we heard some kids on the street daring one another to go walk up on the front porch. They were terrified, and here we were watching television.

"The best thing happened to some students who lived upstairs. They were a young married couple and a bit on the hippy side, a little early for hippies to be in southeast Arkansas. They were eventually asked to move out, for being too noisy, I guess. Anyway, they told us they had a friend visiting them, and they left the friend in the apartment when they went out to get some groceries, and when they came back the friend was not there. They had been joking about the haunted house, and they thought he was playing a trick. They saw a closet door that was slightly ajar and thought, 'Ah, we've got him in there.' And they tried to push the door shut. There was resistance. There was a lot of laughter and screaming and jollity and carrying on, and a lot of resistance from the door. And in the midst of all this their friend, whom they thought they had trapped inside the closet, walked in from the hall. And when they opened the closet door, there was nothing there.

"One time, after that couple had moved out and the apartment over us was empty, my wife and I had gone to bed, and we heard a considerable amount of banging overhead. It sounded like tromping, and furniture being knocked over, and all sorts of things. We called the police, and they showed up. We could hear them out in the parking lot almost daring one another to go into the house. I had to go out on the porch and tell them this was the place, to come in and investigate. One of them pulled his gun and said to me, 'You know your way around; you lead the way.' So I walked up the stairs with the policeman's .38 Special or whatever at my back. We walked all over the place and found nothing.

"A lot of things were not recurring; they were one-shot things. Early one morning we were awakened by the strangest sort of moaning, a sort of continual thing. It didn't go in gasps and spurts; it was continuous. We walked all over the place and found nothing. It was something like the wind going over a chimney, but there was no wind that day. It slowly faded out, and we never heard it again."

Perhaps the Clantons' most striking experience occurred when Dr. Clanton took a picture of his wife looking into a mirror, and in the mirror, reflecting space that would have been behind him, there appeared on the picture a filmy, white human shape. It might have been a trick of light, he says, but it might be something else.

"I still dream about that house," Clanton says, "very frequently. There's always an element of foreboding in these dreams."

Other people who have lived in the house have had unusual experiences, too. Marcia Moffett Daniels, who at the time she lived in the house was director of the county historical museum, recalls: "The most unusual thing that happened was that I thought someone was walking around overhead one night. The girl who lived in the apartment above me was gone. I called the police, and they came and scoured the place and didn't find anybody or anything. I preferred to think it was squirrels, at least while I was living there."

A gothic novel, *Scent of Lilacs*, has been written by Carolyn Wilson, who lived in the house. She denies having seen anything unusual in the house while she was a tenant there but says living there might have influenced her to write a book about a scary old house. In Monticello, it is scripture that *Scent of Lilacs* is about the Allen House.

In early 1985, Judy Ryburn opened a gift shop on the ground floor. Immediately strange things began to happen. She would come in and find things knocked over and money taken from the cash register. Once the mysterious intruders made themselves a salad from some food she had in her refrigerator, leaving her the dirty dishes. Quickly, the word went around town that LaDell Allen was furious about her home being used for commercial purposes and was invading the gift shop at night. It was a cruel blow to dedicated spook aficionados when on the third depredation a window was found open and some screens were slashed, indicating that the problem was not LaDell, but more likely live kids. But hope springs eternal, and it is still suspected in Monticello that at least some of the trouble in the gift shop was caused by the not-quite-departed Allen daughter.

History: The Allen House was built in 1900 by a prosperous planter from the nearby Mississippi Delta, Joe Lee Allen. Stacy Clanton describes the historical-sociological milieu as follows:

"The delta starts about fifteen miles east. You go over Overflow Hill and drop down from rolling pines into flatlands. Up until the late 1920s there was always flooding, and the rich planters would build a house on the nearest high ground. They could build in Monticello and go back to their farms during the week and have their families live in the relative safety of Monticello, which was kind of a snooty town for a small hill town."

The Allen family continued to live in the house until the 1950s, when it was converted into apartments. Ownership of the house remained in the family until very recently.

Identity of ghost: LaDell Allen?

Personality of ghost: Seemingly harmless. As Stacy Clanton puts it, "She just makes a noise now and then, kind of to make her presence known."

Witnesses: The Clantons, Marcia Moffett Daniels, Judy Ryburn, the hippie couple.

Best time to witness: Manifestations seem to have occurred at various times during the day and night.

Still haunted? If not, why not?

Investigations: The only information along this line was supplied by Stacy Clanton, who says: "One time we were visited by a group of parapsychologists who came all the way from Fayetteville, about 350 miles, and asked our permission to set up their instruments. We told them they'd have to see the manager, who told them the owners probably wouldn't let them in since they were not too happy about the ghost association." As a consolation prize, the congenial Clantons took the disappointed parapsychologists out to look for a ghostly light that repeatedly appears along some nearby railroad tracks. It didn't appear that night, Stacy Clanton says, although he says he has seen it at other times.

Data submitted by: Former tenants Stacy Clanton, Marcia Moffett Daniels, Judy Ryburn, Opel Ward, Joe Guenter, Carolyn Wilson Schisler, and Betty Collins, rental agent of the property for many years. William Painton, present owner of the property. Betty Leidinger, a former owner. Fran Franklin, a professor at the University of Arkansas at Monticello. Wyona Jane Watson, former student at the University of Arkansas, who did a historical study of Monticello. Sheriff David Taylor Hyatt and Katharine Hyatt Cordi, neighbors.

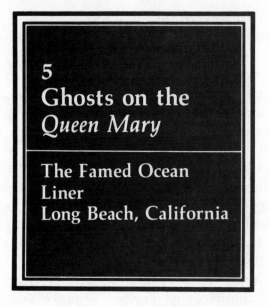

5

Ghosts on the
Queen Mary

The Famed Ocean
Liner
Long Beach, California

Location: The Queen Mary is permanently berthed at the Port of Long Beach.

Description of place: The old British passenger liner is now a tourist attraction, a hotel with 390 staterooms and four restaurants. It is a convention center, and regular tours are run through the ship, one of the highlights of which is a maritime museum. The ship's gross tonnage is 81,237 tons; its length is 1,019 feet; it has twelve decks, three huge funnels, over 1,000 portholes and windows, and an undetermined number of ghostly manifestations.

Ghostly manifestations: The present captain of the immobile *Queen Mary*, John Gregory, is appropriately enough not a seagoing man but a hotel and restaurant executive. Also appropriately, but apparently coincidentally, he is a parapsychologist as well. However, he says, he has not exercised the latter expertise in his present situation. He has not investigated the ship as a parapsychologist, but he has

The Queen Mary

spoken with many former crew members, including the last master of the ship, and passengers who have either had paranormal experiences or heard about them in such a way as to believe them. Many of the people now working on the ship claim to have had such experiences.

In 1983, a columnist for the *Long Beach Press-Telegram,* Tom Hennessy, a pronounced skeptic, decided to check out the ship for spooks. He interviewed many employees and had a scary experience himself during the night he spent on the vessel. He wrote an extended column on his investigations, beginning with the words, "The *Queen Mary* is haunted." Here, with his permission, are some excerpts from his column.

> Bill Thompson, security guard: "On G deck, where we think the ship's morgue was located, lights go on and off and doors slam. . . . And strange things seem to happen around the

artifacts section (a storage area filled with relics from the ship's glory days). We have sensor alarms in there that have gone off. They're like radar. A live body has to go by them to set them off. But the area is padlocked."

Cheryl Zalfini, a secretary: "In the engine room you hear noises. It sounds like clanging, like somebody's working down there, but at 5:30 or 6 at night nobody's working in that area."

Nancy Wazny, a security sergeant: "I was standing alone on the stairs to the swimming pool when out of the side of my eye I saw a woman in her 40s or 50s wearing a striped, old-style bathing suit. She was poised as if about to dive into the pool, which was empty. When I turned full face to stop her, she was gone."

On another occasion, Wazny, then a tour-guide supervisor, was closing the engine-room exhibit for the day. "I was going up the second escalator when suddenly I felt I was being stared at. There was a man on the step behind me. He had black hair and a black beard and was wearing dark blue coveralls. I stepped aside to let him pass and he was gone."

A tour guide, Patricia Salcido, told Hennessy that she has heard a knocking noise in the wall, like the sound of pipe knocking, where there are no pipes. At the same time, she said, she saw two lights—perfect circles, like portholes—on the wall, moving.

Two tour guides, a man and a woman, reported seeing a chain across an entryway in the engine room begin to whip up and down. This was preceded by what sounded like someone clearing his throat. Other people now working on or visiting the ship have reported such phenomena as the sounds of keys

Captain John Gregory and the Queen Mary

rattling, chains dragging, party noises, and shouts and splashing in the pool area.

As the climax of his night on the *Queen*, newsman Hennessy spent a half-hour alone in Shaft Alley, an adjunct of the engine room so named because it houses the ship's propeller shafts. It is known for strange sounds and other happenings. Hennessy writes that he heard clanging noises as though someone were banging on pipes. When he would walk toward the noise, it would stop, but when he retreated, it would resume. At one point he found an oil drum blocking a passageway where there had been no oil drum before, as far as he could recall. Soon after, he traversed the passageway again, and this time he found two oil drums. On a catwalk, he says, he could feel vibrations as though someone were walking toward him. He felt a rush of air in an area that is supposed to be airtight. But the real highlight of his adventure came at 3:33 A.M., when he says he heard what sounded like two or three men talking at once, trailing off into a single voice so distinct that he was able to make out the end of a sentence, ". . . turning the lights off." A security guard subsequently told him that the nearest (live) person to him was two decks away and that other people have also heard voices where he heard them.

History: The *Queen Mary* sailed on its maiden voyage, from Southampton to New York, in 1936. It was a troop ship during World War II. After 1,001 Atlantic crossings it was retired and was docked in Long Beach in 1967.

Identity of ghosts: Presumably passengers and crew of the ship. For example, in one hatchway the sound of rolling metal is sometimes heard. In the early days of the war, a crewman was crushed to death by metal objects in that area. In one of the ship's kitchens, employees report such occurrences as moving dishes, disappearing utensils, and lights going on and off. These may be connected with an incident that happened when the ship was a troop transport. A particular cook was so bad and so unpopular that what seemed an incipient riot developed. The ship's captain was concerned enough to call a cruiser in the convoy to help quell what he felt might turn into a mutiny. Before help arrived, the unfortunate cook was somehow shoved into an oven. He died from the resulting burns.

The aforementioned Nancy Wazny is not the only person who has seen a woman in the pool area. Others have reported seeing an attractive, mini-skirted woman walking toward the pool and vanishing behind a pillar. According to the ship's records, a woman once drowned in the pool. Other apparitions are "The Woman in White," an evening-gowned figure who supposedly drapes herself over the piano in the ship's salon, and "The Poisoned Officer," who reportedly roams an area near the bridge where an officer once died from accidental poisoning.

Personalities of ghosts: No harmful or malevolent ghosts have ever been reported.

Witnesses: Scores of people, including crew and passengers of the ship when it was sailing the seas and employees on and visitors to it now.

Best time to witness: The events seem to occur at various times of the day and night.

Still haunted? Events are still being reported.

Investigations: To the knowledge of people presently associated with the ship, there have been no serious psychic inquiries on board. However, when the *Queen Mary* was launched in 1934, a popular London astrologer, Lady Mabel Fortescue-Harrison, made the following prediction, which was published in British newspapers: "The *Queen Mary*, launched today, will know her greatest fame and popularity when she never sails another mile and never carries another paying passenger."

Data submitted by: Extended column by Tom Hennessy in the *Long Beach Press-Telegram*, issue of March 6, 1983; article by James Crenshaw in *Fate* magazine, issue of April 1984; interview with Capt. James Gregory; material from Wrather Port Properties, present proprietors of the *Queen Mary*.

6

Is John Wayne Haunting His Yacht?

The Wild Goose
Berthed in a Marina at Newport, California

Location: The Wild Goose is anchored in Newport Harbor. It would be advisable before visiting to contact the owner, Lynn Hutchins, at 2412 Wilshire Blvd., Suite 208, Santa Monica, CA 90403

Description of place: *The Wild Goose* was purchased by the superstar movie actor John Wayne in 1964 and became one of his most prized possessions. It was a converted World War II mine sweeper, sister ship to Jacques Cousteau's *Calypso*. Some 140 feet long, with luxury staterooms, it is said to require a crew of six to operate it.

Ghostly manifestations: Wayne sold *The Wild Goose* approximately one month before his death in June 1979, to Lynn Hutchins, a lawyer who lives in Santa Monica. Within four months of his purchase, Hutchins says, he began to experience an apparitional presence, which he believes to be Wayne's surviving spirit. An article about the incidents, which Hutchins says quotes him correctly, appeared in the *National Enquirer*. It quotes Hutchins as follows:

The Wild Goose

"I've seen John Wayne's ghost twice and have felt his spirit nearby many times. I was sleeping in The Duke's stateroom. I remember waking up with a start in the middle of the night. The room was black and the boat was uncannily silent. As my eyes got used to the dark I suddenly became aware of someone standing by the door to the port gangway. I froze because I was alone on the boat. Then I leaped out of bed—and the figure vanished into thin air! Later I talked to Bert Minshall [former captain of the boat] and he said, 'That was John Wayne.' "

Hutchins told the *Enquirer* of another incident that he says happened about a year after Wayne died. He was alone in the main salon, reading a book.

"I had my back to the door and I became aware that somebody was standing behind me. I turned in my chair, and as I did there was a rush of wind. And then Wayne's beer glasses, hanging above the bar, began to tinkle so hard I thought they might shatter. I looked at my reflection in the mirror behind the bar and all of a sudden I saw a second reflection. It was a man with a craggy, weather-beaten face with a twinkle in his eye, a man much taller than I am. I stared in disbelief—because I was staring at the face of John Wayne. I swung around but nobody was behind me. Then I looked back into the mirror but the vision had disappeared."

In January 1983, Hutchins requested Patricia Hayes, a psychic who lives in Atlanta, Georgia, and operates a school for the training of psychics, to attempt communication with the spirit entity. She brought with her three associates, William Clema, Janice Hayes, and Ester-Elke Kaplan, and they did psi scans of the boat on two occasions. Hayes also asked Dr. William G. Roll, a well-known parapsychologist who is head of the Psychical Research Foundation, then located in Chapel Hill, North Carolina, to work with her. Roll is editor of *Theta*, a conservative, scholarly quarterly journal on parapsychology. He wrote an article on the investigation in *Theta* and describes the two previously noted episodes as follows.

In August 1979, at 4 o'clock in the morning, Hutchins had his first encounter with what he later came to regard as Wayne's "ghost." In an interview with. . . Roll, Hutchins recalled the incident: "As I turned from the toilet to walk out of the master bath back to the master stateroom it was just dawn. I could see this big tall figure, this fellow standing right there in the doorway. He took up the whole doorway, the doorway to the master bath, that is. He was standing by the big porthole, about three feet back of the doorway, standing there with a little

John Wayne

bit of a smile on his face. I couldn't make out the features; I couldn't tell who it was, just a big man standing there with a wide hat and a little old smile on his face. Just looking at me. All gray but solid; it wasn't just filmy or anything like that."

Hutchins said he started toward the figure when "he just vanished like that. . . ." He said the figure wore a cowboy hat which prevented his facial features from being seen clearly. The sighting lasted three to four seconds.

Roll describes the second episode as follows in his article:

> The next episode came in October 1979. This time it was 4 P.M. Hutchins was in the main salon sitting at a poker table facing the bar. He got up and went to the bar to pour himself a drink. The bar features mirrored walls."

The *Theta* article then quotes Hutchins as follows:

> I happened to look up. I looked right behind me, right exactly standing by the chair I'd just gotten out of was this tall figure standing there. All gray, wearing a wide brim hat, and Western garb. Couldn't see his face but that was 20 feet away. I thought to myself as I stood there, 'How the hell did he get in here?'

Hutchins told Roll he started to speak when the apparition vanished. The sighting had lasted four to five seconds. Just prior to the sighting, Hutchins said, beer mugs that are tightly bound together on the bar to prevent them from breaking began to clink together.

Hutchins also told Roll that when he spent nights on board he often heard heavy footsteps walking up and down the deck past his stateroom. He would look out quickly but see nothing on deck. Another person, a caterer, who spent a night on the boat, reportedly also, independently, said he heard footsteps. Hutchins said he found out some time later from a crew member that Wayne had a habit of walking twenty laps around the deck in the evening.

History: Since Hutchins seems to be the only person who has reported seeing an apparition, Roll was particularly interested in his relationship to the overall situation. Roll wrote in his *Theta* article:

> Hutchins' emotional attachment to the yacht
> began from the time when he learned of her
> availability. Negotiations for the purchase had
> not been easy. Wayne, working through his son
> Michael as intermediary, interrogated Hutchins
> at considerable length as to his philosophical and
> political views. Finally, these were deemed to be
> compatible with Wayne's own world view; in a
> nutshell, Hutchins was considered 'suitable' to be
> *The Wild Goose's* next owner. Both Hutchins and
> Wayne seemed to regard this changing of hands
> as something of a ceremonial event; Hutchins
> could barely believe his good fortune in
> acquiring *The Wild Goose,* an occurrence made
> more meaningful by his exceptionally deep
> admiration for Wayne. *The Wild Goose* was not
> just *a* boat. It was 'John's boat,' and into it
> Hutchins invested his heart and soul, as well as
> a great deal of money.

Hutchins kept plaques and awards belonging to Wayne hanging in the main salon, and Wayne's books are still in the library. Roll put it this way: "In a sense, *The Wild Goose* is like a floating museum tended by a doting caretaker who takes a very special pride in it. As Hutchins told us, 'It will always be John's boat.' "

In an interview with the author of this book, while discussing the fact that some show business personalities have sued the *National Enquirer* for allegedly making misstatements about them, Hutchins said he had been quoted correctly, adding, "You don't go around making a monkey out of John Wayne; you play it straight."

In assessing the situation, Roll took into account what he termed "the deep emotional triangle created by Hutchins, Wayne, and *The Wild Goose* herself." Roll went on to say: "Hutchins's proprietary attitude, his strong emotional attachment and feeling of steward-ship over something very precious, are attitudes that crop up again and again in haunting cases we have investigated. It may be significant in this connection that no one but Hutchins has reported the sighting

Pat Hayes

of an apparition; his affection for the *Goose* may have created a psi-conducive situation."

A psychological test given to Hutchins by Roll indicated that Hutchins's sighting was not likely to be merely the product of an "overactive imagination," that Hutchins was not particularly a fantasy-prone personality. In the conclusion of his article, Roll, as good parapsychologists usually do, drew no conclusion. "The question of whether an intense emotional 'stake' is critical to haunting-type phenomena," Roll wrote, "and perhaps also to an explanation of why certain individuals have apparitional experiences and others do not, cannot be definitely answered at the present time."

Identity of ghost: John Wayne? During a séance held by the psychics, a message—"Tell Lady I love her"—was received, ostensibly a communication from Wayne. "Lady" was a pet name Wayne used for Pat Stacy, with whom he had a long-standing personal relationship. However, Roll remarks, "In the light of Wayne's fame, it is possible that this term of endearment was. . . generally known."

Personality of ghost: Psychic Patricia Hayes said in an interview that the ghost of John Wayne was indeed there. "What I found," she said, "was that one of the reasons he was there on the boat was because it was one of his favorite places, and he said it still is one of his favorite places to be. He knows he's dead. He doesn't want it to be thought that he is stuck on this side. He just chooses to hang out here. In other words, that's not the only thing he does; when he has some time available he goes to the boat."

Witnesses: Lynn Hutchins, as well as a caterer who prefers to remain anonymous.

Best time to witness: Hutchins has mentioned apparitions during both day and night, as well as the sound of footsteps at night.

Still haunted? "I never feel like I'm alone on the boat," Hutchins says. "There's always a warm feeling of protection there."

Investigations: Psi sessions headed by Patricia Hayes, as well as concurrent research by parapsychologist William Roll.

Data submitted by: Interviews with William Roll, Patricia Hayes, Lynn Hutchins. Articles from the spring 1984 issue of *Theta: The Journal of the Psychical Research Foundation* and from the March 9, 1982, and July 26, 1983, issues of the *National Enquirer*.

7
The Weirdest House in the West

The Winchester Mystery House San Jose, California

Location: The Winchester House and its grounds cover six acres at 525 South Winchester Boulevard, San Jose.

Description of place: This extraordinary edifice, since 1923 a tourist attraction, was built by Sarah Pardee Winchester beginning in 1884. Winchester was heiress to the Winchester Rifle Company fortune. An ardent spiritualist, she had been told by a medium that the ghosts of people killed by the famed Winchester Repeating Rifle were out to get her, but that she could placate them by living in a house in which the construction never stopped. She took the medium's pronouncement very seriously indeed, and the sawing and hammering went on until the day of her death thirty-eight years later.

The building eventually cost $5.5 million, in the days when $5.5 million was $5.5 million. It covers six acres. When the carpentry finally ceased, Sarah Winchester had 160 rooms to hide from ghosts in

The Winchester House

and miles of corridor to roam before she slept. The design is wildly Victorian, intricately ornamental and massive in its woodwork, with balconies, turrets, curved walls, cornices, porches, pediments, arches, wooden balls, cupolas, dormers, and anything else the madly designing minds of that time of architectural frenzy could conceive.

The administration of the Winchester Mystery House is profligate with its statistics. A sampling: 10,000 windows, 950 doors, 47 fireplaces (she had heard ghosts like fireplaces), 17 chimneys (they like chimneys, too), 40 bedrooms, 40 staircases, 52 skylights.

She had a thing about the figure thirteen. A partial statistical rundown: thirteen bathrooms, with thirteen steps into the thirteenth; thirteen windows in the thirteenth bedroom; thirteen windows and doors in the old sewing room; thirteen hooks in her séance room; thirteen glass cupolas in the greenhouse; thirteen stones in the Oriental Bedroom windows. This is a mere scattering of examples of the obeisance to the number thirteen in the house. She signed her will thirteen times.

Ghostly manifestations: Two well-known California psychics claim to have had paranormal experiences in the Winchester House. One is Sylvia Brown of Saratoga, California, who, during a night in Mrs. Winchester's Séance Room, claimed to hear organ music. (Mrs. Winchester played the organ.) No other member of her party reported hearing this, but a tape recorder they had with them is said to have recorded such music. Later, walking through the house, the group reportedly saw moving lights and encountered cold spots. Brown and Antoinette May, a San Francisco newspaperwoman, say that in the bedroom where Mrs. Winchester had died they saw large balls of red light that seemed to explode and then fade.

On Halloween night in 1975, Jeanne Borgen of Pinole, California, a psychic investigator, conducted a midnight séance at Winchester House. Joy Adams of San Jose, a medium, also participated. Mrs. Borgen, it is indicated, was possessed by a spirit, presumably that of Mrs. Winchester. A reporter, Alvin Guthertz, wrote in the magazine *Psychic Guide:*

> It suddenly appeared as if Mrs. Borgen's face
> had aged: her hair appeared to turn gray and
> deep lines creased her forehead. She felt
> staggering pain and was unable to walk. It was
> as if she were having a heart attack and as she
> started to fall she screamed for help.

Mrs. Borgen told the others that she felt a tremendous buildup of energy and that she (Mrs. Winchester) was an over-powering woman, a powerful woman.

Winchester House's well-orchestrated promotional department also provides statements from a number of people who have worked in the building or visited it. These include sounds of invisible workmen, a ghostly photograph of a man in coveralls, cold spots, a shaking floor, piano music, footsteps, a turning doorknob, a soft voice whispering, a window flying open, the odor of chicken soup (smelled by two tour guides, six months apart), a slamming door, lights going on that had been turned off, an office soaked with water. An office manager at the place, Sue Sale, says that while passing a small kitchen she saw a small, gray-haired woman sitting at a table. The woman was dressed like Sarah Winchester, and Sale thought she must be part of a promotion. There was no such promotion going on.

On Halloween night in 1979, a radio station brought a psychic, Warren Capling of Concord, California, to the house. Capling said that in the bed-

The Winchester House from the air.

room where Mrs. Winchester had died he could hear organ music, although the others present did not hear anything. Shortly thereafter, Capling and the others saw a small, glowing light move across the room, stop by the bed, and vanish.

History: Sarah Pardee was born in New Haven, Connecticut, in 1839, and as a young woman was a belle of the town's society. She was an accomplished musician, could speak four languages. She was only four feet, ten inches tall and weighed less than a hundred pounds. In 1862, she married William Wirt Winchester, son of the inventor and manufacturer of the well-known rifle. A daughter was born in 1866 but died a month later. Sarah Winchester never recovered from this loss. In 1881, Mr. Winchester died, increasing Sarah's mental torment. She turned to spiritualism, and a medium in Boston told her that the death had been brought about by the spirits of the thousands of people who had been killed by Winchester rifles. She was told her only escape was to buy a home and build onto it continuously.

In 1884, she came west and bought an eight-room farmhouse in San Jose. Within six months, she had expanded it to a 26-room mansion, and her edifice complex was off and galloping. In her day, the place was known as Llanada Villa. Her project must have been a bonanza for the building workers of the area. Work went on 24 hours a day, every day of the year, for 38 years. It stopped abruptly at her death in 1922. Tour guides point out a row of half-driven nails where carpenters stopped when word came that the 85-year-old recluse had died in her sleep.

The house was sold and was opened to the public a year after Mrs. Winchester's death. Extensive restoration was begun in 1973 and is still continuing.

Winchester House: where ghosts have their own doors and stairs lead nowhere.

Identities of ghosts: Sarah Winchester? People who had worked in the place? Despite Mrs. Winchester's fears, people who were suddenly ejected from this dimension by means of the Winchester rifle seem to take little interest in the house.

Personalities of ghosts: Except for psychic Borgen's feeling that she was being possessed by a powerful spirit, the ghosts seem harmless.

Witnesses: If the Winchester Mystery House publicity is to be believed, scores of people, including staff and visitors.

Best time to witness: Occurrences are reported around the clock.

Still haunted? Administration sources say no events have been reported during the past couple of years.

Investigations: Visits by such psychics as Sylvia Brown, Jeanne Borgen, Joy Adams, Warren Capling, and many others over the years.

Data submitted by: Material provided by the administration of Winchester Mystery House.

8
The Haunted Toy Store

Toys 'R' Us
Sunnyvale, California

Location: The Toys 'R' Us store is located at 130 East El Camino, Sunnyvale.

Description of place: The one-story, 60,000-square-foot modern building was put up by the Toys 'R' Us company in 1970, in Sunnyvale, California, a suburb about thirty miles south of San Francisco. The store building fronts on El Camino Real, the main highway leading south out of the city.

Ghostly manifestations: Strange things were happening in this huge, modern toy store. When employees arrived in the morning, they would find roller skates scattered around. Books would be found on the floor, although everything had been in order when the store was locked up the previous night. Steve Speelman, co-manager of the store, says employees were constantly telling him someone had tapped them on the shoulder—when no one was there! Young women, particularly those with long hair, sometimes felt an unseen hand stroking their locks. "One evening," Speelman says, "we rolled down a metal door at the back of the building, and someone started banging on it, yelling, 'Let me out, let me out!' When we rolled the door back up, there was nobody there. One night I sent two big, husky guys to the rear of the store, and they came back and told me there was someone clumping around wearing heavy shoes. You could hear the thump, thump, thump. It was late at night, and there was only staff in the store, and none of us were wearing hard shoes. One time a customer came to me and said she kept turning the faucet off, but it kept turning itself back on."

Judy Jackson, the other co-manager, who was with the store from its earliest days, says, "A lot of things were happening even then, but it was something we had fun with." By 1978, the story reached Antoinette May, a San Francisco newspaper reporter who liked to write about ghosts. She alerted Sylvia Brown, a psychic who lived near Sunnyvale, and one night, accompanied by a photographer, Bill Tidwell, and some of her assistants, they went to the store to beard the ghost.

They expected the ghost to be John Murphy, a pioneer rancher of the Peninsula Valley. The store had built on part of the huge Murphy Ranch one hundred years before. It turned out to be someone else entirely.

Sylvia Brown says she immediately sensed a tall, thin man wearing a short coat, with his hands thrust into the pockets, looking down at the floor. He told Brown that his name was Johnny Johnson. He urged Brown to move or she'd get her feet wet. Later, as she and the others perused Santa Clara County records, they found that there had been a well where she had been standing in the store.

Photographer Bill Tidwell says that's a ghost standing there in the aisleway, in this photo, which was taken with infra-red film. Tidwell says the photo below was taken by an assistant with ordinary film "at essentially the same moment."

Blow-up of ghostly figure from infra-red shot.

History: Records showed that Johnson was about eighty when he died and had come to California from Pennsylvania during the Gold Rush. He had fallen in love, at a distance, with Beth Murphy, daughter of John, and was devastated when she married a prominent citizen of Sunnyvale. Later he contracted encephalitis, which left him mentally impaired, and during the latter part of his life he was known as "Crazy Johnny." He was tolerated as a marginal employee at the ranch. He died in 1884 when he cut his leg while chopping wood and bled to death. All Bill Tidwell got on this foray was a bright spot on his film. However, in 1980 the TV show "That's Incredible" made arrangements to shoot Johnny for national television and asked Brown and Tidwell to reprise their earlier attempt to contact the ghost. Johnny didn't appear on the TV film, but this time Tidwell says he had better luck. He says he used infrared film and got a likeness of tall, thin Johnny, gazing morosely at the floor. An assistant shooting ordinary film at the same time got a picture of the aisle without any figure, Tidwell says.

Identity of ghost: Johnny Johnson?

Personality of ghost: Johnny seems a lost, sad soul, searching for the young woman he loved hopelessly while he was alive. Some of his antics seem mischievous, an attempt to make contact with the living world. The store employees seem affectionate, even protective, toward him. Very few are frightened.

Witnesses: Many members of the staff of the store, as well as customers, and psychic investigators.

Best time to witness: Johnny seems to spend day and night in the store. For would-be additional witnesses, the store is open for business Monday through Saturday from 9:30 to 9:30 and on Sunday from 9:30 to 6:00.

Still haunted? Yes, and it apparently will be until Johnny moves on.

Investigations: Extensive psychic investigation by Brown and members of her staff, as well as interviews with witnesses by the media.

Data submitted by: Staff of "That's Incredible"; Sylvia Brown and assistants, including Bill Tidwell; staff members of the store.

**9
The Beam That
Split, The Cigar
Lighter That
Floated**

The Former
Bradley House
Denver, Colorado

Location: The former Bradley house is located at 4100 South University Boulevard, Denver. The present owners might not welcome visitors.

Description of place: A Tudor-style mansion in an affluent residential section of Denver.

Ghostly manifestations: In 1962, Dr. Robert Bradley, a nationally known obstetrician, purchased a rambling, run-down, empty house and moved in with his wife and family, planning to renovate the place. He began to realize that he had bought into something unusual when a former caretaker dropped by and asked casually if he had heard the story about the split beam in the drawing room. Some time later, the Bradleys wrote a book about their experiences, *Psychic Phenomena: Revelations and Experiences* (Parker Publishing), in which they said:

> For some time before her death, the former lady of the house had told friends, servants, and

members of the family that when she died she
wanted to lie in state in front of the great
fireplace and that on this night she would split
one of the two large cross beams. She specified
exactly which one. According to the story, the
split occurred exactly in the way she had
predicted. We were to hear this story many
times from many different sources in the years
to come.

The Denver house where the Bradleys lived.

Bradley was not deterred; indeed, he was intrigued, for he was somewhat of an aficionado of
ghosts. Some years before he had belonged to an
amateur acting group that put on their plays in what
appeared to be a haunted theater. Lights kept going
on and off, and so on. Bradley had his first direct
offbeat experience in his new house when one morning he strolled into the drawing room and un-
wrapped a cigar. He reached for a heavily weighted
lighter on a table. As his hand approached it, the
object gently rose and floated about a foot away,
coming to rest on its side. Bradley says he hasn't had

a cigar since. Apparently someone didn't want him smoking, either for his own sake or for the sake of the curtains and drapes. On another occasion, Bradley says, he was lying on a couch in the library, reading a book. It was getting dark, and he thought it might be a good idea to raise the window shade so he would have better light. Suddenly the shade rolled up and stopped a few inches from the top of the windows.

All members of the household heard footsteps, clunks, and thumps. One time, a clear note rang out from a cello standing in a corner. While the house was being renovated, lights kept flicking on and off, and electric sanders would not work, for no discernible reason. Somebody seemed to have objections to changes being made in the house. As time went on, the Bradleys got used to lamps levitating and doors slamming. Strange smells were part of the syndrome. A rotten, fishy smell meant a death in the family was approaching. A smell of roses meant something good was going to happen.

At one time the Bradleys and a local group of people interested in the psychic approached the famous psychic, the late Arthur Ford, to find out what might be causing all this. Ford, through his spirit guide, Fletcher, said most of the spirit activity was being caused by former owners, a man and wife. The man was very well known, Dr. Hubert Work, Secretary of the Interior under President Hoover and Postmaster General under Coolidge. The couple had some differences, according to Fletcher. The woman liked to keep the windows covered during the day. Work would storm through the house turning on the lights, with his wife behind him turning them off. Bradley was convinced Mrs. Work was still around and was using the lights to identify herself. Sometimes all the lights in the house would go on at the same time and go off simultaneously, although there was no master switch to accomplish this in the conventional way. One guest, a decided skeptic, on her first night in the house, heard her bedroom door open and close. She heard footsteps go by her bed and stop in front of the dresser. The top dresser drawer came out and went back in. A second drawer did the same thing. Then footsteps went to a rocking chair standing in the moonlight, and the chair began to rock. Bradley says his guest suddenly stopped being a skeptic.

History: The house was built in 1920 by George Gano, a wealthy department store owner in Denver, for his wife, Ethel. It was built in the Tudor style, and almost everything—windows, beams, furnishings—was imported from England. When Gano died, his wife put the house on the market and went to Europe. Hubert Work, who had known her, bought it. Then he went to Europe and persuaded her to marry him. As a surprise wedding gift, he gave her her own house back. After their deaths, the house fell into a state of disrepair and was unoccupied until the Bradleys bought it.

Identity of ghosts: According to Fletcher, Arthur Ford's spirit guide, they are Hubert and Ethel Work, the former owners.

Personalities of ghosts: Bradley, a most accommodating host, says they are no problem at all. "The ghosts are not causing trouble," he added, "not in the least. They're looking for companionship or perhaps trying to resolve some of the conflicts that may have been involved in their lives." (Such as whether the rooms should be dark or lit up.)

Witnesses: Several members of the Bradley family, as well as scores of people of the community. The

Bradleys, enthusiastic ghost fanciers, welcomed the public to the house. It was written up many times in the Denver newspapers.

Best time to witness: The Bradleys sold the house in 1980, and the present owners are not so welcoming to ghosts *or* live witnesses.

Still haunted? Yes, says Dr. Bradley.

Investigations: Arthur Ford identified the ghosts as Dr. and Mrs. Hubert Work, without being informed they had been the former owners. Many other psychics have tuned in at the house, and various newspaper reporters have milled about.

Data submitted by: Dr. Bradley; various articles in the *Denver Post* were also consulted.

**10
The Lovelorn
Lighthouse
Keeper**

The Ledge Light off
New London,
Connecticut

Location: The Ledge Light is stationed in the waters off New London.

Description of place: The lighthouse is a square block building, remote and inaccessible, stuck in the water where the Thames River, Long Island Sound, and Fisher's Island Sound converge. Built about seventy-five years ago, it serves New London Harbor. It is sixty-five feet high. It is the last lighthouse in the state that is not completely automated, but run by members of the U.S. Coast Guard. Some say this is because of the activities of its supposed resident ghost.

Ghostly manifestations: For the past several decades, until a séance in 1981 that seemed to free the ghost, lighthouse keepers have been reporting a constant succession of phenomena. They called the ghost Ernie, although at the 1981 séance he supposedly revealed his correct name. One lighthouse keeper, identified only as David, told the psychic investigators:

"We found paint cans opened up downstairs with paintbrushes in them. Lights would go on and off. I've seen coffee cups move on the table and the refrigerator doors open and close. I've heard him walking upstairs when both of us [two men are on duty at the light at a time] were downstairs. Doors would open and close. The TV has gone off on me."

The chief lighthouse keeper at the time of the séance, John Etheridge, told of an old radio in the former room of the man who is thought to be the ghost. "If you moved that radio," Etheridge said, "something would move it back."

Etheridge also mentioned a "terrible dead fish odor" in some of the rooms and in the hallway.

Any actual apparition, Etheridge said, has appeared only to women and children. A woman who lived in the lighthouse with her children told of

The Ledge Light
PHOTO BY WILLIAM BURROWS OF *THE DAY*, NEW LONDON, CT

being awakened by something at the end of her bed at night. She described it as a man about six foot one, slender, bearded, wearing a rain hat and a slicker. Her children also reported being awakened by a similar figure.

Etheridge spoke of a lighthouse keeper named Randy who said he would be coming down the ladder at various times and would hear someone calling his name. David spoke of experiences with a cold, clammy feeling. He'd be sitting in a room, and all of a sudden it would become icy cold.

One of the favorite stories in the lore of Ernie is that of the doubting fishermen. Etheridge related, "There were some fishermen who came out to visit the lighthouse keepers. They said they didn't believe in Ernie the ghost. Ernie does not like to be spoken against. When they went out to get into their boat, it was adrift away from the lighthouse. They had to launch a small boat from here to bring their own boat back. And these are fishermen who have been tying up boats all their lives. They know how to tie up a boat."

History: Legend has it that Ernie was a lighthouse keeper whose wife had run off with another man. In despair, he cut his throat and threw himself off the upper level of the lighthouse, leaving a trail of blood down the outside of the structure. His body was never found.

Identity of ghost: In December of 1981, a Connecticut psychic, Roger Pile, was asked to come to the lighthouse and look into Ernie. He brought along his wife, Nancy, who acted as the trance medium, and a mediumship student. Pile had been invited by a marine biologist who worked with the Coast Guard and often visited the light, and the biologist and his wife were also present, as well as the two keepers on duty at the time, John Etheridge and David.

Pile considers his work with ghosts "rescues" rather than "exorcisms." He feels that many ghosts are people who have died and who have lost their way in some manner, rather than going on to the higher spiritual planes as they should in the normal course of events. By gently persuading them, in

Roger S. Pile

effect "opening their eyes" to the higher world around them, Pile urges the spirits to give up their obsessive attachment to the physical world they had known. In Pile's lexicon, an "exorcism" just evicts the ghosts from the premises, without giving them a better place to go.

Pile tapes most of his "rescues." In this case, the ghost came in, supposedly speaking through the entranced Nancy Pile. He said that his correct name was John Randolph. Pile asked Randolph if he would like to be helped over, and the ghost said yes, he would. He then spoke as follows through the medium:

"I was not married. It was my intention, but the idea never reached fruition. We had quarreled. She found solace with another and left. I returned here and realized that the fault was mine. I had thrown it all away. I decided that my method of death would not be the obvious, the jump, but would be more apropos to the crime of having said too much. I took my knife, placed it to my throat, and plunged it in, which resulted in much the same thing as the originally rejected leap. But I thought it much more fitting. Imagine my surprise to find that I remained. And since I remained here, I decided to do what I did best. So I have stayed at the light, and I've made myself known and have enjoyed the companionship of the others. I felt that they were my comrades."

Pile responded with the following ritual:

"Feel the warmth envelop you. Notice off to your right there are two pinpoints of light, coming toward you, to help you across. It will be a very joyful, beautiful experience for you." The ghost said he would go with the lights, and Pile said, "Go in joy and love and peace."

Pile says, "Since we did the rescue it has been very quiet out there, except for one instance when it is believed that Ernie returned very briefly."

Personality of ghost: Pleasant, attempting to be helpful, to make itself known.

Witnesses: Many lighthouse keepers, fishermen, and others.

Best time to witness: While Ernie was there, he apparently manifested at various times of the day and night.

Still haunted? Roger Pile says it's not and produces affidavits from recent lighthouse keepers to that effect. An account in the June 28, 1983, issue of the *New Haven Register* concluded:

> "I guess Ernie is gone," said Coast Guard
> Comdr. Edward Wiegand, with a trace of
> amusement. Some of the men stationed there,
> bored with their duty, "have missed Ernie," he
> said.

Data submitted by: Interview with Roger Pile. Also, an article by Pile in the September–October–November 1983 issue of *Psychic Guide* magazine.

11
The Village of Ghostly Sounds

The Lost Settlement of Bara-Hack near Pomfret, Connecticut

Location: Bara-Hack may be reached as follows: Go to Abington Four Corners (in Pomfret township), which is at the intersection of Routes 97 and 44. Go north on Route 97; take a side road to the left and park just beyond Mashomoquet Brook. Follow an overgrown cow path about a quarter of a mile to the lost village. If any problems, inquire at the library or the general store in Abington Four Corners. The area is uninhabited but is private property, so it should be respected.

Description of place: A deserted village deep in the woods in northeastern Connecticut. Its name was Bara-Hack, Welsh for the "breaking of bread." It was founded around 1780 by two families of Welsh descent. The place, unoccupied since the 1890s, consists of cellar holes and a small cemetery amid the forest.

Ghostly manifestations: Almost since its founding, Bara-Hack has had the reputation of being haunted. In 1927, naturalist Odell Shepard wrote about it in his book, *The Harvest of a Quiet Eye* (Houghton-Mifflin, 1927), as follows:

> Here had been their houses, represented today by a few gaping cellar holes out of which tall trees were growing; but here *is* the Village of Voices. For the place is peopled still. . . . Although there is no human habitation for a long distance round about and no one goes there except the few who go to listen, yet there is always a hum and stir of human life. . . . They hear the laughter of children at play, . . . the voices of mothers who have long been dust calling their children into the homes that are now mere holes in the earth. They hear vague snatches of song. . . and the rumble of heavy wagons along an obliterated road. It is as though sounds were able in this place to get round that incomprehensible corner, to pierce that mysterious soundproof wall that we call Time.

One of the most extensive investigations of the phenomena was carried out in 1971 and 1972 by a group of college students and others, led by college student Paul F. Eno. Eno wrote an account of their adventures that appeared in the October and November 1985 issues of *Fate* magazine. They were escorted to the site by a longtime resident of Pomfret, Harry Chase, who often wandered through the woods of Bara-Hack. Chase had taken many photographs that supposedly show whitish blobs, ghostly streaks, and other characteristics attributed to parapsychological effects on film. The accompanying photos were taken by Chase, although these particular pictures seem normal enough, at least to the

The cemetery at Bara-Hack
PHOTO COURTESY OF PAUL F. ENO

untutored eye. According to Eno, during the course of several visits to Bara-Hack, the students' group experienced many strange phenomena. Although the village site is isolated, well over a mile from the nearest house, they report that they constantly heard the barking of dogs, the lowing of cows, and an occasional human voice from the nearby dense woods. They heard the laughter of children and tried to tape it, but the sounds would not record. In the evening, they saw bluish streaks or blobs. Eno wrote in his article:

> For more than seven minutes we watched a bearded face suspended in the air over the cemetery's western wall, while in an elm tree over the northern wall we clearly saw a babylike figure reclining on a branch.

On a later expedition, one member of the group said his hat had been pulled off and lodged in a tree.

Another, a middle-aged man who had come along as an advisor on cameras and other equipment, and who was a definite skeptic, seemed to be physically restrained by some unseen force. He could move, but not in the direction of the cemetery. He said he felt as though possessed.

As they left, Eno wrote, they heard the rumbling of a wagon and the shouts of a team driver, starting in the cemetery area and moving away through dense, impassable woods.

History: According to tradition, one of the founders of Bara-Hack was Obadiah Higginboth (1750–1803), a deserter from the British army. Another, presumably an acquaintance, was Jonathan Randall. They had both lived in Cranston, Rhode Island. Later a small factory was founded, called the Higginbotham Linen Wheels mill, which made spinning wheels and looms as late as the Civil War. The Randalls had slaves, and according to local sources hauntings were first rumored among the slaves, who claimed that at dusk ghosts could be seen reclining in the branches of a certain elm tree in the burial ground. The factory failed after the Civil War, and the farm owners found greener pastures elsewhere. The last interments in the cemetery took place in the 1890s.

Identity of ghosts: Are they ghosts of the former residents of Bara-Hack? Eno leans toward an explanation that the phenomena are simply sounds that have somehow pierced the barrier of time, through a means not yet known by physical scientists.

Personalities of ghosts: There seemed to be a pervasive sadness about the place, according to Eno. No malevolence was apparent, aside from the snatching of one investigator's hat.

Witnesses: Harry Chase; Paul Eno and his group,

which later became known as the Psychical Research Team of New England; Odell Shepard; and many other visitors to the site.

Best time to witness: Phenomena seemed to occur throughout the day and night.

Still haunted? On one of the group's last visits, in the early 1970s, they prayed and felt somehow a lightening of the atmosphere. As far as the Psychical Research Team of New England is aware, no more ghostly streaks and blobs have been spotted, and "extras" no longer appear on photos taken there. And the voices seem to have disappeared.

Investigations The visits of the psychical research group and many other people, some of them presumably psychic.

Data submitted by: Interviews with Paul Eno, plus information from his article in *Fate*.

PHOTO COURTESY OF PAUL F. ENO

What's left of a house in the ghost village.

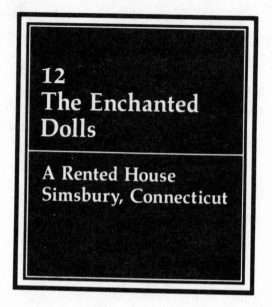

12
The Enchanted Dolls

A Rented House
Simsbury, Connecticut

Location: The address of the Glowackis's former residence is 85B Woodland St., Simsbury. However, the present tenants of the house might not welcome visitors.

Description of place: A yellow duplex house, rented by Richard and Virginia Glowacki from 1977 to 1980, and also occupied by their four young children and friends and relatives.

Ghostly manifestations: The Glowackis lived in the house and had their problems with the supernatural in the late 1970s. One of the first to see an apparition was Richie Glowacki, then nine, who saw a dark, shadowlike image standing at the foot of his bed. It spoke to him, asking where his mother was, then exited through the closed bedroom door. A twenty-nine-year-old cousin of the Glowackis, living with them at the time, began seeing an elderly woman. He said she told him her name was Elizabeth Riley Ames, that she was from Ireland, and that she did not know why she was in the house. He said he also saw an apparition of a one-armed man who wore suspenders over a short-sleeved shirt. He showed Virginia Glowacki and others where the man was standing, and they felt extreme cold there. The young man said he saw the one-armed man toy with a wind chime, and others saw the chimes move, although there was no wind. Several in the house heard moanings and footsteps and saw objects levitate. Richie saw a felt-tip marker go up and come down, as though someone had lifted it. Lights in the basement would repeatedly come on by themselves.

Virginia had a collection of six dolls, which she had arranged on top of a bookcase. One of them, a Spanish dancing doll, seemed to begin to change the expression on its face. Repeatedly, the six dolls would be found facing the wall, instead of toward the room

The Glowacki family at the time of the hauntings.

as they had originally been placed. A picture of Jesus Christ on top of the TV set would constantly turn and face the wall. Once Virginia and her son Jon saw it in the process of turning. Another time, Virginia saw the Spanish dancing doll lift into the air about five inches. It moved through the air above the bookcase, stopping at the opposite end of the book-case. Before it came down, Virginia says, its head turned around on its shoulders so the body was facing forward and the head toward the wall.

At one time, Virginia says, she felt an invisible hand choking her in bed. She prayed, and the hands released their grip. A crucifix came off the wall, and its right arm was broken off when it struck the floor. Another crucifix, on top of the TV set, levitated several times. Doors opened and closed by them-selves; wailing sounds and footsteps on the stairs were heard. And various objects, such as money, a box of nails, a gun and its shells, would disappear. If within some twenty minutes they were not found where they had been, they were never seen again.

History: The house, large, set back from the street, was built in the nineteenth century and may have been expanded from a log cabin. Investigations by the Glowackis and by psychic researchers turned up nothing unusual in its history, except perhaps that at one time it had been used as a halfway house for delinquent boys.

Identity of ghosts: A well-known parapsycholo-gist, Boyce Batey, of a nearby suburb of Hartford, made an investigation over a period of some six months. Working with him was Dr. Brian Riley, also a recognized parapsychologist who lived in the area. Riley, an Englishman, is a nuclear scientist; Batey is an executive with a large insurance company. At one point, they brought a nationally known trance me-

Boyce Batey,
parapsychologist

dium, Paul Solomon, of Virginia Beach, Virginia, into the house. While in a trance, Solomon said that a recently deceased relative of Virginia's had come into the house because she loved Virginia and the children but felt rejected by them. From Solomon's description, Virginia said this was her cousin, a woman who was physically deformed and mentally retarded. She had died shortly before, while Virginia had been recovering from an operation. Virginia had left her bed to go to the funeral home to view the body but had not gone to the funeral. Soon Virginia began to have dreams about this woman. She asked another relative about this, who said this was the dead woman's way of communicating from the other side. "I don't want anyone communicating with me like that," Virginia had exclaimed. "Let her go and communicate with someone else!" The following night the lights in the basement went on, and they continued going on for months. And the dolls started moving.

Solomon and the parapsychologists felt that the deceased woman was doing this. The lights meant, "Notice me!" The turning of the dolls and the picture of Jesus toward the wall meant symbolically, "You're turning your backs on me!" Solomon felt that the elderly woman and the one-armed man had been attracted into the house by the state of consciousness of the dead relative's spirit. Both crucifixes had their right arms broken off when they fell. The one-armed man had lost his right arm, and it was felt by the parapsychologists that this was the ghost's way of communicating his presence symbolically.

Personalities of ghosts: It was felt they were the typical souls who had been confused by death, had lost their way, and were trying to communicate with people on the physical plane.

Witnesses: Many people who lived in the house, as well as visitors and investigators.

Best time to witness: The Glowacki family has moved, and there are not known to be further manifestations in the Simsbury house.

Still haunted? Possibly. The Glowackis moved to a nearby town, and some disturbances followed them for a while. In the Simsbury house, Solomon invoked a blessing asking the ghosts to leave. He also recommended the placing of salt around the lintels of all the doors. This did not seem to have a noticeable effect. Other groups of parapsychologists and psychics came in and urged the ghosts to pass on to a more appropriate afterlife, but the efforts did not seem to be successful. A Roman Catholic priest gave the house blessings, and on another occasion a Mass was said, but the manifestations continued.

Investigations: Many teams of parapsychologists and psychics attempted to analyze the problem and rid the house of disturbances.

Data submitted by: Virginia Glowacki, particularly in an article in *Fate* magazine, issue of December 1979, by Boyce Batey, and by other members of the Glowacki family.

13
The Tippling Ghost and the Hanged Slave Raider

The Governor's House
Dover, Delaware

Location: The Governor's House is located in Dover at 151 Kings Highway.

Description of place: A beautiful old mansion, built in 1790 and considered one of the finest examples of Federal architecture now standing. A three-story building, it is constructed of mauve, weather-mellowed bricks and features large, white-shuttered windows, and a graceful fanlight. It nestles, seemingly peacefully, amid towering pines, crepe myrtles, and trim English boxwoods. The house is called Woodburn.

Ghostly manifestations: Tradition has it that The Governor's House has no less than four ghosts. Two have been seen in times long past; one is reputed to rattle chains on the grounds; another has been known to materialize only once, in the 1940s.

The first is perhaps the most colorful, having a reputation as a wine bibber. Early owners of the house, it is said, routinely filled decanters for the ghost, who, without fail, would have them emptied by morning. One servant swore he actually saw the ghost sitting in the dining room, slowly sipping wine, an old man in powdered wig and Colonial dress. In modern times, the last of Woodburn's private owners, Dr. Frank Hall, used to say that on more than one occasion he would discover a bottle of wine mysteriously emptied.

However, the wino ghost is not believed to have been the first at Woodburn. One who is nicknamed

The Governor's House

the "Colonel" reportedly appeared in 1805 when a family named Bates lived there. They were playing host to an itinerant evangelist named Lorenzo Dow, who was holding a series of revival meetings in Dover. According to legend, coming down to breakfast one morning, Dow passed in the upstairs hall a courtly old man whom he had not seen before. When he mentioned this added starter for breakfast, his hosts were startled, since Dow was their lone guest.

However, when he described the old man, Mrs. Dow said it sounded as if he looked like her father, who had died in the house. Another theory is that the "Colonel" is the ghost of a Revolutionary War colonel who died at Woodburn while the place was being used as a veterans' hospital shortly after the war.

The noisiest ghost is the chain rattler. He is reputed to be a slave kidnapper. Woodburn was once a stop in the Underground Railroad, and a group of raiders attacked the place. They were driven off by forces led by a Quaker named Daniel Cowgill, who then owned the house. This particular raider supposedly hid in a gnarled old poplar tree and, according to one version of the story, accidentally hanged himself. Whether he was hanged accidentally or on purpose, the clanging of chains is purported to well up out of the hollow of the ancient tree. Moans are said to be audible, too, especially when the wind is high and the moon is bright. These are traditionally considered to be cries of slaves who were killed or captured at Woodburn.

The fourth ghost is a little girl wearing a red-checked gingham dress. An apparition of such a child was reportedly seen playing by the pool in the garden, but her identity is a mystery. A footnote to this anecdote is a report stemming from the 1985 inauguration party of the current governor of Delaware, Michael N. Castle. A number of women guests said they were aware of tuggings at their skirts, the way a child would tug.

History: The house was built in 1790 by John Hillyard on a tract of land given to his great-grandfather by William Penn. It was lived in by many families over the years. In 1966, the state bought the place and renovated it as Delaware's first official executive mansion.

Identity of ghosts: According to legend, the wine bibber, the "Colonel," the slave raider, the little girl, and possibly fugitive slaves.

Personalities of ghosts: There have never been any reports of malevolence.

Witnesses: A variety of people who have lived in, worked in, and visited the mansion.

Best time to witness: Most, although not all, phenomena seem to occur at night. The mansion is open to visitors on Saturdays from 2:30 to 4:30 P.M. Special group tours at other times may be arranged.

Still haunted? Some of the reports are relatively recent.

Investigations: In May 1985, some sixth-grade students in the gifted and talented program at Warner Elementary School in Wilmington were reading about ghosts. They wrote to Governor Castle, asking if they could make an investigation of Woodburn, and he assented. The students—Holly Forbis, Taryn Morrow, and Faith Truman—spent a night in the mansion, accompanied by their teacher, Connie Malin. They brought along a tape recorder, a video camera, a large thermometer, and a Ouija board. They came loaded for ghosts, but they were anything but credulous.

"The girls were not willing to believe," says Ms. Malin, "that these things did not have scientific explanations. They were hunting for the scientific truth behind this. They weren't willing to accept that it was just spiritual phenomena or anything of that nature." However, Ms. Malin says, "Strange things happened to our equipment. A lot of things malfunctioned, and we don't know why."

Although the tape recorder was relatively new and had been tested, parts of the tape seemed to have been erased; there was nothing on it.

"My husband is a science teacher," Ms. Malin says, "and he gave us a very large laboratory thermometer. We had it set up in a room downstairs, on the floor. The girls were working the Ouija board there. I went upstairs; I let them do their thing. One of them came upstairs frightened and told me it had gotten very cold in the room downstairs. I went down, and it was very, very cold. The temperature on the thermometer remained constant, yet it seemed freezing in the room. It didn't register on the thermometer."

The camera, it turned out, reproduced objects clearly, but people were transparent. "The girls," says Ms. Malin, "looked like they were ghosts."

Data submitted by: Shirley Bailey and Natalie Loughran of The Governor's House staff, Jeffry Welsh of the governor's staff, and Connie Malin. Material used from the book *The Haunting of America* (Houghton-Mifflin, 1973), by Jean Anderson, and from an article in the April 24, 1966, issue of *The Sunday Bulletin Magazine*.

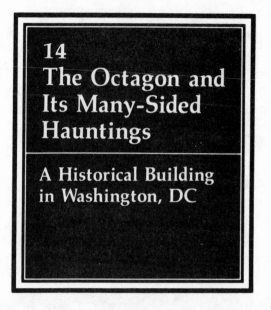

**14
The Octagon and
Its Many-Sided
Hauntings**

A Historical Building
in Washington, DC

Location: The Octagon is at 1799 New York Avenue,
NW, in Washington.

Description of place: This landmark of architecture in the nation's capital has since 1899 been
headquarters for the American Institute of Architecture. Although called "The Octagon," it is actually
six-sided. The four-story structure, a classic example
of the American Federal style of architecture, was
built from 1798 to 1800 at the corner of New York
Avenue and 18th Street, two blocks from the White
House. The unusual shape of the building was pre-
scribed by the sharp angle of the intersection of the
two thoroughfares. The building now houses a museum of architecture, open to the public.

Ghostly manifestations: Revenants—the rather
elegant term The Octagon seems to favor in referring to its ghosts—have been part of the building's
history from its early days. In fact, The Octagon
provides researchers with some twenty pages of

typewritten material on such matters, much of it a study done in 1982 by Alicia Clarke as part of the George Washington University Museum Studies Program. The folklore is broken down into such categories as The Bells, The Quadroon, The Whipping, The Staircase, Dolley Madison, The Man in Black, and Miscellaneous Revenant Activity, as well as new legends. Some of the material is as follows:

The Bells

An excerpt from a family memorate by Virginia Tayloe Lewis, a granddaughter of the builder of The Octagon, Col. John Tayloe III, states: "The [service] bells rang for a long time after my Grandfather

The Octagon—a contemporary photo.

Tayloe's death, and everyone said the house was haunted; the wires were cut and still they rang. . . . Our dining room servant would come upstairs to ask if anyone rang the bell, and no one had."

By 1889 the bell ringers had been given an identity, as in this account: "The story goes that the spirits of the slaves whom death released from their chains visit the old home and announce their coming by the ringing of the bells."

In 1952, Jacqueline Bouvier wrote in an unpublished manuscript that Mrs. John Tayloe had the bell wires cut after her husband's death in 1828 because she felt "that enemies were trying to drive her from the house."

Another account attributes the bell-ringing to a gambler who with his retinue of women occupied the upper floors of the then-decaying mansion. One night he was assaulted by a hard-drinking farmer. He supposedly grabbed a bellpull to steady himself as he reached for his gun, but the farmer had the drop on him and fired his own gun. Thus ended one more gambler and entered one more ghost. This version holds that the ghost of the gambler is still clutching the bellpull while he reaches for his gun.

The Quadroon

This person, a female slave sometimes referred to as an octoroon, was according to legend a favorite of Colonel Tayloe. A variety of versions of the story, one juicier than the next, picture Tayloe as jealous of a friend, an English army officer, sometimes said to be a navy officer, over the lissome lass. Varying accounts have Tayloe killing the officer, the officer killing the woman, the crazed officer committing suicide by leaping off a top landing to the stone floor below, the finding of the officer's body in a closet, the slave girl's being sealed in a closet, the girl's committing suicide, and various combinations of the above. Bouvier, in her essay of 1952, identifies the killer of the English officer as "one of the Tayloe boys, a young blood with his father's passion for horses and a few passions of his own for gambling and wenching." In any case, any or all of the actors in this historical melodrama have been suspected at one time or another of roaming the building.

The Whipping

Another Octagon legend is built around a cruel slave owner during the early part of the 1800s who whipped or starved slaves to death in the house. One particularly colorful version cites the ghost of a jockey who made the mistake of throwing a race while astride a horse owned by one of the masters of the Octagon and was whipped to death for his duplicity.

The Staircase

The Octagon has two staircases, the main one of which spirals up three floors, an irresistible temptation for any imaginative young woman who would like to become a romantic revenant. At least three young women are given credit for haunting the Octagon because of marriage problems. One is identified as Colonel Tayloe's eldest daughter, who jumped or fell two flights after her father supposedly refused to let her marry an Englishman. Another is the beautiful slave girl we have already met, who in this version was thrown from the top of the spiral staircase by the same English naval officer, whom in this account she refused to marry. A very bad loser, in this tale, he then jumped after her. And finally, we come to the case of Tayloe's second daughter, Betty. Tayloe, said to be a difficult parent, opposed her contemplated match also. According to a 1969 article by Jacqueline Lawrence in the *Washington Post*, "In the course of a bitter argument he pushed the girl away from him; she fell over . . . the staircase, breaking her neck on the floor below." Then again, some say she dived head first; still others say she merely tripped over a cat.

Dolley Madison

When the British burned the White House in 1814, President James Madison lived for a time in The Octagon, where his First Lady, the redoubtable Dolley, made the place the center of Washington revelry. Dolley is said to haunt The Octagon, which is only fair, since she is also said to haunt several other buildings in Washington. At midnight she is said to hold court again, to the sound of silver and the clink of glasses. According to legend, Dolley has been sighted several times, and the smell of lilacs is often noticeable when she is about. Aaron Burr, a friend of Dolley's, has also been a popular apparition at the Octagon.

The Man in Black

A modern legend derives from a doctor who was summoned to the Octagon in the 1940s by a caretaker, James Cyprus, to treat Cyprus's ailing wife. The doctor asked Cyprus if there was a costume party going on. There wasn't. The doctor then told of encountering on the stairs just a few moments before, a man dressed in a military uniform of the 1800s.

Miscellaneous Revenant Activity

People who work at The Octagon seem to be still hearing and seeing things. In an interview recorded in 1982, a former curator, Allison MacTavish, tells of a number of instances. They involve such things as a ghostly woman's voice, a guttural moan; the rustling of silk skirts; a white specter. The most interesting accounts, said MacTavish, come from the maintenance men, each of whom has heard or seen something. In the late 1970s, Walter Rush, working late at night, told of seeing a man in late-nineteenth-century black clothing, with a tall hat, walk up the stairs past him, tip the hat, continue on, and disappear. In 1981, another maintenance man told substantially the same story. A young woman employee tells of a dog who appeared to be terrified when taken down to the basement. And Helen Dawes, a hostess who was leading a group of tourists through the house, tells of seeing something white disappear as she entered a room.

History: The builder of the house, Colonel Tayloe, was a rich Virginia plantation owner who is said to have built the house at the suggestion of his friend, President George Washington. The extraordinary building was designed by Dr. William Thornton, who was also an architect of the United States Capitol. Among visitors to the house have been Thomas Jefferson, James Monroe, John Adams, Andrew Jackson, Stephen Decatur, Daniel Webster, Henry Clay, the Marquis de Lafayette, and John Calhoun. The Tayloe family lived in the house until 1855. Other families lived there afterward, then it served as a girls' school and later as the United States Hydrographic Office. In 1899, it was taken over by the American Institute of Architects, which renovated the deteriorated building.

Identity of ghosts: Readers are invited to make their choices from the foregoing nominations.

Personalities of ghosts: No violence or other unpleasantness seems to have occurred.

Witnesses: Seemingly a significant proportion of

people who have lived in, worked in, or visited the house.

Best time to witness: Happenings seem to occur at various times of the day and night.

Still haunted? Many of the incidents reported are quite recent, although the present staff denies awareness of any unusual events.

Investigations: The administration of The Octagon says there have been no formal psychic inquiries.

15
The Haunted Powder Room

Ashley's Restaurant
Rockledge, Florida

Location: Ashley's Restaurant is at 1609 South U.S. Route 1, Rockledge.

Description of place: A two-story restaurant, dating from the late 1920s, on U.S. 1, a busy four-lane highway. The exterior is constructed of wood and stucco, with huge cypress doors.

Ghostly manifestations: A variety of parapsychological incidents have been reported in this restaurant for many years. A number of psychics have visited the place—some many times—and declared that the building is host to several entities. Some of the most bizarre incidents have taken place in the ladies' room.

A prime witness is Judi Cowles, who was manager of the restaurant from 1979 to 1984. One night after closing she went into the ladies' room to check it out. There are two stalls. She was using the facilities herself when she happened to note an unusual pair of legs and feet under the opening to the other stall.

They were wearing high-heeled, high-button boots—quite uncontemporary. When she came out of her stall, the door to the other stall was open and no one was there, although she did not hear anyone leave, a series of sounds that would have been unmissable.

Malcolm Denemark, a photographer for Florida Today, *took this photo inside Ashley's Restaurant to accompany an article on the place's ghosts. When he processed the film, he says, he was startled to note the figure of a man in dark pants and white shirt, possibly a waiter's or busboy's uniform. Denemark says: "When I took the photo from the second floor balcony, there was no one in the area. Please note the absence or lack of shadows from the 'person' in the photo."*

The ladies' room has two doors. One leads in from the lobby of the restaurant. Then there is a short corridor to an inner door. Several women—both waitresses and customers—have reported a choking sensation while traversing the little corridor. Judi says that one night after closing she went in to check the place and turn off the lights. As she was coming out, she found herself immobilized in the corridor. "I put up my hand to hit the outer door," she says, "and my hand just would not hit the door. I was stuck. I tried hard, and all of a sudden the door flew open and I went plunging out, landing on the floor in the lobby."

A number of women have reported seeing the image of a young woman, wearing 1920s clothing, in the mirror of the ladies' room. And the water in the wash basins sometimes comes on unexplainably.

But the ladies' room does not have exclusive rights to the folklore of the restaurant. Things seem to happen all over the place. There is a stairway where people often feel as though they are being bumped or pushed. Judi Cowles says quite a number of husbands over the years have been admonished by their wives to stop shoving on this stairway. Jean Stevens, a psychic who has visited the restaurant many times, tells of a vision she experienced, and which she says other psychics have, too. She says she saw a man being dragged down this stairway by two law enforcement officers and being thrown into a police car. A witness to this was the man's teenage daughter, who was screaming uncontrollably. The girl, the psychic said, was possibly retarded. This violent incident, Jean Stevens says, is what is causing the turbulence experienced by some people on this spot. "That energy is there," she says. "Traumatic events and tremendously emotional moments can leave a residue, and if people are sensitive or psychic they can pick up on those incidents."

The place has the usual manifestations of a haunted restaurant. Glasses and dishes fall and break, untouched by human hands—or at least that's what the waitresses, bartenders, and buspersons insist. And the sneeze guard—the glass contraption that hangs over the salad bar in many restaurants—sometimes starts swinging.

Many people tell of hearing whispering in the restaurant, usually when the place is closed. Judi Cowles tells of experiencing this, and so do other members of the staff. In 1982, reporter Billie Cox of a local newspaper, *Florida Today*, researched the restaurant over a period of several months. He mentions picking up whispers on his tape recorder. He also speaks of a "loud, angry buzz" recorded on the tape while he was traversing the stairway where people feel they're getting shoved.

"Everybody knows this place is haunted," Billie says. He interviewed many policemen; the Rockledge police station is across the highway from the restaurant. The police tell of burglar alarms going off with no forcible entry, of lights going on and off inexplicably, of at least one incident of a very loud female scream coming from the place in the dead of night. The officers often hide out in the restaurant's parking lot while watching for speeders, and this must be very unsettling for them.

History: The place was built in the late twenties and has had many owners. Its name keeps changing. Cox recalls some of the names, such as the Loose Caboose, the Mad Duchess, the Sparrow Hawk, Gentleman Jim's. It has been known as Ashley's Restaurant for the past couple of years. This constant turnover bemuses Cox. "The place has an optimum location," he says. "It's on U.S. 1 and it's a stone's throw from the intersection of another four-laner. It's a premium location."

Jean Stevens suspects there is something ominous about the site itself, which rubs off on the restaurant. "I think that's the reason it changes hands constantly," she says. "Owners don't last there." She said that a man told Judi Cowles that he had been in the construction crew when the building was put up. When it was almost finished, a fire broke out for no apparent reason. All of the glass in the bar area— mirrors and drinking glasses—shattered. Repairs were made, and the restaurant opened. "I think," Jean says, "that there are some places that are prone to, and actually attract, this kind of activity, and the land this building is on is one of them."

Identity of ghosts: The powder room ghost is believed to be a young woman named Ethel Allen, who came to grief one night about fifty years ago. She was last seen at the restaurant. Her body was found mutilated and burned, on the banks of the Indian River, nearby. She was identified by a tattoo on her thigh, a rose with a noose around it. No one was ever arrested. On one of her visits, Jean Stevens went into a trance and tells of a very disquieting experience. "I saw a murder take place, very clearly," she says. "I saw the death take place in an area that that storage room is now. [There is a storage room in the building that somehow makes people nervous.] I saw a man chase a woman down the stairs. She was bleeding. He had a knife. The place is now a dead end, a service area, and I wondered why she would flee this way. Later on we found out that this was where the front door of the building used to be. She was trying to get out. He caught up to her, put both hands on her shoulders, shoved her to the floor, and finished the murder there. They were dressed in clothing of the late twenties or early thirties." This, Jean says, was Ethel Allen, and she suspects it is her ghost that is haunting the ladies' room. Jean says she knows who the murderer was but cannot reveal it. He is now dead, but his family is still in the area.

Another entity, Jean says, is a little girl—about

Ashley's Restaurant

six—who was killed in an automobile accident on U.S. 1 just outside the restaurant. She died on the road, according to the psychic, but her spirit wandered into the restaurant, possibly attracted by the other spirits that were there. The girl has been seen by a number of psychics.

When Billie Cox was doing his story, he took with him one of the paper's photographers, Malcolm Denemark. Denemark took a number of photos inside the restaurant. On one was a man in dark pants and a white coat who, Denemark says, was not there when he took the picture. In addition, the figure casts no shadow. Later, in a test, he had a person stand in the same place to see if he would cast a shadow, and he did. Denemark says the camera would not work right after his second expedition to the place. The film would constantly be scratched.

Jean Stevens suspects the image is that of an elderly man who did odd jobs at the restaurant at one time. He was given a room upstairs, where he lived. "I think his presence in the photo is a statement," Jean says. "He's saying, 'This is my place.' "

One story that might point to this entity is told about a woman customer who gave her order to an elderly waiter, who took it and departed. When her meal was not forthcoming, she complained and was told the restaurant had no old waiters.

Personalities of ghosts: No one has ever been injured, but some people might well think they have been harassed.

Witnesses: Many staff, customers, and investigators at the restaurant.

Best time to witness: Judi Cowles says things seem to happen predominantly at night or early in the morning, possibly because they are quiet hours in a restaurant and incidents are more readily observable.

Still haunted? Psychics have made efforts to calm the place down, and it seems to have quieted somewhat.

Investigations: Billie Cox worked with two psychics—Jean Stevens and Rose Joya—during his investigation of the place. Many other psychics have visited the place. For a while one worked with the staff once a week after closing, a fringe benefit not offered by many restaurants.

Data submitted by: Billy Cox; Judi Cowles; Jean Stevens; Malcolm Denemark; Greg Parker, present owner of Ashley's Restaurant; the Rockledge police. Article by Nancy Osborn in *Florida Style*, issue of summer 1984.

**16
The Doctor Who
Killed Himself
and Returned To
His Aunt's House**

Atlanta, Georgia

Location: Mrs. Milam's address is 4065 Pierce Rd.,
College Park, GA. It would be advisable to write in
advance to inquire if she would welcome visitors.

Description of place: The house was built in the
late 1970s. Its style is Mediterranean, its exterior
apricot stucco. It has two stories, six bedrooms. It
was designed and built by Frances Milam, a successful Atlanta builder. Divorced, her son grown, she
lives there alone.

Ghostly manifestations: In 1983, Mrs. Milam's
nephew, Dr. Bob Mabry, committed suicide by shotgun. Within a day or two, she says, he was in touch
with her. "I could feel him like tapping on my
shoulder," she says, "saying to pick up my pen and
write." Mrs. Milam had been a student of Patricia
Hayes, a well-known psychic who trains people in
parapsychology, and she knew about automatic writing, although she had never done it.

She had been close to Mabry and had thought his

100 The Ghostly Register

life was going well. "We don't know why he committed suicide," she says. "It was a real mystery to all of us."

Mrs. Milam picked up her pen and wrote, with Mabry supposedly guiding her. She wrote letters to about ten people, only two or three of whom she knew. He put things into each message that only that particular person would know. "I typed them," she says, "and sent them to Florida with his former wife. The people were very skeptical when I told them how the messages had come about, but when they read the letters they found there was a message in there for each of them that was just characteristic to them, things no one else would know about, so they had to believe what had happened."

Mabry told her he had tried to approach two or three other people but had not been able to get through to them. Mrs. Milam was open to him. Most of the activity takes place in an office off her bedroom. "Sometimes I'll come in at night," Mrs. Milam says, "and if I don't take time to recognize him, directly behind my bed it's like somebody is just sort of pecking on the wall. I'll say, 'Yes, I know you're around. Are you willing to write tonight?' "

There are various other parapsychological happenings, observed by Mrs. Milam and sometimes by her son and his wife. "I'll be upstairs," she says, "and you'll hear something fall downstairs, and you'll go downstairs, and there's nothing out of place." Sometimes objects are moved mysteriously.

According to Mrs. Milam, the chief subject of her nephew's correspondence is suicide. "He says suicide is not an ending," Mrs. Milam says. "It's just a continuation of life. He says he realized that the instant he pulled the trigger. He advises very definitely against suicide. He wants particularly to reach young people who think by committing suicide they're ending their lives. He wants them to know that they still will have the same problems, for the soul is eternal."

Mrs. Milam says she has written about twenty-five pages with her nephew. Now, she says, she has also had other spirits coming through her through her automatic writing, people she doesn't know.

History: Mabry's mother had died in his youth. Mrs. Milam says, "I was his second mother." Mabry was thirty-two when he killed himself. He was engaged in a successful medical practice in Florida, specializing in emergency medicine. He had problems with his contemporaries, Mrs. Milam says, which she attributes to his brilliance. "He had a hard time relating sometimes," she says. He was divorced, but the divorce had been five years before, and Mrs. Milam does not think this was a factor in the suicide.

Identity of ghost: Supposedly Dr. Bob Mabry.

Personality of ghost: Mrs. Milam says, "He's a very loving person, so I have no fear about his being in the house here."

Witnesses: Frances Milam and occasionally her son and his wife.

Best time to witness: The manifestations happen when Mrs. Milam is at home, usually in the evenings or on weekends.

Still haunted? Yes.

Investigations: Patricia Hayes and several of her students have visited the house a number of times and, Mrs. Hayes says, are always aware of energy there. Her assessment of the situation is as follows: "He wants to be acknowledged, and he also wants to get some of his thoughts on suicide across. It's a comfortable environment, he had good feelings with the person [Mrs. Milam], and he wants to stay close to this physical vibration simply because that's what he's writing about."

Data submitted by: Frances Milam, Patricia Hayes.

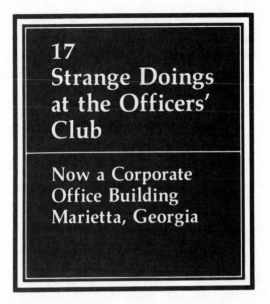

**17
Strange Doings
at the Officers'
Club**

Now a Corporate
Office Building
Marietta, Georgia

Location: The office building, although currently used by a private corporation, is located on General Road on the grouds of Dobbins Air Force Base in Marietta, and is not accessible to the public.

Description of place: This three-story wood and brick building, built in the early 1800s, originally was a private home. In modern times it became an officers' club for Dobbins Air Force Base. In more recent years, it has been used as an office building by the aircraft company Lockheed Corporation.

Ghostly manifestations: The building has long had a reputation for being haunted, and the sightings and other phenomena seem to be continuing. In 1984, Nick Joiner, a Lockheed employee, was performing his early-morning duty of unlocking the front door of the old officers' club when he says he saw an image at the foot of some stairs. "It was a blonde woman in her late twenties," he says. "She paused at the foot of the stairs and then started to float upward." According to an October 1984 article by John Rossino, in the Lockheed local publication, *Southern Star*, Joiner is one of about twenty Lockheed and Air Force personnel to have had strange experiences in the old house.

One of the choice stories, about ten years old, was related by Geneva Perry, now retired, who was a cashier at the club at the time of her encounter. She was working alone on a Saturday morning, she says, when she heard the front door of the building open and close. She left her office to see who had come in, but there was no one there. She went back to her desk and continued to work. Soon after, she says, she heard footsteps. Looking up, she saw an elderly couple standing in the doorway of her office. She was aware immediately, she says, that they were not of this world. They stayed there several minutes, she says, then left the room.

The most recent manager of the club, Joe Goss, testifies that one day when he was supposedly alone in the building he heard footsteps upstairs. "I ran

PHOTO BY JOHN ROSSINO

The former Officers' Club on Dobbins Air Force Base.

upstairs to see who was there," he says, "but there was no one." Air Force security personnel Art Cleveland and Earl Martin have had the duty of checking on the building after closing hours. "The house is unbelievable," Cleveland says. "Lights we know we turned off would be on again when we passed by on rounds." Martin says, "Once I drove by and saw an upstairs window that I knew to be nailed shut, open. The light was on in the room when I got upstairs, but there was no one present, and the window was still open."

Not long ago, a group of people working in the kitchen on the first floor heard what sounded like furniture being moved upstairs. When they went upstairs, they found the furniture moved, but there was no one there. Also, toilets are sometimes flushed by an unseen hand.

History: In its early days, according to Air Force records, the house was known as Cottage Hill, and later as the Gardner place. The first record of the place shows its sale from the original owner in 1862. Legend has it that the house was spared in Sherman's March to the Sea during the Civil War because an Englishman living there at the time had the forethought to hang out an English flag. Sherman apparently figured it didn't make sense to ask for trouble and left the house alone. However, bombs were bursting all about, and two servants are reputed to have been killed when a storage building close to the house was hit. The Englishman committed suicide around 1880, giving further possible fuel for ghostly phenomena.

Identity of ghosts: No one seems to have an inkling.

Personality of ghosts: No one seems to have been harmed, only titillated and/or scared.

Witnesses: Nick Joiner, Joe Goss, Art Cleveland, Earl Martin, Geneva Perry, and a number of other Air Force and Lockheed people.

Best time to witness: Things seem to happen around the clock.

Still haunted? Probably.

Investigations: No formal investigations have been undertaken.

Data submitted by: Interview with John Rossino, and use of his article in *Southern Star*.

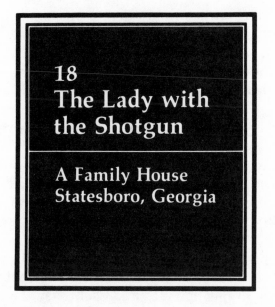

18
The Lady with the Shotgun

A Family House
Statesboro, Georgia

Location: The address of the house is 9 Cetterower St., Statesboro. However, Mrs. Hollingsworth says she does not think the new owners would welcome visitors.

Description of place: A one-story, white frame house, built in the 1930s, on a street in Statesboro.

Ghostly manifestations: In the early 1970s, Stothard Hollingsworth, a roofing contractor, and his wife, Mary Ann, moved into the house, then about forty years old, with their three teenage daughters. Before long, Mrs. Hollingsworth began seeing a woman with long hair, wearing a long, white gown that seemed to date from the past century. All the other people in the family also saw this woman several times. "My husband saw her one night," Mrs. Hollingsworth says, "standing by the side of my bed staring down at me. He said it scared him so badly that he couldn't move. He says she just stood there for a while, then turned and walked away toward the living room."

The woman seemed to hang out mostly in the living room. The Hollingsworths thought that if they added to the original parts of the house perhaps the ghost would not invade the new territory, but they quickly found that it did. One night, Mrs. Hollingsworth says, she woke up to find the barrel of a shotgun touching her nose. The ghost was holding it, but the gun seemed very real. "I had never smelled a gun barrel," Mrs. Hollingsworth says, "so I didn't know how they smelled, but it was so real I could smell this one. It smelled like burnt firecrackers, and I can still smell it. It scared me very much because I thought we were being robbed and shot. Then I saw her turn and walk away. I woke my husband up, and I just sat on the side of the bed, trembling all over. He looked all over the house, and there was no one there except the family. And all the doors were locked." Sometimes at night, Mrs. Hollingsworth says, as they lay in bed they would hear footsteps walking from one end of the house to the other.

History: The Hollingsworths bought the house from an elderly widow (not the ghost). They lived there for five years, then sold it and moved to another house in town. The Hollingsworths know nothing further about the history of the house.

Identity of ghost: Unknown. Mrs. Hollingsworth says none of the neighbors had any idea who it could have been.

Personality of ghost: Not particularly hostile, except for her one act of gunslinging.

Witnesses: The Hollingsworths and their three daughters.

Best time to witness: The ghost was seen only at night.

Still haunted? Mrs. Hollingsworth says she doesn't know and plans no efforts to find out.

Investigations: None known.

Data submitted by: Mary Ann Hollingsworth.

19
The Ghost of the Mummified Rat

An Old Downtown
Building
Genesee, Idaho

Location: The address of the building is 206 Walnut St., Genesee. Before visiting, it might be advisable to get permission from the present owner, Heidi Linehan, Sara Joyce's daughter. Ms. Linehan's address is Route #1, Genesee, Idaho 83832.

Description of place: This is a building on the main street in Genesee, a town of some eight hundred people in the farmland of northern Idaho. It was built in the 1880s, first the central part and over the years two wing sections. It is constructed of brick, and the front has large windows all the way across. There is one story and no basement.

Ghostly manifestations: In 1974, Sara Joyce came from Pocatello, the second-largest city in Idaho, and bought the building from people who had lived in one of the wings for many years. The middle section had served as a storage place for construction equipment belonging to these people. It also housed an extensive collection of rocks, crystals, and gemstones, an interest of the former owner, as well as many Indian artifacts, which he collected. Ms. Joyce came to the area because her son, Bill Coccia, had been attending the University of Idaho in Moscow, fourteen miles away. Also with her was her daughter, Heidi Coccia, and baby granddaughter, Solara Fern. A fact that may be pertinent to this account is that Sara is a very psychic person who has had parapsychological experiences much of her life. "I have an Indian heritage," she says. "My father's mother was Indian. The psychic orientation is quite

Sara claims that she never felt anything or heard noises in this part of the building, above the construction business office.

All of the hauntings took place in this area of the building.

The museum was in the middle section of the building.

Sara Joyce lived in this section of the building.

Sara Joyce's building

strong, or at least I pick up on it every so often very strongly." She wrote this account of her experiences:

"The first thing we noticed, during both the day and night, was the sound of doors opening and footsteps. I was forever going through the entire building, looking for intruders, checking all the doors, making certain they were closed or locked. There were other things, like waking up at night to feel the presence of someone in the room, seeing movements out of the corner of my eye, feeling like someone was passing me in the hallways.

"My son was soon leaving for a job in Hawaii, and before he left he put in a very secure lock system that gave us assurance that we would be safe. Not long after he left, my daughter, who had met a young Genesee farmer, married him, and she and her little girl went to live on his farm. This now left me alone in the building. I wasn't really afraid to be alone there. I had a very comfortable living space in the east third of the building. During the two years there with my daughter we had become quite accustomed to the noises. We laughed and joked about the ghosts, made all manner of reference to their possible personalities, gave them names like Jasper and Earl, and generally accepted them as harmless. It seemed that the more active the ghosts became, the more interested I became in them. I wanted to understand what all this was and how it could be that this building could be so thick with them. I have chosen to tell about two of my own experiences that seemed more dramatic and extradimensional. As follows:

"One evening as I was preparing to go to bed

[the bedroom was a little upstairs room up over the kitchen], I heard the most tremendous racket going on in the museum part of the building. I was certain that I had locked all doors earlier, but here was a huge, noisy, rushing racket going on, like someone shoving furniture or heavy equipment back and forth across the room. I felt my heart beating; I had never really felt fear there before. I called out, 'Who is there?' I also propped a chair up against the connecting door to the museum. I couldn't believe my ears—this wasn't a little racket; this was a loud, angry racket. I finally called my daughter on the phone. She said, 'Call the police.' I didn't want to call the police, but soon decided to do it. The minute I called them and hung up the phone, the noise stopped. Not a sound could be heard. Three policemen came; they went through the entire place, checked every room, every window and door, and also searched the surrounding area of the building, finding nothing suspicious or out of place. I thanked them for their trouble, and they left. They had not been gone for five minutes when the racket began again, louder and more insistent than before. I couldn't believe this. . . . I wasn't really afraid now; I just thought, this is the strangest thing I have ever heard of. I sat up the entire night, pondering what it could be, and the noise kept going. Every so often I called out, 'Who is in there?'

"Along about early morning the noise quieted, finally stopped altogether. I began to feel fairly calm and also very tired. As it was now almost morning, I decided to go upstairs and lie down. As all was quiet and dawn approaching, I was almost ready to close my eyes, when all of a sudden I looked up to see a man standing in the doorway of my bedroom. This was an old man, tall, thin, bathed in a sort of gray-blue light, a transparency about him but still a recognizable person. My entire body came to alert. I sat up and looked at him. I saw him raise his left arm and throw something at me. It was lightning-quick. Something hit me smack in the chest. Sparks flew into the air. I screamed out. But he still stood there looking at me, his eyes saying, 'Do you see me? Do you see me?' I yelled back, 'I see you! I see you!' At which time he faded away, leaving me in a state of wonderment about him and why he put on such a display for me. I still think of this man, and I still wonder about him.

"One morning early, I came down the stairs, turned the corner into the kitchen doorway, and quick as lightning something jumped up onto my arm. It was a rat! A huge, silvery, shiny, golden, transparent rat. It had an abundance of hair, and I felt its claws on my skin as it climbed up my arm. When I screamed, it disappeared. I stood on the spot several minutes in disbelief. How could this have been? I began to doubt whether I had really seen it, looking at my arm to see if there were marks on my skin. There were no visual marks, but I could still feel the sensation of claws pricking my skin.

"After I had moved out of the building to a house in Genesee, a very calm and quiet house, so far completely free of noises and presences, my son Bill had returned from Hawaii and had moved into the old apartment to do some remodeling and restructuring of the space. When he lifted up some of the floor boards in the kitchen under the sink, there lay a huge rat mummy, complete with a quantity of hair and a long, bushy tail. We theorized that this rat had long ago died under the floor boards there and that somehow its spirit had released itself at the very moment I entered the kitchen, using my arm on its upward path, up and away!

"Bill's ghost experiences were different from mine. He felt that they were hostile and aggressive forces, harmful and even dangerous.

Sara Joyce

He found himself jumping up out of sound sleep many times, ready to do battle for his life, almost like a survival situation. Of course, he was disturbing *their* habitat by tearing out old partitions, rearranging space, pounding nails, and ripping into old floors. Maybe they didn't like it.

"While he was in Hawaii he had asked an Oriental exorcist about how to get rid of ghosts. The exorcist gave him several formulas for so doing. These involved chanting, talking and scolding, and throwing salt throughout the rooms, into every corner and opening. Ghosts didn't like salt, he said. Bill did this ritual several times, and for several weeks there were no wandering presences and no sudden jolts in the night. He felt quite assured that the ghosts were gone, so he now proceeded to concentrate happily on his work. But one night as he was bent over some work he was doing on the floor, he suddenly felt the sensation of someone hovering over him. Or, as he said later, 'Something was ready to leap up on my back!' He whirled around, ready to fight. No one was there. He then realized that the ghosts were still in the building and that they were not going to leave by way of salt or chants or being cussed at. So he came forth with a very calm and logical lecture to them that ended with the words, 'All right, you can stay here if you want to, but just don't go creeping up on a guy when he's sleeping or working.' Bill moved himself out of the building and never slept there again, going there only in the daytime to do his work.

"Another story concerns a young woman, Joanna Byrne, a ballet dancer from Australia who was visiting us. She had spent the summer camping and floating the wild Idaho rivers, so when she arrived she was very tired. Without hesitation, she unrolled her sleeping bag on the living room floor and climbed in and went to sleep. I had already moved from the building by then, but she was staying in my former apartment. Here is how she described her first night there:

"In the night she awoke to the terrifying awareness that someone was hovering over her. She thought it was a woman with long, black hair. She was terrified because she thought the woman was trying to get into the sleeping bag with her. She tried to jump up but found her movements hampered by the sleeping bag, which sent her stumbling and falling around the room. She told me she had never been so frightened in her life, and she spent the rest of the night sitting up with the sleeping bag wrapped tightly around herself. She didn't want to leave the building after this. She wanted to find out more about this kind of goings-on, so she stayed for a while. But this one experience was the only time she was contacted by the ghost or ghosts there."

Mrs. Joyce then wrote of a young woman friend of hers, Ellen Vieth, who had planned to open an antiques shop. One evening before the opening of the store, she went there to do some arranging and cleaning. "She had just finished vacuuming the entire place," Sara wrote, "and was standing in the center of the floor when she suddenly felt the presence of someone standing beside her. She told me, 'The strangest feeling came over me. The hair on the back of my neck stood up. I dropped the vacuum cleaner. I looked down, and there was a puddle of water on the floor. Now it couldn't have been there before, because I had just run the vacuum over there.' "

Ellen decided not to open the store, although in an interview she said considerations other than the ghosts contributed to that decision.

History: The building, put up in the 1880s, was for much of its existence used for commercial purposes. At one time or another, it is known to have housed a general store, a post office, an ice cream parlor, a restaurant, a hand-rolled cigar store, a cleaning establishment, and a laundry, and it probably was home to other, long-forgotten enterprises. For about thirty years before Sara Joyce bought the building, it was owned and used by a local family. The man of the house was a builder and contractor, and the central, original part of the building was used to house machinery employed in his business. He also kept his collection of artifacts, rocks, crystals, seashells, and bottles there. The family lived in the easternmost part of the building. In 1984, Sara sold the building to her daughter, who expects to use it as a community arts center. Sara, who inherited the collections when she bought the building, donated many of the artifacts to the University of Idaho. A company from Spokane, Washington, bought some of the other collections.

Identity of ghosts: Sara Joyce says she has seen many apparitions in the old building, some of whom she could identify. One was a young man who used to visit her, who was killed in a car accident. Another was a young woman visitor who died in a fire.

Sara wonders whether the Indian artifacts might be a reason for some of the happenings. There were bones, teeth, arrowheads, stone tools. For example, she says: "When I was cleaning up the place, I found a coffee can in one of the rooms with fragments of a skull. I felt a personal objection to people going into Indian graves and gathering up these things, so I took this skull and went out on the back hillside and buried it. I felt it was proper to bury it. I made a mound with some rocks and things. My son thought maybe all that rushing around that you could hear was somebody looking for the rest of his body."

(The author of this book speculated as to whether the presence of large amounts of crystal, combined with Indian bones and artifacts, might be a factor. Shahannah Lindman is proprietor of Crystal Vision, a shop in Brookline, Massachusetts. She also happens to have a Native American grandmother, like Sara Joyce. She felt the proximity of crystals to the Indian material could indeed be significant. She said: "Crystal does hold on to energy. They give off vibrations of energy, and they also are receptive to it. Crystals need to be cleaned regularly, because they do hold on to these energies. Quartz is used in technology for communication because the oscillating vibrations carry and amplify and transmit. It's a channel when you have it around.")

Personality of ghosts: They can be noisy, disturbing, sometimes seemingly hostile, although some are not.

Best time to witness: Incidents have taken place at all times, but mostly at night.

Still haunted? Sara says, "The building may or may not still be haunted, but I am never going to sleep there again in order to find out."

Investigations: Sara Joyce herself is very psychic, but there have been no outside investigations.

Data submitted by: Sara Joyce, Ellen Vieth.

20
The Lady Who Haunts a Bar

The Country House Restaurant Clarendon Hills, Illinois

Location: The address of the Country House Restaurant is 1041 West 55th St., Clarendon Hills.

Description of place: A wooden frame building, on a busy thoroughfare in Clarendon Hills, a suburb about twenty miles west of Chicago. The co-owner, David Regnery, describes the place as looking like an old roadhouse. It has two stories, with a gabled roof. The first floor is divided between a bar and a restaurant, the latter seating about seventy people. The second floor is used as office and storage space.

Ghostly manifestations: David Regnery had been co-owner of the restaurant for two years when, in 1976, he first became aware of strange doings about the place. One morning about ten he came in with another man to do some measuring in the kitchen. They went into the bar to have a drink. The room has interior shutters, and suddenly the shutters on one window opened by themselves, letting in sunlight. As Regnery recalls, "I had just said, 'Randy,

121

what kind of a beer do you want?' We didn't have a beer there. We left pretty quickly."

That was the beginning of Regnery's awareness that he might have an unseen customer. "After that," he says, "we began to notice doors opening and closing by themselves. I had other experiences. At night I'd be up in the office, after hours, and I'd hear people downstairs. I'd think someone had left the door open, and I'd go down to say we were closed, and there'd be nobody there, and the door would be locked. People on the staff had the same sort of experiences.

"Sometimes at night three or four of us would be sitting around having a drink before going home, and all of a sudden a door would open or slam shut. Sometimes a jukebox would go on by itself. The first time it happened I called up the people who take care of the jukebox and asked if it could be some kind of mechanical time delay, and they said absolutely not.

"One of our night cleaning crew refuses to work alone, ever since he heard a woman crying all night."

Regnery asked the previous owner of the place, Richard Montanelli, if things had happened while he owned the place, and Montanelli said he had noticed nothing, even though during his ownership he and his wife and mother had lived upstairs. But Regnery tells of giving a room to a policeman friend who was going through a divorce and needed a temporary place to stay. It was on the second floor. The policeman moved a bed into a storage room. One night he heard footsteps coming up the stairs and grabbed his gun and flashlight. But no one appeared. "This happened a number of times," Regnery says, "so after a while he didn't bother anymore."

Regnery says customers have seen unusual things, too. One seems to have seen an apparition. "I was at the hostess station," he says, "and this man walked in with his wife and started joking with me. He said, 'What are you guys running here, a bordello?' I asked him what he meant, and he said when they came in he could see a blonde young woman at one of the upstairs windows, motioning to him. I ran up the stairs, but nobody was there."

History: According to David Regnery, the building was put up in the early part of this century and was probably originally a farm house. "I think it was a speakeasy at one time," Regnery says. A family named Kobel owned the place until about 1957, when Montanelli bought it. In 1974, Regnery and his brother Patrick bought it.

Identity of ghost: When offbeat things began to happen at the Country House Restaurant, David Regnery remembered that he knew a man who specialized in this sort of thing. He is Richard Crowe, a folklorist who is fascinated with the occult to such an extent that he has established the Chicago Ghost Tour, possibly the country's only regularly scheduled tour of haunted places. Regnery asked Crowe if he would check out the restaurant. Crowe showed up with a psychic named Evelyn Taglini. She immediately began to get startlingly accurate impressions. Regnery recalls:

"This psychic said, 'Yes, there is someone here; I feel it. It's a woman twenty-eight years old who used to be a customer here. She came in, was very upset, possibly had an affair with a bartender. This was in 1957. She left here very distraught and committed suicide right after she left, within a half a mile. She is the one who is haunting the place."

Regnery continued: "I'd never heard about anything like that happening, but I called the guy [Montanelli] we bought the place from, and he said yes, that did happen, but it happened in 1958."

Crowe remarks that the psychic's performance was particularly impressive because, "None of us there knew about this, so she couldn't have picked it up telepathically."

Montanelli, who now runs a tailoring business in Chicago, said: "The story about that woman leaving our place and apparently committing suicide is true. She came in with her child, about three or four years old, on a Sunday about 1:00 P.M. She wanted to leave her child with us to watch. I refused, and she walked out with the child, and the next thing we heard is that she had hit a tree about five blocks down the road. The child was not hurt. There was a story that she was involved with one of our bartenders, but I don't know anything about that. She and her husband used to frequent our place. They were friendly, nice people. Her husband came in shortly after the accident and was trying to figure out why she did it. I had no idea she was distraught. My wife was with me, and we both talked to her. She tried to tell us that she had an errand to run and would we please watch the child for an hour. I didn't want to take the responsibility for watching the child; after all, it was a tavern and a restaurant. My wife didn't want the responsibility either. The woman—I can't remember her name—hadn't been drinking. It seems impossible that it could have been an accident because she ran off the road and headed directly into a tree, as though she was aiming for it. What got everybody all upset was not only that she killed herself, but that she had the child with her. We think that's why she wanted to leave the child. I don't know what she was so distraught about."

Personality of ghost: No reports of anything hostile or harmful.

Witnesses: David Regnery and staff and customers of the restaurant.

Best time to witness: Usually at night, but sometimes during the day. Regnery says, "These things are more noticeable at night, since this is a very busy place during the day."

Still haunted? Apparently. Regnery says that recently, just after closing at night, a hostess felt a cold draft and was aware of the scent of lilacs. These phenomena have also been noted at other times.

Investigations: The session with Evelyn Taglini. Crowe has brought in other psychics, too, who have come up with similar conclusions.

Data submitted by: David Regnery, Richard Crowe, Mr. and Mrs. Richard Montanelli.

21
The Haunted Fraternity Headquarters

The Executive Offices Building of Sigma Pi Fraternity
Vincennes, Indiana

Location: The Sigma Pi executive office building is situated on Old Wheatland Road, Vincennes. The staff people there enjoy their spooky building and would probably be pleased to show it to visitors.

Description of place: A thirteen-room, brick mansion built in 1916, on a thirteen-acre site timbered with hundreds of oak trees. The architecture is Georgian.

Ghostly manifestations: About a dozen people work in this building, the national headquarters of Sigma Pi Fraternity. Most of them are young; five are men not long out of college, serving as consultants, who fan across the country visiting the various chapters of the fraternity as advisors and troubleshooters. The women working in the building are secretaries. One of them, Becky Crowley, has worked there for six years and has become quite used to the strange shenanigans. "The first time it happened, though, I was really startled," she says.

She works a lot at night, and one night the copying machine turned itself on. "I left everything as it was, and I went home," she says.

But soon she was used to the ghostly antics. "I've had the front door open on me," she says. She'd be coming in at night, reach for the door handle, and it would open. She's so used to this that she actually goes in and goes to work, often alone in the building. "I've heard my name called out," she says, and she thinks it's a male voice. The first time she heard her name called she thought it was a fellow worker, but on investigation she found nobody else in the build-

The haunted headquarters of Sigma Pi Fraternity.

ing. Becky and many other people hear footsteps, see lights going on and off, and witness equipment, such as the copying machine, turning itself on and off. Sometimes all the lights in the building go on simultaneously. The consultants feel the main problem is that the psychic chill caused by the ghost turns the coffee cold in a matter of seconds.

No one seems to have seen an apparition, but Larry Rovira, a consultant, says there used to be a dog who seemed to see things. "He'd stare at empty space, and the hair on his back would rise," Larry says. "And about the same time your coffee would suddenly turn cold." Another working problem, Rovira says, is that papers on one's desk move. "You don't see it happen," he says. "They'd just be in a different place from the last time you looked."

History: The house was built by Col. Eugene C. Wharf, a successful Vincennes businessman. He acquired his military title during the Spanish-American War. His family lived in the house, which he called Shadowwood, and the place became a center of Indiana social activity. At one time the land on which the house stands was called Rebel Hill, because southern sympathizers used to meet there prior to the Civil War. At the same time, a mansion across the road was a prominent stop on the Underground Railroad, and many escaping slaves were made welcome there. Understandably, there was a great deal of tension in the immediate area. The Wharfs, who died in the 1950s, left the estate to Vincennes University, but the university had no practical use for the place, and through the intervention of prominent members of Sigma Pi it was given to the fraternity as a national headquarters in 1962.

Identity of ghost: Judging from Becky Crowley's experience, it could be male, and most of the live inhabitants of the building assume it is Colonel Wharf. In fact, Rovira says that when lights go on or the temperature suddenly goes down, "The guys say, 'Don't worry, Colonel; it's just me.' "

Personality of ghost: Nothing harmful, or even very frightening, has ever happened. It seems like a spirit who just wants to register his presence on the premises. "We're used to it," Rovira says, "although it gets kind of eerie at times."

Witnesses: Dozens of people who have worked in the building over the years.

Best time to witness: The manifestations seem to step up at night, but there have been many during the day, too.

Still haunted? Yes, the tradition continues.

Investigations: "We haven't had any psychics come in," Rovira says. "It doesn't bother us. When I go on the road and talk with the undergraduates, it's entertaining. We're the only national fraternity that has a haunted headquarters."

Data submitted by: Larry Rovira and Becky Crowley, as well as printed material from the fraternity's headquarters.

**22
The Gray Lady
and the Spanish
Opera Singer**

Resident Ghosts at
Liberty Hall
Frankfort, Kentucky

Location: Liberty Hall is located at 202 Wilkinson St. in Frankfort.

Description of place: Liberty Hall, now a museum under the auspices of the National Society of Colonial Dames of America, was the private home of the family and descendants of John Brown, one of the first senators from Kentucky, from its erection in 1796 until 1937, when an heir deeded it to become "an open, semi-public property." It is maintained for tours much as it was during the residence of the Brown family. A handsome, three-story building, its front features an elegant Palladian window above the door, a white front gate, and a brick-paved walk.

Ghostly manifestations: The chief ghost of Liberty Hall is "The Gray Lady," who is believed to be Mrs. Margaret Varick, an aunt of the first Mrs. Brown to live in the house. The story goes that the Browns' eight-year-old daughter had died in 1817. Mrs. Varick, a New York society woman, had come to comfort them. The sixty-five-year-old woman traveled over eight hundred miles, much of the way on horseback. Three days after arriving, she died of a heart attack. She was first buried in the garden but later was removed to a cemetery. For over a century and a half, sightings have been reported of a small, trim woman dressed in gray, usually doing some household chore or gazing out a window.

In recent years, the manifestations apparently have not included sightings of an apparition. For example, about twenty years ago, after a fire, a fireman and an employee of a local newspaper remained in the building for three nights to guard against vandals. They reported doors closing behind them and candles being snuffed out by sudden drafts of cool air.

More recent happenings are reported by Eugenia Blackburn, a former curator of the museum of the Kentucky Historical Society, in Frankfort. A distant cousin of the Brown family, Mrs. Blackburn lived in rooms in Liberty Hall for a couple of years in the early 1970s. Sometimes, she says, doors would open with no visible opener. Once, she relates, when she was taking a shower the door of her bathroom was open, and she thought of closing it because of coolness. She put her head under the shower to wash off the soap, and when she came up for air she looked and saw the door had just been closed. There was no breeze to close it, she says.

Another time, she says, she woke up in the middle of the night and began to think of an old beau who had given her a music box, which she hadn't played for years. Suddenly it came to life, playing "Auld Lang Syne" from beginning to end. This piece was one of several on the music box but was the only one that played. "The next day," Mrs. Blackburn says, "my children came to visit me, and I told them what had happened. They jumped and down on the floor to see if they could make the music box play by the vibration, but it didn't make a noise."

Two subsidiary ghosts figure in the lore of Liberty Hall. More-or-less true believers in "The Gray Lady" tend to look down their noses at these two, although they can hardly be called Johnny-come-latelies. In fact, they slightly antedate Mrs. Varick, the official ghost. One is purported to be the spirit of a Spanish opera singer who came from New Orleans to give a concert in a neighboring house. After her concert, she went to a party at the Browns'. During the course of the evening, she wandered out into the garden alone and never was seen again. It was suggested that the Indians got her. This was in 1805. The other ghost is believed to have been a soldier in the War of 1812 who was enamored of a young woman who was visiting the Brown family. The romantic legend is that he comes to the windows, peers in wistfully, and then turns and walks away.

History: John Brown was very much a VIP in his day, and many VIPs visited him at his home. A guest list would include Lafayette and presidents James Monroe, Andrew Jackson, Zachary Taylor, and William Henry Harrison. Aaron Burr, a close friend, also visited him. Brown, who came from Virginia, studied law under Thomas Jefferson, who counted among his other talents a proficiency in architecture. Jefferson suggested that Brown build a one-story house, since he had plenty of land, but Brown had already begun building the place with two stories and an attic.

Identity of ghosts: Mrs. Margaret Varick is the popular choice for "The Gray Lady," but the Spanish opera singer and the lovelorn soldier also have their adherents.

Personalities of ghosts: Mrs. Blackburn's ghost, the opener and closer of doors and player of a nostalgic strain on the music box, seems quite congenial.

Witnesses: In recent years, Mrs. Blackburn, and the fireman and the newspaperman, whose names are Lies Barber and Bob Watson, respectively.

Best time to witness: Incidents seem to occur mostly at night.

Still haunted? Mrs. Blackburn thinks it is. However, Mary Smith, curator for the past ten years, says she hasn't seen or heard of any ghosts around the place during her tenure.

Investigations: Ms. Smith says that in 1985 a group of about twelve student psychics came with their leader to check out the place. "They seemed to think there were some different people wandering around the house," Ms. Smith says.

Data submitted by: Eugenia Blackburn, Mary Smith, Ann McDonnell of the Kentucky Historical Society, articles in the *Louisville Courier-Journal* and *Lexington Herald-Leader*.

**23
Ghosts on the
Old Plantation**

Destrehan Manor
House
Destrehan, Louisiana

Location: Destrehan Manor House is situated at
9999 River Road, Destrehan.

Description of place: Originally a West Indies-
style manor house, completed in 1790, it faces the
Mississippi River, about thirteen miles above New
Orleans. In its early days, there were many outbuildings, including nineteen slave cabins. During the
mid-1800s a great deal of remodeling was done to
make the house conform to the Greek Revival style
popular in the South at that time. The original
columns—brick on the first floor, cypress above—
were covered over with brick Doric columns. The
curving staircases leading to the upper floors as well
as a curving rear wall were added, and all of the
ceilings, originally exposed beams, were plastered. In
recent years a great deal of restoration has been
done.

Ghostly manifestations: Sporadic stories of
hauntings have surfaced in connection with Destre-

han Manor for many years. The majority of anecdotes seem, however, to be of recent origin, after major restorations had been undertaken and tours were instituted on a systematic basis. All of this might make a cautious haunting buff suspicious, especially since the current proprietors of the mansion go so far as to issue a flyer telling of recent sightings of apparitions, titled, *Ghost Sightings at Destrehan Plantation? You Be the Judge.*

But the sheer number of apparent witnesses—many of them employees of the place but many others tourists—does give pause even to the hardened skeptic. Perhaps the prime witness is a teenage girl, Annette Roper, a daughter of a family that works at the manor. She says she has often seen a white figure. In an article in a local newspaper, *River Parishes Guide*, reporter Leonard Gray wrote:

> Ghosts at Destrehan Manor? Doesn't every plantation house claim its own resident ghost? Isn't this just a publicity put-on? But if you talk quietly to Annette Roper and you see the fear in her eyes and the tremor in her voice, you know she was frightened very badly by something. You don't have to believe in ghosts to realize that.

And in a story in the November 4, 1984, issue of the *New Orleans Times-Picayune*, Kristin Gilger wrote,

> . . . Annette, a slender, frail girl with dark hair and dark eyes that suit her sweeping purple gown with a hoop skirt, turns pale and shaky at the mention of Henderson's [the putative ghost's] name. She said she refuses to sleep by herself or walk outside alone at night anymore.

The way Annette tells it, her introduction to the apparition occurred one night in 1984, when she was reading in bed in her bedroom in a trailer her family was occupying just behind the manor house. She looked up, she says, and saw a white, transparent shape seemingly sitting in a nonexistent chair, within arm's reach. She passed her hand through it. Terrified, she lay in bed till morning, until she heard her father in the kitchen. Then, she says, the shape vanished. Within the month, she saw the shape again; once while outdoors around dusk she looked up and saw it in a second-story window; another time she saw it crossing the driveway. A cousin, Glenn Williams, supposedly ran into the shape in the ballroom of the house. It is said that he refuses to return to the manor. Annette says that while outdoors near the manor house she has heard a male voice call, "Annette."

A popular current theory concerning this particular Destrehan Manor apparition is that it is the ghost of one of the early owners, Stephen Henderson, who lived there with his wife Elenore, née Destrehan, in the mid-1800s. Elenore died at age nineteen, and Henderson, bereft, died a few years later. They are both buried in a cemetery nearby. Annette Roper is said to resemble Elenore Henderson.

Other staff members and volunteer workers over the past several years have reported seeing a similar apparition. But there also seem to be many subsidiary spooks about. There is the story of the former owner who attended a reception at the manor, the unusual aspect of this visit being that he had died in New Orleans, earlier that day.

A most intriguing but abundantly questionable theory of the identity of at least one of the apparitions is that it is the ghost of Jean LaFitte, a pirate

PHOTO BY KATHY ANDERSON OF THE NEW ORLEANS TIMES-PICAYUNE

Annette Roper poses in front of Destrahan Manor House.

who made good in New Orleans in the early nine-teenth century. He owned ten ships that preyed on Spanish merchantmen in the Gulf of Mexico and was also into slave-running and smuggling. He dealt with plantation owners and was a friend of Stephen Henderson. He often visited the place. In fact, the manor's publicity handouts call LaFitte "one of Henderson's business allies and close comrades," referring to LaFitte as "the pirate-patriot." During a time when the manor was empty in the 1960s, the place was constantly broken into by vandals looking for LaFitte's treasure, although there never had been any indication that the pirate-patriot left any there.

Aside from Annette and her startled cousin, an apparition is reputed to have been spotted by others of Annette's relatives, as well as a deliveryman bringing in pralines. And photographs taken in and around the house often, it is said, have "extras," unexplained blotches of light and even the occasional face or figure.

History: The house was completed in 1790 by Robert Antoine Robin de Longy. In 1802, his daughter and her husband, Jean Noel d'Estrehan, purchased the house and 1,050 acres from the other de Longy heirs. Sugarcane was coming in, and the place became a prosperous sugar plantation. When Stephen Henderson died, a widower, he left a will freeing his slaves and providing for establishment of a factory to manufacture clothes and shoes for blacks. Surviving relatives protested the will, which was declared ambiguous and was nullified in 1838. Descendants of the family owned the property until the early twentieth century, when it was purchased by an oil company, and through a succession of mergers it became the property of the American Oil Company (AMOCO). A refinery was built on the site but closed in 1958, and the house was left to suffer the ravages of time and vandals. A group of local people formed a nonprofit group in 1972, called the River Road Historical Society, to restore the manor, and the property was given to them by the oil company. A great deal of work has been done on the place in recent years.

Identity of ghosts: Although Jean LaFitte is the most colorful candidate, cooler heads consider the chief apparition to be Stephen Henderson, distraught by his young wife's death and the preemptory manner in which his surviving relatives dealt with his will. And there are a number of added starters.

Personalities of ghosts: Harmless, it would seem, but a pretty sad lot.

Witnesses: Apparently a good portion of the parish's population, not to mention tourists.

Best time to witness: Around the clock. The house is open for tours from 10:00 A.M. to 4:00 P.M. except for major holidays.

Still haunted? Seems to be.

Investigations: No psychics or parapsychologists have been invited in as yet, says the current administrator, Joan Douville, who adds, "We like things the way they are."

Data submitted by: Joan Douville; article by Leonard Gray in the June 16, 1985, issue of the *River Parishes Guide*, published in Boutte, Louisiana; article by Kristin Gilger in the November 4, 1984, issue of the *New Orleans Times-Picayune*; article by Darlene LaBranche in the November 22, 1984, issue of *L'Observateur*, published in Laplace, Louisiana.

**24
A Haunted Castle**

Beckett's Castle
Cape Elizabeth, Maine

Location: The address of Beckett Castle is 1 Singles Road, Cape Elizabeth. However, the present owner prefers to remain anonymous, and possibly would not welcome visitors.

Description of place: This house is not really a castle, but it has been called "Beckett's Castle" since it was built in 1871 by Sylvester Beckett, prominent in Portland in the arts, a publisher, an attorney, and, most intriguing for our purposes, a dedicated spiritualist. The structure is actually a stone cottage with a picturesque three-story tower. Additions have been made in recent years by the present owner.

Ghostly manifestations: Beckett was author of several books, among them a lyric poem titled, "Hester, the Bride of the Islands." A passage from that poem reads:

> If the soul dieth, if our years
> On earth, of discord, joys, and tears,

Be all of life, then life is vain,
And Heaven's great work imperfect!
No! Death is but a second birth—
And man, immortal, oft returns. . .

According to many witnesses and established local tradition, since his death in 1882 Beckett has systematically gone about trying to prove that he wasn't wrong. No less an authority than the eminent psychic, Alex Tanous of Portland, has investigated and gone on record that Beckett is the chief ghost in that castle.

Twice in 1982, Tanous toured the place with journalist Lynne Campbell. They interviewed the now-deceased Robert Lins, who was living there. Lins said that four times he had hung a painting above the kitchen stove, and each time he found it wedged behind the stove, reversed. (There must have been something about that painting Beckett or some other entity didn't like.) Once, Lins says, he was stopped and held in place while crossing the living room. The door between the tower and Lins's bedroom refused to stay shut. "In desperation," he said, "I nailed the door shut. As I left the room, the nails flew out of the wall, just missing my head." Lins said he constantly heard footsteps and felt sudden chills, and doors were wont to burst open with no visible physical impetus.

The present owner, who moved in in 1984, asked to remain anonymous and prefaced an interview with the familiar disclaimer, "I'm not a believer in this kind of thing. But," she continued, "there have been two incidents since I've been here. One was when a young man was working outside doing some landscaping. An outside door leading to the tower, which he thought was closed, came open, and there

Beckett's Castle

PHOTO BY LYNNE CAMPBELL

was this sort of bluish curtain that blew out, like a piece of material that seemed to be billowing out the door. He ran in, thinking I would kill him because something was blowing out the door, and it was actually nothing, no piece of blue material was there.

"The other incident was that I was lying in bed ready to go to sleep, and I kept feeling this bed sheet sliding back and forth across my neck. Eventually it was so much that I turned on the light and tried to see if there was any wind blowing or something that could have blown the sheet. And then I decided there wasn't, and maybe it was one of these things that people were calling ghosts that was doing that. It was very gentle, whatever it was."

History: In Beckett's time, the castle was a gathering place for artists, journalists, and influential Portlanders. He lived there with his family, a widower in the later years of his life. Col. Walter Singles bought the place in 1933 from Beckett's grandson. Lins lived there with Singles's late daughter, Edna. The place was empty for a short time until purchased by the current owner.

Identity of ghost(s): Tanous said, "There are perhaps an endless number of entities here that will appear to different people at different times." These entities, Tanous said, ranged from an elderly man to a child. Two of Beckett's children died in childhood. Also, Tanous felt that many artists, painters, had worked there and were still doing so. He also said he was aware of a beautiful woman with dark hair, dressed in lace, who was grieving over a dead child. However, he said that Beckett was the dominant entity in the place.

Personality of ghost(s): "The vibes are excellent," Tanous said. "There is no evil in this house." The present owner is, as noted above, a skeptic. However, she says, "Before I moved in I asked Lynne Campbell to ask Alex Tanous if at least it would be safe to live here, and he said not only would it be safe but they would also be very protective. And that made it OK."

Witnesses: The late Robert Lins, Alex Tanous, the current owner, a landscape worker.

Best time to witness: Manifestations appear to occur both day and night.

Still haunted? The present owner says things are still happening.

Investigations: Two visits to the place by Alex Tanous.

Data submitted by: Alex Tanous; Lynne Campbell, in interviews and from an article by her in the January 12, 1983, issue of *The Chronicle*, a Portland publication; the present owner of the place.

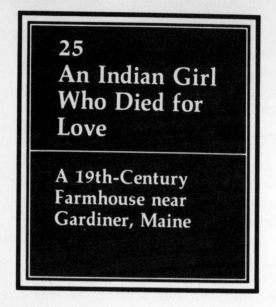

25
An Indian Girl Who Died for Love

A 19th-Century Farmhouse near Gardiner, Maine

Location: The Swain house is on Route 197 in Litchfield. Visitors are welcome, but call ahead.

Description of place: A wooden frame house, built sometime during the 1800s, near Gardiner, Maine.

Ghostly manifestations: Mary Swain, a nurse, bought the old house in 1959 and says she soon became aware something odd was going on. A painter working in her bedroom on the second floor came down, a bit shaken. The door to the room kept opening and shutting by itself, he said, which rather unsettled him. Mary was inclined to credit it to too many beers, but when her mother, Pat, who was psychic, first entered the house, she announced that she felt a presence. Things constantly turned up missing; windows went up and down by themselves. And so Mary's younger sister, Diana, and two friends broke out a Ouija board. They quickly contacted a supposed spirit, which called itself "Ajax." Ajax said the spirit was an Indian girl, and the

144

Swains often talked with this spirit through the board. They named her Beatrice. She said she had died tragically, many years before. Now her spirit, she said, lived in a maple tree in a nearby pasture.

No one seems to have actually seen Beatrice, except possibly Phraya, Pat Swain's Siamese cat, who constantly followed something with her eyes, but a number of humans say they sensed her. Mary's late father, Fritz, felt she hovered over him as he read his newspaper each evening, particularly when he was perusing the obituaries. Mary had problems with the constant removal of a ceiling panel in her bedroom.

Mary Swain's house

Mary's brother, Dwight, was very much the macho skeptic, until one morning when he was shaving in the bathroom a picture came off the wall with a horrendous crash. "The hook was still in," says Mary. "The only way it could have come down was if someone lifted it and dropped it. My brother stopped making caustic remarks when we talked about Beatrice."

In spring of 1977, the contact with Beatrice seems to have ended. During one of the Ouija board sessions, Beatrice said harm was heading their way and that she was going to try to prevent it. Soon afterward the tree in which her spirit supposedly resided split with a crack that resounded over the fields. The tree had been struck by lightning years before and was rotten and weak, but the Swains felt it was unlikely to split on a calm, windless day. Ajax, through the Ouija board, said Beatrice would not be back. However, a few months later there was a strange occurrence that the Swains can't decide whether or not to attribute to Beatrice. To keep animals from getting at the garbage, Mary had taken an old millstone from the barn and put it on top of a trash can. One morning she found it split into multiple pieces. No one admitted to having touched the stone, let alone shattering it.

History: Mary Swain bought the house from an elderly couple, now deceased, who had lived there for many years. They made no mention of any psychic events.

Identity of ghost(s): According to the Ouija board operators, the ghost was an Indian girl whom they called Beatrice, who said she had died tragically. The Swains invited a well-known psychic, Alex Tanous of Portland, to visit the house. He said there were a number of entities inhabiting the house but that Beatrice was indeed the most active. He said that Ajax, the controlling spirit of the Ouija board, was an Indian who had known Beatrice in life. Tanous agreed with what had come through the Ouija board. The girl the Swains called Beatrice was, he said, an Indian girl who had fallen in love with a

Alex Tanous

white man named Gordon, who had probably been a missionary to an Indian tribe not far away. They had decided to marry, very much a taboo as far as the Indians were concerned. But they eloped, helped in their escape by none other than Ajax, and had fled to the area where the Swains' house now stands. The Indians pursued the fleeing lovers, caught them, and burned Gordon before the girl's horrified eyes. The execution had probably been done near the maple tree. "The energy of her spirit is still here," Tanous said. The girl herself was later executed. Tanous felt that the spirit of the Indian girl had been activated by the strong psychic energy of Pat Swain.

Personality of ghost: There seemed to be nothing hostile about the Indian girl's spirit. It gave the impression of an entity who wanted to register its presence with the living.

Witnesses: The Swains and a number of visitors to the house, not to mention Phraya, the Siamese cat, now deceased.

Best time to witness: Beatrice seemed to manifest herself throughout the day and night.

Still haunted? There have been no overt manifestations since the late 1970s.

Investigations: A visit by Alex Tanous, as well as many Ouija board sessions by the Swains and their friends.

Data submitted by: Alex Tanous and Mary and Pat Swain.

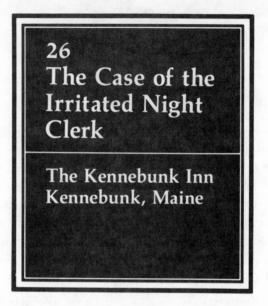

26
The Case of the Irritated Night Clerk

The Kennebunk Inn Kennebunk, Maine

Location: The Kennebunk Inn is at 45 Main St., Kennebunk.

Description of place: The part of the building that fronts on Main Street in the middle of this resort town on the coast of Maine was built as a home in 1799 and was used as such by various families throughout the 1800s and early 1900s. It was turned into an inn in 1926. In the 1940s it was expanded, and the current owners, Arthur and Angela LeBlanc, have further enlarged it to twenty-two rooms. The original part of the structure is built in the Colonial style; the extension in the rear blends with the old architecture. The entire building is painted yellow.

Ghostly manifestations: As far as can be determined, all was quiet here until the LeBlancs bought the place in 1978 and began to make a few changes in the building. The LeBlancs came from Salem, Massachusetts. He had recently retired from the Air Force with the rank of major, having flown as a navigator in Vietnam and later with the Strategic Air Command. But he'd always had a yen to be an innkeeper, and they bought the place, which had gone downhill since its World War II glory days, at an auction. Early employees included Dudley Donovan, a bartender, and Janet Cipriani, a waitress. Janet still works there.

The ghost seems to be selective with the people he twits, and Dudley and Janet have been prime candidates for his attentions. Early on in the LeBlancs' stewardship, small hand-carved mugs behind the bar were wont to fly off their shelf and strike Dudley while he was mixing a martini or Manhattan.

The Kennebunk Inn

Angela LeBlanc says she once witnessed a mug fly through the air and mug Dudley. Glasses on shelves behind the bar have been known to shatter when no one was nearby.

Janet had a shattering experience herself with a crystal goblet. A special party was being held, and expensive crystal water goblets were broken out for the occasion. Janet, who has the reputation of never dropping or spilling things—at least without help— had arranged the crystal goblets in the center of a large tray and surrounded them with lesser glass goblets. She had brought the tray into the dining room and was about to put it down on a table when one of the crystal goblets went up in the air, flew across the room, and shattered against the far wall. The glasses that had been surrounding it were undisturbed.

These are just highlights. "A lot of quirky little things were constantly happening," Janet says. "We'd set up the dining room tables, and they'd be disheveled in the morning. Silverware would be askew; chairs would be moved."

History: The original part of the building was built as a home in 1799 by Phineas Cole. It remained a private dwelling until a man from Portland, a Mr. Baitler, turned it into an inn, which he called The Tavern. James and Walter Day expanded the place in the 1940s and changed the name to Kennebunk Inn. Later, under various owners, it fell into decline, until the LeBlancs bought it and did considerable expansion and renovation.

Identity of ghost: Somewhere along the way, LeBlanc hired a waitress named Pat Butler. "She's sort of psychic," LeBlanc says. "She said, 'That's a ghost.' She felt it was centered in the basement. She said, 'The name Cyrus keeps coming to me.' So we named the ghost Cyrus.

"Then," says LeBlanc, "a really strange thing happened. A man came in—just for one night—from Taiwan. He had been out of the country for thirty-five years. He said he had a lot of memories of this inn. He said his grandfather was more or less the night clerk, night watchman, night auditor of this place for years. He took care of the inn at night, sort of a clerk-of-the-works type. The man said that one morning he was called to the inn because his grandfather had died here. I took a deep breath and asked the man what his grandfather's name was. "He said, 'Cyrus.' And we had been calling the ghost Cyrus for over a year! There were rooms at one time in the basement. There were when we bought the place; we've taken them out. Some of the people who worked here lived in the rooms down there. Cyrus must have lived in the basement. He's still there."

Personality of ghost: For months, he'll be quiescent; then the manifestations will flare up. They usually coincide with any renovations. "Apparently," LeBlanc says, "he doesn't like the changes we make in the building. He was used to it the other way. When we begin changing things, that's when the activity starts." And when Cyrus wants to, he can be quite mischievous and disruptive. About six months before the LeBlancs were interviewed, Cyrus was really quite indiscreet. LeBlanc tells the story:

"Janet was working," he says, "and Janet has never spilt anything in her life. Two of our regular custom-

Waitress Janet Cipriani
PHOTO BY ARTHUR MYERS

ers, a doctor and his wife, were in the dining room. They come here about four times a year while traveling. Janet was holding two wine glasses on a tray while talking with them. The tray was absolutely level; the wine glasses were perfectly level. But all of a sudden they fell off the tray and dumped into the lady's lap."

Witnesses: The LeBlancs, Dudley Donovan, Janet Cipriani, Pat Butler, the doctor's wife, and many other employees and customers of the inn.

Best time to witness: Cyrus usually seems to come to life in the evening.

Still haunted? LeBlanc says things have been relatively quiet for the past few months, but there haven't been any renovations for the past few months.

Investigations: There haven't been any formal psychic investigations, but psychic people, such as Pat Butler, and visitors who profess psychic abilities agree there is something going on.

Data submitted by: The LeBlancs, Janet Cipriani; case suggested by Robert Ellis Cahill in his book, *New England's Ghostly Haunts*.

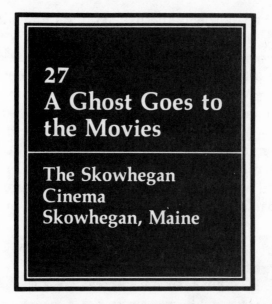

**27
A Ghost Goes to
the Movies**

The Skowhegan
Cinema
Skowhegan, Maine

Location: The Skowhegan Cinema is situated at 15 Court St., Skowhegan.

Description of place: The theater, built in the 1920s, is typical of movie theaters of that era—ornate, gilded, with stuffed chairs and a sweeping balcony. It seats about a thousand people. It is a red brick building on a side street in the business section of Skowhegan, an industrial town of about seven thousand.

Ghostly manifestations: Bob and Joanne Perry bought the place in 1972. Perry is a distribution manager, and they operate the theater as a sideline. Perry says he often felt strange in the place, as though someone were watching him, but overt manifestations did not begin until the Perrys built an apartment into the theater building and moved into it, a couple of years after they had bought the place. While the renovations were going on, a helper who was cleaning the theater after an evening perfor-

153

mance had all the lights turned out on him, although he and the Perrys were the only people in the building, and the doors were locked. Quickly, the strange doings were stepped up. While Perry was applying plaster to the ceiling of the new apartment with a trowel, the trowel was torn out of his hand. It shot downward, hit the countertop, and put a dent in the Formica that is still there. An even more bizarre thing happened soon afterward to Mrs. Perry. Her husband had painted white the walls of a room in the new apartment. Mrs. Perry was alone and preparing

The Skowhegan Cinema

to cover the woodwork with a stain. She had placed an unopened can of stain in the middle of the room, when the doorbell rang. She went downstairs and found a friend at the door, and the two went back upstairs. When they entered the room, a roll of masking tape rolled toward them on the floor, stopping at their feet. Then they saw the wall. There was a dark stain splattered across the newly painted white wall. Yet the can was still resting in the middle of the floor, unopened, its contents intact.

While Perry was working on the wiring of the apartment, he would get shocks, even though the electricity was disconnected. He called in a professional electrician, who also got shocked, even though he was sure he had disconnected the current. Perry had carefully piled rows of firewood in a room behind the theater. One day he found the wood spilled, but not haphazardly. It was spread across the floor, leaving not a foot of space to walk on. Once Perry thought he momentarily saw a black vision in the theater, and another time a chunk of the ceiling above the theater's balcony was torn out and flung into the lower part of the theater, although no one was hit by it. A Halloween film was being shown at the time, whatever significance that might have.

History: The building was put up in 1929, by Blin Page, a prominent Skowhegan businessman, and a partner, Joseph Dondis of Rockland. They owned the theater for several years, then sold it to a theater company based in Boston, who sold it to a similar company, and that company sold it to the Perrys. When the theater building was constructed, it displaced a house on the property, which was moved next door, where it still stands. The house changed hands many times and is now an apartment house. The Perrys bought the theater in the early 1970s and within two years began renovating the upstairs as an apartment, where they still live.

Identity of ghost: Leslie Bugbee, a parapsychologist who specializes in recording voices of ghosts and taking photographs of them, feels the disturbed and disturbing entity is probably someone who worked in the theater or possibly someone who had lived in the house that originally stood on the property and became upset when the Perrys began to alter the familiar arrangement of the theater.

Personality of ghost: Definitely angry, hostile, and mischievous.

Witnesses: The Perrys and some of their friends and employees.

Best time to witness: The phenomena seem to occur during both the day and the evening.

Still haunted? There still seems to be a presence in the place, the Perrys say.

Investigations: In late 1984, Leslie Bugbee of Cornville, Maine, spent a day trying to record electrical voice phenomena, often called *EVP*, at the theater. No voices were recorded, although Bugbee says there are rappings on the tape that were not heard by the people present. He plans to stay overnight at the theater to make further recordings and take photos with infrared film.

Data submitted by: Bob and Joanna Perry; Leslie Bugbee; Don James, Skowhegan attorney; Elizabeth Sealey, daughter of Blin Page; chapter suggested by an article in the November 1984 issue of *Yankee* magazine, by Michael Kimball.

28
Why on Earth Shouldn't Edgar Allan Poe's Old House Be Haunted?

The Poe House
Baltimore, Maryland

Location: The Poe House is situated at 203 North Amity Street, Baltimore.

Description of place: The curator of Poe House, Jeff Jerome, describes the place as "a very plain, two-and-a-half-story house of brick, wood, and plaster." It was built around 1830, one of a series of working-class homes. There are four-and-a-half rooms, with two bedrooms upstairs. Poe's room was in the attic. The present neighborhood is low-income housing, predominantly black.

Ghostly manifestations: In its issue of November 10, 1985, *The New York Times* printed a United Press International story with the headline, "Ghost of 'Mr. Eddie' Bars Intruders at Poe's House," the gist of which was that street gangs in the inner city Poe Project do not invade this little museum for fear of the ghost of the famed writer of horror stories.

Curator Jerome says the identity of the spirit or spirits is undetermined but that there seems to be something paranormal going on at the place. Jerome is sensitive about any implications that he is putting out stories of hauntings to boost the tourist trade. "Many of these things happened in the sixties," he says, "long before I came on the scene."

Jerome cites an event that took place in 1968, during riots at the time of the assassination of Martin Luther King. "The police were called to Poe House," Jerome relates, "because lights were being seen inside the building. It was thought that someone had broken in and maybe was going to torch the place. Police didn't have a key to the house, and they didn't want to break down the door, so they surrounded the place and waited till the next day when a tour guide showed up and let them in. There was no one in the house. But the police too had seen a light in the house during the night, a light that moved from the first to the second floor to the garret. It's one thing when a neighbor says he saw things, but when the police surround the house and see the same thing it makes you wonder.

"In the early sixties, there were several instances of people being tapped on the shoulder. This happened in a room that was the bedroom of Poe's grandmother. The visitors would mention this to the tour guide. This happened over a period of months, and the people were tourists, from all over the country, so it's not likely to be some sort of conspiracy.

"Something happened to me recently," Jerome says, "and when it actually happens to you, it really makes you wonder. On Halloween in 1980 we held a séance at the house. It was held at midnight and was a publicity stunt by a radio station. The station was obviously looking for a gimmick, but they did make an effort to get legitimate psychics involved. Among

The Poe House

the group of psychics was a man and wife team.
After the séance they came up to me and said they
were upset with me. They said, 'You told us there
wouldn't be any tricks. You can tell your friends
upstairs to come down now.' They had been in the
grandmother's room, and Poe's garret room was just
above them. The woman said she heard voices and
noise going on up there, and they thought it was a
joke or a publicity stunt. So we went upstairs and
nobody was there, so they then felt it really was
spirits.

"In 1984, we were doing a dramatic presentation of
Berenice, Poe's first horror story, which he wrote

here. The actress was getting ready in the back room, Virginia's (Poe's wife's) room. I was downstairs, and I heard a loud crash. I ran upstairs, and her face was white. She said the window had fallen out of the frame and smashed on the floor. The shutters were closed, so there was no gust of air. And the window was snug. There was no way it could have accidentally fallen out. Someone would have had to physically pull it up out of the grooves it was resting in and then drop it on the floor. Psychics have told me it was a spirit just making its presence known. I don't think the actress could have done it, because it really shook her up. She gave a bad performance after that, she was that shaken."

In addition to these specific incidents, Jerome mentions the usual paranormal events such as doors and windows opening and closing without any seeming live human energy. He mentions in particular a time an English psychic visited unannounced, just a tourist, and told Jerome that he had picked up many sensations in the rooms. The next morning, when Jerome arrived he found doors and windows open. "Psychics have told me," Jerome says, "that when a psychic goes into a place it tends to bring out spirits. They draw on the psychic's energy and make these gestures."

History: The house was new when Poe lived there, from 1832 to 1835. When he came there, three people were living in the house, Elizabeth Poe, his grandmother; Maria Clemm, his aunt; and Virginia Clemm, his cousin, who later at the age of thirteen became his wife. She married him when he was twenty-seven. Poe had left West Point and was at loose ends. He was twenty-five and was just beginning to write short stories. "He knew he had family in Baltimore," Jerome says, "and it was a matter of his knocking on the door and saying, 'I'm related to you,' and they took him in."

The house was lived in, sometimes quite briefly, by a number of people over the years. In 1922 it became vacant, and it remained so until 1949 when it was opened as a historic house by the Edgar Allan Poe Society. Until 1977, when Jerome became curator, the house was looked after by volunteers, students at a nearby law school, who acted as tour guides.

Identity of ghosts: Jerome says, "If there are ghosts in the house, we have no idea who they are, but psychics have claimed to have gotten a vision of an old woman, dressed in period costume. They couldn't make out facial features, but she had gray hair and was heavy-set. More than one person has said this. There are two places that seem to be more sensitive than others, and that's the back bedroom, which was Virginia's, and Poe's room in the attic. Poe did not die in the house; he died at Church Home Hospital in Baltimore, which is still standing, in 1849. The grandmother died in the house in 1835. But other families have lived in the house, and I'm sure other people have died in the house."

Personality of ghosts: Nothing hostile or harmful seems to have happened. Mostly the typical manifestations of spirits who want to make their presence known.

Witnesses: Jeff Jerome, the Baltimore police, many visitors to the house.

Best time to witness: Except for the 1968 riot incident and the 1980 radio show, most of the reported happenings are noted during the day, since ordinarily there is no one in the house at night. The house is open to visitors Wednesdays through Saturdays, from noon to 3:45 P.M.

Still haunted? Some of these events are fairly recent.

Investigations: Many psychics have visited the place, both informally and for specific inquiries.

Data submitted by: Jeff Jerome, curator; some information from a UPI story in *The New York Times*. Suggested by Beverly Quint of Rockport, Massachusetts.

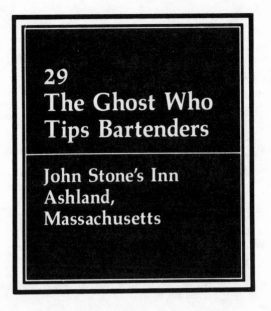

**29
The Ghost Who
Tips Bartenders**

John Stone's Inn
Ashland,
Massachusetts

Location: The address of John Stone's Inn is 179 Main St., Ashland.

Description of place: A three-story building constructed of chestnut and granite in 1832, on the main street of the village of Ashland. Ashland is a small place, about twenty miles west of Boston, a working-class town well outside Boston's ring of affluent suburbs.

Ghostly manifestations: A veritable smorgasbord of paranormal events seems to have been laid on at this old restaurant. Some suspect that a rash of happenings in the past few years is related to the fact that the restaurant is in the throes of a new lease on life, with extensive alterations, often a stimulant for sluggish spirits. The most refreshing manifestations are the $10 bills that constantly materialize in the tip jars behind the bar. This beneficence has occurred several times, always a $10 bill.

Bartender Eileen Streitenberger, one of the beneficiaries, tells of coming on for an evening shift with another barkeep and both of them finding bills in their tip jars. The day bartender testified that she had taken all her tips at the end of the shift, and her word doesn't seem to be doubted.

(It might be worthy of note that an old photograph of John Stone hangs behind the bar.)

Almost every employee of the restaurant seems to have a story, many of them first-hand experiences.

John Stone's Inn

PHOTOS BY ARTHUR MYERS

For example, Kyle McDonald, a young cook, says: "One day I was down in the storage room, putting things away. I was stacking big metal cans on a counter. Three times cans fell off. There was no reason for them to fall off; they weren't on the edge or anything. That was my ghostly experience."

One of the standard stories around the place is about the time the owner, Leonard "Cappy" Fournier, sent a bartender named Tony down to the cellar

A photo of John Stone that hangs behind the bar.

to bring up some ice. Tony, the story goes, leaned over to scoop some ice out of the machine, when he felt a tap on the shoulder. Looking around, he saw no one there. Fournier went down to get the ice himself, and the same thing supposedly happened to him.

At least one of the ghosts seems to hang out in the cellar. Debbie McClain, the manager, tells of a waitress's reaching into the ice machine and having something hold her arm in there for a moment. "These are the sort of prankish things he—or she—does," Debbie says.

Debbie tells of a strange photograph taken by a patron at a party in the upstairs lounge. He was taking pictures of his woman companion. In one photo, there seemed to be a disembodied, floating hand and the silhouette of a head. "He brought them back and showed them to us," Debbie says. But even more striking, behind the living woman's head was a picture on the wall, the startling aspect being that there is no picture on the wall. "It was an old-fashioned cameo shot of a woman," Debbie says, "with an oval matting."

The customers also seem to get into the act, at least according to the legends of the restaurant. Fournier says: "A woman was in the dining room with her back to the wall. She said she felt two hands around the back of her neck. She started to yell, 'Get my check!' At least she paid the bill."

Butch Adams, the general manager, relates: "One day a gentleman was asking Cappy about the ghosts. He started raising his voice, saying that there were no such things as ghosts, that he didn't believe it. He said we were making it up. All of a sudden, at the table they were sitting at, the ashtray cracked right in front of them. He didn't say much after that."

No respectable haunted restaurant would be complete without a little girl ghost, and John Stone's Inn has one. A girl about nine or ten has appeared several times in a small room off the kitchen, according to one of the cooks. She is there, the cook says, early in the morning when she opens up. She is looking out the window, and as the cook enters the room the girl turns her head, smiles, and fades away. One morning Fournier and the cook arrived to open up and found the window smashed—with the glass outside on the ground, indicating it had been broken from the inside. The place had been locked for the night, nothing was stolen, and there was no other damage. At least one neighbor has said he sees a little girl staring out this window.

History: The inn was built in 1832 by Captain John Stone, a wealthy land owner and entrepreneur. A railroad was about to be built through town, and he reasoned that an inn next to the tracks would be a profitable investment. The tracks, now part of the Boston & Albany Railroad, are still in use. Speeches abounded when the inn opened, the most celebrated orator being Daniel Webster. In Stone's day, the place was called The Railroad Boarding House. Stone ran the place for only about two years, but he retained ownership, finally selling it to his younger brother, Napoleon, many years later. The place has

gone through many changes of ownership. At one time a secret room in the cellar, discovered only recently, was a way station for the Underground Railroad, housing many runaway slaves.

In modern times, until Fournier bought the place in 1976 and named it after its first owner, it was called the Ashland Hotel. A good many years ago the Boston Marathon started in Ashland. It now starts three miles away in Hopkinton, but the marathon runs past the inn. For years it was a gathering place for spectators and runners on the day of the race and the night before. Many runners took rooms at the inn.

Until Fournier took over the inn, it had been a rough place, avoided by a genteel clientele. It was called euphemistically a workingman's bar and was also frequented by motorcycle gangs. "There was a shooting here once," says Butch Adams. But Fournier has turned the place into a class act, complete with the quaint original wooden rafters. He is planning to remodel the upstairs so the place can be used as a hotel again, and the staff is eagerly awaiting a wild flurry of ghostly activity when this alteration of the environment begins.

Identity of ghosts: In 1984, Raffaele Bibbo, a parapsychologist from the Boston area, arranged a séance at the inn. It must have been one of the least private séances in the history of parapsychology. Bibbo, who runs a school of the psychic in Waltham, a suburb of Boston, brought along three of his mediums and about fifty of his students. A TV crew from a Boston station was also present to record the proceedings. And about a hundred of the staff and clientele of the inn also crowded into the upstairs lounge, where the séance was held, swelling the audience to some one hundred fifty incarnate souls. According to the mediums, there were a few discarnate ones on hand, too.

One of the mediums drew a blank, but two others seemed to come up with hits. The spirit of John

Stone supposedly came through medium Terry Pendleton. "The main spirit is John Stone," Bibbo says. "He came though Terry, saying this was his place and he didn't want anybody in that building. He still owns it as far as he's concerned."

Bibbo had no suggestions as to why John Stone was so intent on keeping people out of "his" inn, but another medium at the session, Henry LaFreniere, may have come up with a good indication. The spirit of a traveling salesman supposedly came through LaFreniere. He said he had come from New York and was staying at the inn. Late at night, he had gotten into a card game with John Stone and some of Stone's cronies. The salesman was accused of cheating. Stone went into a fury and hit him on the head with a gun, more or less accidentally killing him. The others in the room were sworn to secrecy, and the luckless salesman was buried in the cellar. "We've dug at random," Bibbo says, "searching for the bones, but we've had no luck yet."

According to medium LaFreniere, the salesman's ghost said that the others took his money and hid it in a safe underneath the bar. Fournier was quite intrigued by this information, for when he had bought the place there was indeed an ancient safe underneath the bar, and he had removed it.

Bibbo said there was evidence of several ghosts, including a woman innkeeper, a child, and others.

About four weeks later, Bibbo and his group returned to try to calm things down. Stone came through Terry Pendleton again, and this time she—supposedly controlled by Stone's spirit—swept a group of glasses off a table in front of her.

Personality of ghosts: The usual mode of expression seems to be prankishness. John Stone seemed angry and inhospitable at the séances, but he—or someone—is certainly nice to bartenders.

Witnesses: Dozens of employees and customers of the place.

Best time to witness: The happenings seem to occur both day and night.

Still haunted? Flying glasses, falling china, and $10 tips are still occurring.

Investigations: Two séances conducted by Bibbo's group.

Data submitted by: Cappy Fournier, owner; Eileen Streitenberger, bartender; Robin Drohan, waitress; Butch Adams, general manager; Debbie McClain, manager; Kyle McDonald, cook; Raffaele Bibbo; Terry Pendleton; article by Joanne Derbort in the *Middlesex News*; article by Leila Dunbar in the January 21, 1985, issue of the *Tri-County Advertiser*.

**30
The Ghost of the
Salem "Witch"**

Witch Hollow Farm
Boxford,
Massachusetts

Location: The address of Witch Hollow Farm in 474 Ipswich Road, Boxford.

Description of place: A beautifully maintained Colonial farmhouse in northeastern Massachusetts, built in 1666.

Ghostly manifestations: The house has been known as a haunted place for many generations. The chief ghost is believed to be Mary Tyler, who was condemned as a witch in Salem in 1693 and had lived in the house as a young woman. The most enthusiastic observer of Mary in recent times has been the late Arthur Pinkham, who lived in the house in the mid-twentieth century. He spoke and wrote extensively in his memoirs of continually seeing the ghost of Mary. Pinkham was the grandson of Lydia Pinkham, the inventor of the famed women's tonic. He was president of the Lydia Pinkham Company, based in Lynn, not far from Boxford, for thirty years.

From 1958, the place was owned by Ed French for

twelve years. The Frenches moved to New Hampshire when living in this chic pocket of northeastern Massachusetts got too expensive. French says he saw Mary "a couple of times" walking from the carriage house toward the main house. This was by night, by the light of the moon. He didn't try to speak to her. "I was too dumbfounded," he says. He says she appeared as a young woman.

Currently living in the house are Steve and Jean Rich and three of their children. The children are in their early twenties. The elder Riches have not seen any ghosts, although they feel presences and hear

Witch Hollow Farm

PHOTOS BY ARTHUR MYERS

unexplained noises. Their daughter, Sarah, however, a college student, has had more explicit experiences. At night in her bedroom she would hear rustling. When she turned the light on, nobody would be there. Once she heard a voice whisper her name. "One night," she says, "I turned the light out and felt something come down on top of me. I couldn't move my arms or legs, as though somebody was holding them down. I tried to speak, but something came down over my mouth. I just prayed that it would go away, and after about ten minutes it did." Another time while lying in bed she felt as though somebody were poking her, but when she turned the light on no one was there. Sometimes she would see a green light as she approached her bedroom, but when she opened the door it would go away. The Frenches also spoke of seeing green light in that room. The elder Riches and Sarah and her brother Bill sometimes would hear a bang in the attic. Sarah says she feels cold spots in the house. On one occasion, she and a friend heard unexplained noises in the kitchen, as though the cupboard doors were being opened and banged shut. The noises stopped when they went into the room. When they returned to the living room, the fire in the huge fireplace had inexplicably blazed up, and the room was full of smoke.

History: The house was built in 1666 by Moses Tyler. Mary, his sister, lived there until she married

Richard Post. She later was accused during the witchcraft hysteria in nearby Salem, but she confessed and was not hanged.

Identity of ghost(s): Mary Tyler seems the most likely ghostly occupant, but psychics have said there are other ghosts in residence. Sarah Rich feels some of the manifestations of which she has been aware were caused by a male ghost.

Personalities of ghosts: The current owners feel very much at home in the house, ghosts and all. They feel they are welcomed by the ghosts, although some of Sarah's experiences seem rather negative. There is no record of anyone ever having been hurt by a ghost in the house; however, some visitors to the house have felt they were unwanted, that there were presences that were unfriendly to them. One visitor said she felt ghostly hands pushing her out the door.

Witnesses: The Riches, Arthur Pinkham, Ed French, and various visitors.

Best time to witness: The Riches say the ghosts walk by night, when the lights go out.

Still haunted? Seems to be.

Investigations: Various professional psychics have felt presences in the house, as have other people who claim psychic sensitivities.

Data submitted by: The Riches; Ed French; Charles Pinkham, son of Arthur Pinkham; the Essex Institute, a historical museum in Salem; and various others who desire to remain anonymous.

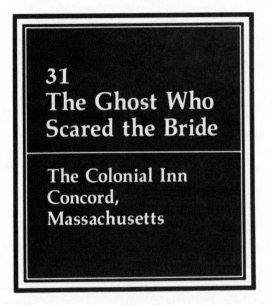

31
The Ghost Who
Scared the Bride

The Colonial Inn
Concord,
Massachusetts

Location: The Colonial Inn is situated at 48 Monument Square, Concord.

Description of place: The Colonial Inn might be considered a proper landmark of New England quaintness, situated as it is on Monument Square in historic Concord, a short walk down the road from the "rude bridge that arched the flood," where the Colonists and the Redcoats had one of their first encounters of the Revolutionary War. The attractive Colonial architecture that fronts the building combines three houses that date from the eighteenth century. In the 1960s and 1970s, a sizable addition of conventional brick and cement block was put up behind the Colonial structure.

Ghostly manifestations: In 1966, a newlywed couple, M. P. and Judith Fellenz of Highland Falls, New York, registered at the inn and were given Room No. 24, a large room on the second floor of the old part of the building, overlooking the square. The next morning the bride looked rather peaked. About two weeks later, Loring Grimes, the innkeeper and part owner, received an intriguing letter from her, herewith quoted in part:

> I have always prided myself on being a fairly sane individual but on the night of June 14 I began to have my doubts. On that night I saw a ghost in your inn. The next morning I felt too foolish to mention it to the management so my husband and I continued on our honeymoon. I wondered whether or not any other sightings of a ghost had been reported or if any story of one was involved in the history of the inn.
>
> The incident sounds very melodramatic. I was awakened in the middle of the night by a presence in the room—a feeling that some unknown being was in the midst. As I opened my eyes, I saw a grayish figure at the side of my bed, to the left, about four feet away. It was not a distinct person, but a shadowy mass in the shape of a standing figure. It remained still for a

The Colonial Inn at Concord.

PHOTO BY ARTHUR MYERS

moment, then slowly floated to the foot of the bed, in front of the fireplace. After pausing a few seconds, the apparition slowly "melted" away. It was a terrifying experience. I was so frightened I could not scream. I was frozen to the spot. . . .

For the remainder of the night I could not fall asleep. It was spent trying to conjure a logical explanation for the apparition. It was not a reflection of the moon as all the curtains were completely closed. Upon relating the incident to my husband he said the ghost was included in the price of the room.

History: Room No. 24 is in the oldest part of the inn. It was a room in a house built in 1716 by Capt. Joseph Minot, a soldier and physician. The Minot house became part of the inn, along with two neighboring houses, in the latter part of the nineteenth century.

Identity of ghost: Mrs. Fellenz's letter was promptly answered by Loring Grimes. He wrote in part:

Neither I nor any New Englander born of these historic and memorable parts has any reason to doubt your story. Our inn lives in the past as well as the present, and I am delighted to learn that there is now a resident "character" (besides myself). That the "ghost" was a polite and dignified one fits in well with the policy of the inn. We are indeed sorry that you were frightened by him, especially on such an occasion as your honeymoon. We are also sorry that your husband was not awake to share your frightening, if unique, experience. It is a

Concordian's belief that a man should be well scared on his wedding!

The room in which you shared your nuptial bliss was originally in the home of Dr. Joseph Minot, a surgeon in the Revolutionary War. It may, in all sincerity, have been the good doctor making his rounds. And if you are a literary inclined person, I am not so humble as not to

Postcard of the Colonial Inn.

suggest it may well have been the good Ralph Waldo Emerson trying to sum up the courage to give a newlywed advice on achieving a good marriage. If, Mrs. Fellenz, you are of the independent nature, I might also ponder on the reappearance of Henry David Thoreau, the kind of man who might like to give wisdom to young New Yorkers entering the sea of matrimony rather than contemplating Walden Pond. There are, of course, scores of personages in the 250 years of the Colonial Inn's history who might well appear on such a honeymoon night, if only out of deviltry. In the inn they break dishes, creak the planks, melt the butter, and sometimes even overstimulate our cocktails.

Personality of ghost: "Polite and dignified"?
Witness: Judith Fellenz.
Best time to witness: Apparently at night.
Still haunted? Paul Barry, current manager of the inn, says that recently he had another report on Room 24. A frequent guest of the inn, a businesswoman from Virginia, told him that she felt a presence in the room and that she would never stay in that room again. Lois Parker, sales manager of the inn, who has worked there some twenty-five years, says that a woman who worked in the dining room was sure there was a ghost in Room 24. However, Mrs. Parker adds, "I stayed in that room one time, and I didn't see a ghost."

Investigations: None that the management is aware of.

Data submitted by: Paul Barry and Lois Parker; copies of the Fellenz and Grimes letters were provided by the inn's management; the incident was suggested by an article by James Willert in the March 1983 issue of *Fate* magazine.

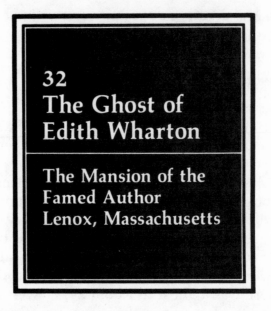

32
The Ghost of Edith Wharton

The Mansion of the Famed Author Lenox, Massachusetts

Location: The entrance to the grounds of The Mount is at the intersection of Route 20 and Plunkett Street, in Lenox.

Description of place: Called The Mount, it is a neo-Georgian mansion, built between 1900 and 1902 by Edith Wharton, one of America's great literary figures, as a country retreat in the Berkshire hills of western Massachusetts. Set on an estate of over a hundred acres, there are a number of outbuildings, originally used as servants' quarters. Gardens that date from Wharton's time are still kept up.

Ghostly manifestations: The place has for some time had a reputation of being haunted. For a number of years a now-defunct girls' school, Foxhollow School, owned the property and used The Mount primarily as a dormitory. Rumors of ghosts, particularly that of Edith Wharton, abounded. "There were lots of stories," recalls an alumna. "Of course, girls' boarding schools will be girls' boarding schools." In 1978, a very high-powered acting troupe called Shakespeare & Company moved into The Mount. It was headed by Tina Packer, an eminent Shakespearean actress from England, and the group has become one of the most praised practitioners of the Bard in America. Very quickly, the actors began to feel they were not alone.

Dennis Krausnick, a former Jesuit priest turned actor and director, was one of the founders of the company. He was the first of the group to enter the building. "It was locked up and boarded up," he recalls. "My brief was to measure all the rooms in the building." As he worked, supposedly alone in the building, he heard constant footsteps, but an exhaustive search revealed nobody. This was only a beginning. Many members of the company have their stories. Some are willing to talk; others prefer not to, at least for publication. Tina Packer is willing.

"I had been living at The Mount for four years," she says. "I was sleeping in what was called the

Edith Wharton's mansion, The Mount.

Henry James Room at that time, the largest of the bedrooms. I was very troubled that night, anxious about this and that, and there was a huge storm outside, and the wind was whipping around, and the shutters were rattling. I woke up, and I could see and feel that there was somebody in my room. I could see the outline of a man who was standing in the center of the room with his back to me. I thought it must be the person I live with. We live in the same house but don't share the same bedroom. I spoke to him, and the man turned around slowly and looked at me, and it wasn't him at all. It was some gentleman of staid face, with his hair pulled back in a ponytail. I realized it was a ghost, and I got very frightened, and I went back underneath the covers again. I had a conversation with myself about how I shouldn't be so silly; having never seen a ghost before, I should definitely look at it again. And I came back out from under the covers again, and it had gone. But then I realized that if I changed my mental state back to what it was, I'd see it again. Which then I did, and don't ask me how I did that. So then I refocused it again. And then I looked at it again, and he just turned and looked at me, and then I got frightened again and went back under the covers."

Andrea Haring is an actress and voice teacher. She reports an even more startling experience, as follows:

"It was in the winter, about 1979. We had had a meeting, and a lot of feelings had come up, and people were really excited and disturbed. I went up to Edith Wharton's writing room because a couple of people were having a discussion in my bedroom. There was an extra mattress in Edith Wharton's room, and I thought

I'd just lie down till they were done. I stoked up the wood stove in the room so that it should have stayed warm until about noon the next day. This was around midnight. I slept till about four in the morning. Then I drifted awake because it was very cold in the room. My eyes were still closed, but I was awake, and I sensed there was someone in the room. I opened my eyes and saw three figures in the room, and where the room had been bare of furniture there was now a small divan and a desk with a chair. I thought I must be dreaming, but I sort of pinched myself and slapped myself, and I thought, No, I'm awake; I must be seeing ghosts.

"One was Edith Wharton, whom I recognized because I'd been reading her biography. I could see the details in her dress and in her face and the way her hair was done, even though it was dark outside. She was kind of half seated, half lying on this divan. At this little desk was a man who was writing. I could see the muttonchops and his face and his outfit. I didn't recognize him, but he appeared to be gesturing to Edith. Although I couldn't hear any sound, they appeared to be talking to each other. He would stop and make a gesture like, 'Oh, yes' or 'Aha,' and then he'd start writing again. It almost appeared as though she were dictating to him. It was interesting because this was her writing room. And then there was a third figure who was standing with his arms folded, and I recognized him as Teddy Wharton, her husband, whom she eventually divorced. He was standing there with his arms crossed, looking at the two of them. I thought to myself, I wonder if I can leave. The minute that thought crossed my mind, all three of them turned and looked at me. I looked from one to the other. I have no reason for why I did this, but for some reason I just kind of smiled at them and nodded my head, kind of like, 'Hi, I'm here. I see you, and I guess you see me.' Edith Wharton gave me a kind of short, dignified nod. Teddy Wharton gave me a kind of brusque acknowledgment, with a nod. But I felt that that was his way, not that he was malevolent toward me or anything. And the guy at the desk, whom I didn't recognize, beamed at me and nodded his head quite vigorously. And then they all turned back to what they had been doing.

"I felt absolutely free to go at that point, which I did. As I closed the door, I still saw them there. I left the room and went across the hallway to my proper bedroom and found that the girl who was supposed to have slept in there where the ghosts were was in my bed. So I went back to the other room. I didn't feel scared. Whereas the room had been freezing, freezing cold, it was now warm. The stove had been going the whole time, but I had woken up because the room was so freezing. I found no one in the room—no furniture, no anything. The feeling that I got from it was that past, present, and future were all happening at the same time, that for some reason time as we know it was irrelevant. That somehow I was a part of their time and they were a part of my time.

"The next day I told a friend of mine in the company who had been doing a tremendous amount of research on Edith Wharton. She had this wonderful book that had pictures of all sorts of people who had been friends of Edith Wharton's. My friend thought maybe the man I didn't recognize was Henry James, because it was known that he was there a lot. So I looked through the book and identified the man from his picture. It turned out to be a guy who they suspected was Edith Wharton's lover and who had also helped her in a secretarial way in some of her works. The details of Edith Wharton's dress, which I had never seen before, I later saw in this book."

Haring did not hesitate to relate her experience to others in the company, and she says that the day after, one of the other people, Josephine Abady, told her she too had seen ghosts and she was very relieved that Haring had too, because up to then she was sure no one would believe her. Josephine Abady is a well-known figure in American regional theater. She is now artistic director of the Berkshire Theater Festival in nearby Stockbridge. At the time of her sighting of ghosts, however, she was head of the Theater Department of Hampshire College. The Mount was in a state of disrepair when Shakespeare & Company moved in, and Abady led a group of students from Smith, Hampshire, the University of Massachusetts, Amherst, and Mount Holyoke in helping to recondition the place. Abady relates:

"I lived in The Mount on the top floor in what I imagine was one of the servant's rooms. Once I was down on the second floor, and I saw a figure in the hall in turn-of-the-century dress. It was a woman. It disappeared. A few nights later I was upstairs and I saw the same figure. I have a very active imagination, so I thought it must

be something I was making up. A couple of
weeks went by, and I saw it again, standing in
the hall with a man. The woman looked very
much like Edith Wharton; the man looked like
Henry James. I found out later that Henry James
had indeed spent a lot of time at The Mount. I
didn't know that when I saw this figure.

"One of the things I heard all the time while I
was at The Mount was this rustling sound, as
though someone in a long dress were walking
by. One night I heard that sound, and I went out
in the hall, and I saw the figure that I had now
seen three times before walking away from me.
After you see something over and over, you
realize that it's a phenomenon that you probably
can't explain, but it's not your imagination at
work. I'm perfectly willing to believe that Edith
Wharton was so fond of The Mount and left it
so regretfully that she might have come back."

Some of the members of the Shakespeare company had frightening experiences in which a ghost
seemed to restrain them forcibly. Dennis Krausnick
tells the following incident, which is similar to experiences related by others in the house:

"Once I was asleep in a double room in the
servant's quarters, which served as my office
and bedroom. One night while in bed, I heard
someone come into my office. I thought it was
one of the actors, who wanted to talk about
something. I said 'Who's there?' The footsteps
stopped. I got up and went into the office and
turned on the light. There was no one there. So
I went back to bed. Sometime after, I was aware
of a large figure standing next to the bed, a tall

human being's figure, dressed in a kind of cloak
with a hood on it, open in the front but closed
down enough so that you couldn't see any face
within it. I felt at some level that it was
antagonistic to me. It took me what seemed like
a full ten minutes of struggle to actually raise
myself. I felt it was trying to press me back
down on the bed. When I finally did overcome it
and get myself to a seated position, it was gone.
It dissolved. A cat at the foot of the bed that had
been purring had stopped purring. That scared
me even more. It would have been more
comforting to think that I was hallucinating and
the cat knew there was nothing there."

Krausnick also tells of hearing, during the first
two years the company had taken over The Mount,
when he was alone much of the time, what sounded
like young people's voices outside. "They would
always be on the side of the house that I wasn't," he
says. "I would look, and there would be nothing. The
sound would stop when I would actually look out the
window. There were never any tracks in the snow or
anything like that. This experience recurred many
times in the course of the first two years. Finally I
just got used to it and ignored it. It was like listening
to a small playground, fifteen or twenty kids."

Was it the sound of girlish laughter from the
former students of Foxhollow School, somehow im-
printed on the atmosphere? For very few of these
young people could have died yet. While they lived at
The Mount, the girls were acutely aware of scary
stories, recalls Dorothy Carpenter, an alumna who
now lives in New York City. "People used to talk
about it all the time," she says. "I don't think Edith
Wharton ever typed, but they used to say she was

typing in the basement. Every time we'd hear a creak, we'd say it was Edith Wharton's ghost, but nobody really thought it was. Nobody gave it any credence."

Later, she changed her mind. Foxhollow School stopped using The Mount when enrollment shrunk, and the place fell into disrepair. Carpenter wanted to preserve the ornate ceiling of the ballroom and returned in the early 1970s to do the work herself. "When I was working on the ceiling, I was living there by myself for two months," she recalls. "I probably was inhaling a lot of plaster dust at the time, but, in any case, I saw a ghost on the terrace. It was during the day. The ghost looked like somebody in an off-white summer dress, sort of maybe lace but not real gauzy. I think it was Edith Wharton. In fact, I didn't have any other thought at the time. I didn't wonder who it was; it was her. I've seen pictures of her, but not pictures looking like this. It was alive. My feeling was that I wished she wouldn't see me. I was looking out onto the terrace. I was just looking out the window, and she was walking on the terrace. She walked up to the edge and then walked back, and I was very quiet. At the time I thought maybe I'd been inhaling too much plaster dust. I didn't tell anybody except a good friend. I said I thought I'd been around there too long, that the other day I saw Edith Wharton's ghost on the terrace."

History: Edith Wharton was born in 1862 into the New York society she portrayed, often scathingly, in her books. Her maiden name was Jones. The Joneses were Very Important People in the city's upper crust. It has been said that the term "keeping up with the Joneses" refers to these Joneses. She married a fellow socialite, Edward Wharton, sometimes described as "charming but dim." She eventually di-

vorced him, preferring literati and intellectuals to
rich conventionals. One of her favorite people was
the writer Henry James, who often visited her at The
Mount. Wharton, who died in 1937, left The Mount
in 1908 and sold it in 1912. It is said that she had
found that her spiritual home was really Paris.

Edith Wharton

The Mount passed to the ownership of various
private individuals, one of them being a well-known
journalist, Carr van Anda, managing editor of *The
New York Times*. Foxhollow School owned the property for several years, then sold it to a developer,
who turned the school buildings and campus into a
country refuge for well-to-do city escapees. The
Shakespeare company has owned The Mount since

1980. The company produces its plays outdoors during the summer, although it operates as a going concern all through the year. The building is being further restored, and plays based on Edith Wharton's life are put on there throughout the summer.

Identity of ghosts: According to witnesses, Edith Wharton and various other people around her, including Henry James, not to mention the girlish laughter that seems to suggest a cluster of Foxhollow girls astray in time.

Personality of ghosts: Varying. Often the apparitions seem aloof, unaware. But sometimes, as in the experience of Andrea Haring, they seem to interact with the living, in a not unfriendly manner. However, the experiences of Dennis Krausnick and others seem to indicate a rather menacing, unfriendly spirit.

Witnesses: Many members of the Shakespeare group, some of whom are still connected with the company, others of whom are not. Also people involved with Foxhollow School.

Best time to witness: The ghosts seem to appear around the clock, with some preference for the darker hours. Tours may be taken of the house during the summer, but apparitions and ghostly rappings are not guaranteed.

Still haunted? The ghosts seem to have no intention of quitting the premises for a gaggle of actors.

Investigations: No psychics or parapsychologists have been brought in.

Data submitted by: Tina Packer, Dennis Krausnick, Andrea Haring, Josephine Abady, Dorothy Carpenter, and others.

33
The Inn With a
Nonpaying Guest

The Plaza Guest
House
Provincetown,
Massachusetts

Location: The Plaza Guest House is located at 11 Pearl St., Provincetown.

Description of place: A Greek Revival, three-story frame house with thirteen rooms, now used as a guest house, on the tip of Cape Cod. It is known to have been built before 1830.

Ghostly manifestations: The place has been a guest house only since 1981, when a former chef, Franz-Josef Patzwald, bought it. Strange things had been happening in the house for a number of years, and Patzwald got an early initiation. "Just after I moved in," he says, "a door started rattling like crazy. The windows were closed, so there was no wind. I told 'him' off, to be quiet; it's my house now." But the ghost has a mind of his own. Patzwald still hears steps, particularly on the stairs. Some people hear voices, he says. The main haunt of the ghost seems to be Room No. 6, on the second floor, although Room No. 7 runs a close second. A strange light sometimes appears in the latter, and once when Patzwald was ripping up linoleum in the room he found spots on the floor that he suspects might be dried blood. One night, Patzwald relates, he rented No. 6 to two Canadian girls. That night he heard one of the girls screaming. She had gone to the bathroom next door and had been chased back to her room by a strange light. Also, a closet in the room keeps opening without visible help.

Lee Faroba, who has lived next door for some time, has a number of interesting tales about the house. Speaking of Room No. 6, she says, "You can't

The Plaza in Provincetown

get an animal into that room for love or money. Not a cat or dog will go across the threshold, nor can you drag them in. They stop dead at the door and whine and cry, and if you try to drag them in they snap at you."

Faroba was a close friend of the people who owned the house for ten years before Patzwald. She recalls, "A friend of theirs from New York was going to stay a week after they left in the fall, and I was going to close up. He stayed one day and came over to tell me he was leaving. He said, 'I went to bed last night. [Not in Room 6 or 7, but downstairs.] Everything was fine. I didn't have a drink; I didn't smoke a joint. I woke up about three in the morning, and I was two feet above the bed.' It terrified him. He sat up the rest of the night. And he was a sensible architect type, who I don't think even believed in this sort of thing. He was the coldest, most levelheaded sort of person."

Faroba's best story concerns a small gathering in the living room. "One evening," she relates, "we were all sitting around. There was a desk in a corner. One of the house guests had once been tested for ESP and been told he had a high degree of it. All of a sudden he said, 'There's someone sitting at the desk.'

The Plaza in Provincetown

We didn't see anything. This man, his name was Eddie, said he got the name Zeke Cabal. He said the person was feeling out of place, that he didn't know why he was there, that he meant no harm and was just confused. The name meant nothing to any of us."

A couple of months later, Faroba and one of the owners of the house were at a local museum and were talking with the elderly curator. They asked him if that name meant anything to him. According to Faroba, the old man said, "Sure, Zeke Cabal is the one who burned to death." Faroba adds, "Cabal was a sort of town drunk. I guess it was in the 1920s. He burned himself up in a little shack at the other end of town one night. What he was doing in my friends' house nobody seems to know, but the name was authenticated."

History: The house was built in the early nineteenth century by a sea captain named Higgins. His family lived there for generations, and the place was long known as the Higgins House. Faroba has known at least the past four owners of the place. She lives in a similar house next door, which she calls "a big ark of a house."

Identity of ghost: Zeke Cabal might be a good guess for starters, although Patzwald's suspicions about the floor stains in Room No. 7 give one pause. Sometimes, it is said, a spirit that "belongs" in a place will set up vibrations that draw in other wandering confused spirits.

Personality of ghost: The ghost reported by the guest with ESP was, the observer said, confused and feeling out of place, but was not at all malevolent. The Canadian girl and the dogs and cats might have different opinions.

Witnesses: Patzwald and other owners, as well as guests in the house.

Best time to witness: Most of the heavy occurrences seem to have happened at night, although Patzwald says he has observed some strange things during the day, too.

Still haunted? Patzwald says he thinks the occurrences are lessening, but two guests who are psychic and who stayed there recently say they could feel the energy of the spirit(s).

Investigations: No formal investigations, aside from the observances of guests who happen to be psychic.

Data submitted by: Franz-Josef Patzwald, Lee Faroba, and Ann Valukis and Gail Howatt, the guests who recently felt the energy.

34
Was It a Troll That Flooded the Cellar?

A Turn-of-the-Century House Somerville, Massachusetts

Location: Karen Robinson's house is situated at 35 Hall Ave., in Somerville. It would be advisable to contact Ms. Robinson before visiting.

Description of place: A three-story, wooden house in the lower-middle-class Boston suburb of Somerville, a town that is partly ethnic, partly young people on the way up, and partly overflow from academic, intellectual Cambridge, next door. The house was built in 1894, and was probably a single-family dwelling until the 1920s, when it was converted into a two-family house. It is set on a field-stone and brick foundation.

Ghostly manifestations: Two young women live in the upper apartment, which comprises the top floors of the house. One, Karen Robinson, is the owner of the house, having bought it in 1983. She is an actress and a model and also works in the public relations field. Her tenant, Julie Verrier, moved in in 1985. She is a customer services representative for a computer firm. Several months after Julie had moved in, the two women were going out in the evening. As they were leaving in Karen's car, Julie said, "I'm beginning to think this place is haunted. I keep putting things in places, and they disappear or show up someplace else." This struck a chord with Karen, for she had had a strange feeling about the place since she bought it. "There were things about the house from the very first that I did not feel comfortable with," she says.

For one thing, she was troubled with flooding in the cellar, which seems a prosaic enough problem for a householder, but further developments indicate there might have been more to it than that. Karen has been psychically sensitive throughout her life. She particularly got an uncomfortable feeling when she went near the back wall of the house, in bedrooms on the second and third floors. "I kept a lot of clothes in the room on the third floor," she says, "and I would hate to go up to that room at night, which I would do if I were going out and I needed clothes." For a while, she slept in the back room on the second floor, but she felt uncomfortable there. "I had," she says, "a feeling of a presence at night, of its being almost like an animal, as though it had claws or wanted to bite me."

When Julie moved in, she took the back room on the top floor. The bed was set about six inches from the wall. Repeatedly, she would wake up in the morning to find that the bed had moved up against the wall. She would find belongings in a different place than she had put them. She would find slippers that she had left in the bedroom downstairs in the living room. "Lights that I'd shut off would come on again," Julie says, "the front hall light, the bathroom light. This was when I was alone in the apartment.

PHOTOS BY ARTHUR MYERS

Karen Robinson's house

Sometimes I'd get a funny feeling that mischief was in the air."

Not long after Karen and Julie had their talk in the car, Karen went to a Cambridge psychic, Chaya Sarah Sadeh, and told her what was going on. On visiting the place, Chaya felt there was a troll trapped in the cellar. She felt that the troll had been involved in a spring that was covered over and blocked when the house was built, almost a hundred years ago. "Sometimes," Chaya says, "what we think of as ghosts—human beings who have died—are instead what might be called noxious rays, earth energies that are blocked. I felt this troll was stuck there. We did a ritual releasing of him. What came to me to do was to send him to another plane, where his energies could be transformed into a more positive and fruitful existence. That's what I often do."

Karen says: "We traced an energy from the basement all the way up through the back wall of the house. I could feel it when Chaya showed me where it was along the back wall. If you put your hand up there, it was very hot. Chaya thought there was a troll living under the house."

The ghostly manifestations, Karen says, became much more active when Julie moved in and began sleeping almost against the back wall. "He felt she was really invading his space," Karen suggests.

Karen Robinson

On the evening following the exorcism, Karen feels, the troll came to her. "After Chaya left," she says, "I could feel his presence. I was washing up in the bathroom. It was like a little voice was saying, 'Please don't make me go. I want to stay here.' I told it that it really had to leave, but it was very emotional for me, because I felt this little spirit had suddenly become very vulnerable. I got a real image of this furry little creature with claws. It didn't seem to have the intelligence of a human being; it seemed very naive. And the night that it left and was begging me to let him stay it seemed very childlike."

History: Karen is not aware of any psychic manifestations in the house before she bought it. She purchased it from a couple who had lived there some thirty years. During Karen's brief time in the house, however, she has been aware that various unpleasant things have happened, usually to young men who lived there. A young man who lived downstairs was killed in an automobile accident. A young couple broke up. Her own marriage broke up. Skeptics might say this is par for the course in Somerville, or anywhere else, but Karen's feelings are worth noting.

Identity of ghost: A troll?

Personality of ghost: Julie felt it was "very mischievous." Karen felt it was "a little more nasty than that."

Witnesses: Karen Robinson, Julie Verrier, and Chaya Sarah Sadeh, the psychic who performed the exorcism.

Best time to witness: Most of the manifestations seem to have taken place after dark.

Still haunted? The exorcism seems to have been successful. "That was the last connection we've had with it," Karen says. "There's been a wet patch on the cellar floor, but even through the horrific rains that we've had, the sump pump has never been full, and there's been no flooding."

Investigations: The exorcism performed by Chaya Sarah Sadeh.

Data submitted by: Karen Robinson, Julie Verrier, Chaya Sarah Sadeh.

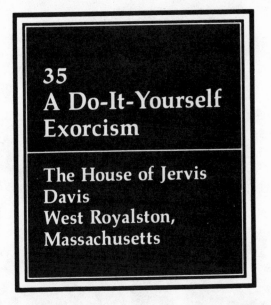

**35
A Do-It-Yourself
Exorcism**

The House of Jervis
Davis
West Royalston,
Massachusetts

Location: The Cooks no longer live in the house. The present owners would prefer no visitors.

Description of place: A two-story white farmhouse built in the late 1700s, adjacent to farmland, in north central Massachusetts.

Ghostly manifestations: The house appears to have been inhabited by the ghost of Jervis Davis, the original builder and occupant. For decades it has been considered haunted by residents of the neighborhood. People moved in and out, usually leaving within a year or two, frightened by glimpses of Jervis Davis and by various poltergeist activities. A woman who lived there in the early 1960s said sometimes all the shades in the house would fly up at once, making a horrendous clatter.

In the mid-1960s, a young couple, Ernie and Lynn Cook, moved in, determined not to let Jervis chase them out. Lynn occasionally would see Jervis. Many people felt cold spots, particularly in the kitchen. The

The house of Jervis Davis

Cooks's boarder, Steve Butterfield, would sometimes see Jervis sitting on the stairs when he was
about to go up to his bedroom for the night. On
these occasions he would come back to the kitchen
for another cup of coffee. Once he found an old-
fashioned knife in his bed, which later disappeared.
Clunks and bumps abounded; cutlery would unac-
countably disappear or be changed in position. The
hot water valve in the cellar would sometimes be
tampered with. The Cooks felt they had an unwelcome guest, but the ghost obviously felt *he* had
unwelcome guests. Eventually, the young people,
the Cooks and Butterfield, began to get annoyed
with Jervis's antics. They would talk about him in

the kitchen when they felt he was around, questioning whether he was really married to the mother of his children—Lynn could find no marriage record in the town's files—and blaming him, as an early selectman, for the present problems of the town. When they did this, the poltergeist disturbances escalated markedly.

By this time, the Cooks had three small children, and Jervis was making the house too crowded. One evening they had a brilliant idea—they would find Jervis's grave and escort him there. In a mood of

The grave of Jervis Davis

high hilarity, the three adults and the three children piled into a car, urging Jervis to come along. After searching several old cemeteries in the area, they came across Jervis's grave. Lynn felt a twinge of guilt about having twitted Jervis about not having made an honest woman of the mother of his children when she saw his wife's grave situated chastely beside his own. But to business: "OK, Jervis," Lynn said, "stay here and don't bother us anymore. Fun's fun, but it's over with." And they haven't been bothered by Jervis since.

History: Jervis Davis was a farmer and prominent citizen—a selectman—in the rural village of West Royalston in north central Massachusetts. He built the house during the 1700s and lived in it with his family throughout his life, tilling adjacent acreage. As far as the Cooks know, no one except themselves had worked the farmland since the death of Jervis. People had just used the house as living quarters. Lynn Cook suspects that irritated Jervis, who decided to drive out these interlopers. And he usually did.

Identity of ghost: Probably Jervis Davis.

Personality of ghost: Jervis was mischievous at best; at his worst, he expressed distinct hostility. However, although he attempted to frighten people out of "his" house, there is no record of his ever actually having hurt anyone.

Witnesses: Dozens of people who have lived in or visited the house over the years. Lynn Cook says she

Lynn Cook

sometimes would feel Jervis sitting on her bed and that one night he materialized and tried to pull her out of bed. Lynn reports, "I said, 'Oh, will you leave me alone!' And he just vanished." Lynn attributes her bravery to the fact that she was brought up in a house in Barre, Massachusetts, that was haunted, and she got used to ghosts at an early age.

Best time to witness: Jervis seems to have gone back to his family plot.

Still haunted? Apparently not. Lynn has a theory about why Jervis gave up his haunting routine. "I think," she says, "that what made him leave was that we were doing with this land what he wanted to do. We were farming; we were homesteading it. Since his day, no one else had done this. They were just living in the house and going out to their jobs. I think in a way we were making him happy, and he decided to leave us alone."

Investigations: The author interviewed the Cooks and Steve Butterfield extensively.

Data submitted by: The Cooks and Steve Butterfield, as well as Dick Davis of Pittsfield, Massachusetts, a descendant of Jervis.

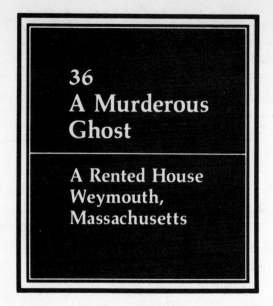

36
A Murderous Ghost

A Rented House Weymouth, Massachusetts

Location: The account was given to the author by Rev. Schultz some years after the occurrence. The address is not available.

Description of place: A two-story house, converted from a barn, with a stairway down the middle.

Ghostly manifestations: In 1973, Edd and Ruth Schultz moved into this house with their baby son, Christopher. Schultz, just out of an Episcopal divinity school, was a part-time assistant in a parish in the village of Hanover for the summer. It was a hot summer that year, but they found that the stairway that split the house was always very cold. One day, while Edd was out, Ruth happened to be standing at the top of the stairs, holding the baby in her arms. Suddenly she felt hands on her back, pushing her. With the baby, she fell down the stairs, about twenty steps. As she was falling, she could feel a cold chill all around her, but from the baby she felt a warm glow.

She was not hurt, and neither was the baby. She did not tell her husband at the time what had caused her to fall. About a week later in the middle of the night, the baby, who slept in another room, woke up screaming, for no apparent reason. Ruth got up to go to him, and Edd awoke as she was leaving their room.

Edd recalls: "When I woke up I had what I can only describe as the most tremendous feeling of fear and panic, for no apparent reason that I was aware of. I felt almost as though there were some evil presence that was there and was holding me down—almost, I guess, trying to possess me. As my wife was going through the corridor, she said that again she felt these icy cold hands on her shoulders. She felt these icy hands around her neck as though they were trying to choke her. We picked up the baby, and the baby calmed down after a while, and this feeling of panic we had began to go away. The morning after, I performed an exorcism on the stairway. This was the first time I had ever done it. I had done some lecturing about the church and the occult but had never done any of that kind of thing myself. It was a simple form of exorcism that is described by the Bishop of Exeter, Church of England, in a small book. After the exorcism, there was still a little bit of chill in the stairway, but it didn't seem to be quite as strong, and we didn't have any occurrences after that."

History: About a month later, the landlady mentioned that the place had once been a barn and that a man had committed suicide by hanging himself from the rafters in the area that had become the stairway when the building was converted into a house.

Identity: Possibly the man who committed suicide.

Personality of ghost: Obviously malevolent and murderous.

Witnesses: The Schultzes—although there may have been others before and since.

Still haunted? Not known.

Investigations: The author interviewed the Rev. Edd Schultz, now an Episcopal pastor in Philadelphia. He is a psychic and has had extensive experience at exorcism and in teaching parapsychology.

Data submitted by: The Reverend Edd Schultz.

**37
A Weird Chopin
Concert**

A Deserted Mansion
near
Gulfport, Mississippi

Location: This account was given to the author recently by Fran Franklin, who was 11 at the time of the occurrence, and who does not know the exact location of the house.

Description of place: It looked like a traditional plantation house, constructed of brick painted white, on the Gulf Coast of Mississippi near Gulfport. However, it had been built only ten years before the incident recounted here took place.

Ghostly manifestations: In 1941, Fran Franklin, now a professor in the Department of Communication Arts at the University of Arkansas, was a girl of eleven. She had a favorite aunt, who was unusual in that she was only four feet tall and also in that she was the editor of a newspaper, the *Laurel* (Miss.) *Leader-Call*. Her name was Harriet Gibbons, and she was a woman of very definite opinions. One of those opinions was that there are no ghosts.

Aunt Harriet knew the wealthy couple who had built the imitation plantation house. About two years before, their teenage daughter had committed suicide. Soon afterward, the couple had moved out hastily, taking only their clothes, leaving the furniture and other possessions behind. Harriet Gibbons often bemoaned what she considered her friends' superstition. Once, while visiting Fran's parents, she said that this had become a challenge, that she planned to stay overnight at the house and prove there was nothing unusual going on there. Fran heard her and asked if she could go along on this ghost hunt, and her aunt agreed.

One evening soon afterward, Aunt Harriet, with Fran in tow, let herself into the house with a key her friends had given her. They arranged chairs in the front hallway and sat down to wait. Nothing happened for some time, but near midnight they heard a noise that seemed to come from the upstairs hall. It sounded, says Fran, like footsteps. They heard a door close, presumably an upstairs bedroom door, and the footsteps seemed to be coming down the hall.

Fran says she looked at the top of the stairs, half expecting to see a dim, ghostly figure, but there was nothing there. However, the footsteps then began coming down the stairs. As they reached the foot of the stairs, Fran could see a depression in the carpet. Then the footsteps reached the marble hallway and clicked across the foyer. They went down a hall to a set of double doors that opened into a music room. The doors opened.

Fran recalls that she was terrified, but her aunt did not show any reaction, so she didn't either. The footsteps continued across the floor of the music room until they reached a piano, which was within their vision with the double doors open. As they watched, the piano stool came back. The top covering the piano keys was raised, revealing the keyboard. Then the music began. Three pieces by Chopin came from the piano.

Then the music stopped. The keyboard cover was lowered again, the piano stool was put back in its original position, and the steps came back out of the room. The double doors were closed, and the steps tapped across the marble foyer back to the foot of the staircase. There they hesitated, as though the unseen performer were momentarily observing her audience of two, then the footsteps ascended the stairs, went back down the hall, and went into the bedroom, and the door was heard to close.

Aunt Harriet turned to Fran and said, "It's now time to go." As they were driving back to the Edgewater Beach Hotel, where they were staying, Fran asked her aunt what she thought of all this, and her aunt replied with one sentence: "There is no such thing as a ghost."

To Fran's knowledge, her aunt never spoke of the evening's expedition again except once, many years later when Fran and her husband were having dinner with her. "My husband had always suspected this story," Fran recalls, "and he related it to my aunt. Her only comment was 'There are no such things as ghosts.' "

History: After their daughter's suicide and their precipitous departure from the house, the couple had gone to Europe, where they stayed with friends for some time. They never returned to the plantation house. When they eventually came back to the United States, they built another house and lived there.

Identity of ghost: Presumably the young woman who killed herself.

Personality of ghost: Possibly confused, seemingly not hostile.

Witnesses: Fran Franklin and Harriet Gibbons.

Best time to witness: This incident took place around midnight.

Still haunted? Fran Franklin does not know if the house is still standing.

Investigations: Only known one is that of Fran and her aunt.

Data submitted by: Fran Franklin; first suggested by an account in the book *Ghost Stories from the American South* (August House, 1985) by W. K. McNeil.

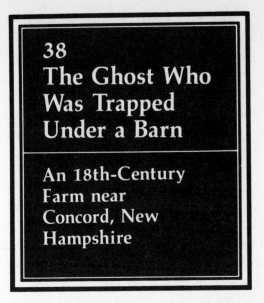

**38
The Ghost Who
Was Trapped
Under a Barn**

An 18th-Century
Farm near
Concord, New
Hampshire

Location: The current owners of this farmhouse wish to remain anonymous, and prefer the exact location of the place not be revealed.

Description of place: Manifestations were occurring in an eighteenth-century farmhouse. They were also, it appeared on psychic inquiry, happening around the property, particularly on a spot where there had once been a barn.

Ghostly manifestations: Roger and Nancy Pile have taught mediumship in Connecticut. One of their students—who asked to remain anonymous in this account—had lived as a girl with her parents in this New Hampshire farmhouse. As a child, she constantly heard a thumping noise and felt presences in the house, particularly in the attic. Currently, she is a research chemist in Connecticut. She was becoming worried about her parents, who still live in the house and were increasingly becoming aware of paranormal manifestations, which were making them edgy. She asked the Piles to accompany her to her childhood home and see what could be done about laying the ghost, or ghosts. Roger Pile reports:

"We found several pockets of what we call 'trauma residue,' energies created by a trauma at that point. In the attic, with several people present, the torn wallpaper began to move back and forth. There was no air up there; it was completely still. When we said, 'Yes, we know you're there,' the movement stopped. We were picking up psychic impressions that the entity, whoever he was, had met with an accident and that we would find out if we investigated around the grounds, which we did.

"There were two main areas of traumatic energy. One was in a sort of hollow on an old road leading off into the woods. The other was in a field near the house. There was a lesser thing in the nearby cornfield. While I was there I saw a small boy running with an arrow through him. I didn't know what it meant at the time, but I was later to find out that it was an interesting adjunct to this whole situation.

"We investigated the field first and found that this was perhaps the most powerful area. The psychic impression that came was that the entity had been working in a barn that had been there and that the timbers of the barn had collapsed on top of him, pinning him there. This would account for the loud thumping noise that was heard from time to time.

"When we investigated the other area, the picture came of a young woman coming back from visiting friends in a horse and wagon and finding her husband pinned underneath the barn wreckage. She turned the horses around and whipped them up the hill to get help. As she went up the hill, the wheels struck a rock, she was thrown out and instantly killed.

"Since there was nothing we could do about that situation, we went back to where the barn had been. I went into trance and psychically levitated the timbers off this entity. The reason for this was that the entity died with the mind-set of being pinned there, even though there was nothing there now. The time and place were fixed in his consciousness, and therefore he was still pinned there some 170 years later. This happened in 1814."

History: Pile says that the investigative group later checked town records and found that a barn had indeed stood on the spot in question, even though there was no physical sign of it now. In further trance work, Pile said, he found that the boy he had sensed who was pierced by an arrow was the son of the entity. Some years before, the boy and his mother had been killed by marauders. The woman who was killed driving the horses to get help was the entity's second wife. According to Pile, his student, the young woman who had lived in the house as a child, was a reincarnation of the woman killed in the wagon incident.

Identity of ghosts: Pile attempts to "rescue" earth-bound entities; that is, to send them on to higher spiritual planes. In this case, he says, "It was necessary to psychically levitate the timbers off him and give him a healing before he was ready to be rescued." This done, Pile urged the entity, whose name was Charles, to look to the light, and the entity gratefully moved away from the prison he had made for himself for so many years. The little boy, the entity's son, whose name was Ben, went with his father. There was also a little girl there. Pile asked Charles who she was, and the entity replied, through Nancy Pile, who was acting as trance medium, "I knew her by Missy. I don't know what her name rightly is." Guided by Pile, the little girl also moved into a higher dimension.

Personalities of ghosts: Says Pile: "The personality of Charles was that of a Scottish farmer; a good, hard-working, very kind, thoughtful man." He had a rather archaic way of speaking, which Pile says he believes was prevalent in New England in the early 1800s. "The personality of the little girl," Pile says, "was exactly that of a little girl. While my wife was in trance her feet were sort of going over one another as a little girl's would do, and she sat in the chair just like a little girl would do, and indeed her voice was similar to a little girl's."

Witnesses: The Piles, their student, and their student's parents, who lived on the place.

Best time to witness: When there were manifestations, they seemed to come at various times of day and night.

Still haunted? No manifestations have been noticed since the "rescues."

Data submitted by: Roger Pile, Nancy Pile, and their student.

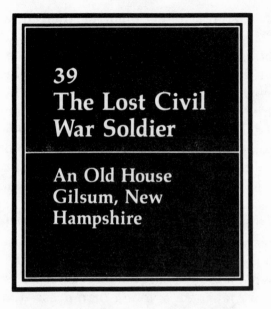

**39
The Lost Civil
War Soldier**

**An Old House
Gilsum, New
Hampshire**

Location: This account is a reminiscence by the late Charles Hapgood. He did not pinpoint the address, other than Gilsum.

Description of place: A two-story wooden house dating from the early nineteenth century in the town of Gilsum, New Hampshire.

Ghostly manifestations: Mr. and Mrs. Alfred Cutler (not their real names) moved into this old house in the late 1960s. He was a student at Keene State College. Very quickly they became aware they were not alone. Mrs. Cutler was a sensitive and could feel a presence. On the physical level, heavy steps could be heard, lights would go on and off when no one alive was switching them, household objects would be inexplicably moved. Teaching at Keene was a professor of anthropology, author of several books, who was also known as a mystic. His name was Charles Hapgood. The Cutlers asked Dr. Hapgood to come to their house and see what he could do about ridding them of their unwelcome guest. Hapgood often dealt with ghosts through automatic writing. He would hold a pen over paper, and the ghost would supposedly guide his hand. Writing, the ghost said he had been in the house for a hundred years and that his name was George. He said he did nothing but sit on the cellar steps or the steps going up to the second floor. He also often sat in the kitchen. Hapgood asked him why he stayed there, and the spirit replied that he didn't know how to get away. At this point, Hapgood went to the phone and called Elwood Babbitt, a well-known clairvoyant who lives in central Massachusetts. He told Babbitt there was an energy in the room and asked what it looked like. Babbitt said it was standing very near Hapgood, a young man dressed in a Civil War uniform. Trying to break the spirit loose from its physical-plane bondage, Hapgood asked the spirit if it prayed. It wrote in capital letters, "YES, I PRAY EVERY DAY." Hapgood asked what sort of a physical life he had had. The ghost wrote "I DID EVERY-THING I SHOULD HAVE." Hapgood by this time had deduced that this was a very self-centered, self-absorbed spirit, unconcerned with anyone but himself. So he launched on a bit of psychotherapy with this ghost. "I said," Hapgood related, " 'In this town of Gilsum there are a lot of people who are in trouble, people who have lost things. You could help them. Look around this town and see if there's anyone you can help, a person maybe who has lost a ring. Perhaps it's under a rug. Give her the idea of looking under the rug,' and so on. If you will do that, your prayers will be answered.' " Hapgood said George may have taken the suggestion, because he never, to anyone's awareness, turned up in the house again.

History: By checking deeds, Hapgood and the Cutlers found that a hundred years before there had been two Georges living in the house, father and son. It was during the time of the Civil War, and Hapgood suspects the young man had been killed in the war and this was his spirit.

Identity of ghost: Possibly a young man who had lived in the house before going away to war a hundred years before.

Personality of ghost: George seemed confused, helpless, and concerned only with himself. Hapgood says, "A ghost is usually trying to communicate with someone on the physical level—sometimes a specific person, sometimes anyone. The ghost is hardly ever trying to annoy; that's not its purpose. They want attention, because they can't find their way in the astral plane, and for some reason they can't get the help they need there. So they try to find someone sensitive to communicate with on the physical plane."

Witnesses: The Cutlers, Hapgood, and—at a distance—Babbitt.

Best time to witness: The ghost seems to have found other haunts, on this plane or another.

Still haunted? Apparently not.

Investigations: Clairvoyance by Charles Hapgood and Elwood Babbitt.

Data submitted by: Charles Hapgood (now deceased).

**40
Some Cats Aren't
Satisfied with
Nine Lives**

Victorian Mansion
Midland Park, New
Jersey

Location: This house is located at 15 Franklin St., Midland Park. Before visiting, please contact the present owners, James and Anita Ford.

Description of place: An elegant Victorian mansion, built during the Civil War, with a pillared porch, three stories, and a mansard roof. It has eighteen rooms, including eight bedrooms, and ten-foot ceilings. There are many floor-to-ceiling windows.

Ghostly manifestations: A number of ghosts seem to be hanging around this old house, but the most intriguing is the apparent spirit of a cat. Several people have said they have seen it—a yellow and white kitty. Many others have felt it—or some sort of furry critter. And probably hundreds have felt warm spots where it had been—possibly still was—lying. The present owners of the house, James and Anita Ford, are pretty much skeptics, but they and their two grown children report feeling the warm

SKETCHES BY ETHELYN WOODLOCK

The Haunted House of Midland Park

spots. A New Jersey writer, David Anderton, a friend of the former owner, reports having felt the warm spot, as did his wife, Katherine. Katherine got an extra dividend the night she was visiting in the house when she was poked, nudged, or elbowed at the foot of a flight of stairs, reportedly the favorite station of one of the human ghosts.

The former owner, and most enthusiastic aficionado of the house's ghosts, is Ethelyn Woodlock, who lived there for some twenty-seven years. She is an eminent realist painter, and after moving into the house she began to consider herself somewhat of a psychic painter. She believes that much of her painting has come from a higher source, and at one time she painted a portrait of her favorite ghost. She lived there with her late husband and her two daughters, now grown. Her husband and one daughter were confirmed skeptics, she says, although the other daughter had an open mind on the subject.

Mrs. Woodlock is convinced that each ghost has its own preserves and sticks to them. The cat ghost, for example, hangs out in a small, third-floor room. Mrs. Woodlock says during her time she had four different beds in the room, but the cat adjusted nicely, leaving its warm spot on each of them in its turn.

Another ghost, who frequents the downstairs hallway—possibly the nudger of Katherine Anderton—is believed to be a wealthy businessman who lived in the house from 1906 to 1911, when he shot himself in the barn. His name was—is?—Max Crayhay. Mrs. Woodlock feels she has seen an apparition of Crayhay.

One of his sons had a friend named Rose, a teenager who somehow got involved with one of the house servants and became pregnant by him. She wanted to marry him, but her family objected because of the class difference. According to tradition, Rose was locked in an upper room at the house and was killed while trying to climb out of a window and join her lover for a romantic elopement. Her domain, according to Mrs. Woodlock, was the upstairs hallway.

Other house ghosts are reputed to be an old woman, once owner of the house, who was shot and killed in a robbery, and a small boy, visiting one of the Crayhay children, who died in an accident in the house, whom Mrs. Woodlock calls a free spirit. She says she once woke up at night and saw the ghost of an old woman hanging over her, and the ghost then proceeded to hit her on the nose.

Despite the anecdotal nature of much of this information, the haunting of the house seems quite

Ethelyn Woodlock painting entitled "The Yellow Room."

well established. Ghostly lights and sounds have abounded for years and seem to have been experienced by scores of people.

Ethelyn Woodlock painting entitled "Stairway to Starlight."

History: The house was built in 1864 and in its early days was the summer home of a wealthy New York lawyer. A succession of owners followed. The Crayhay family occupied it from 1906 to 1934. The house then changed hands again a number of times, till the Woodlocks bought it in 1952, selling it to the Fords in 1979. It has long been one of New Jersey's favorite haunted houses.

Identity of ghosts: Most of them seem to originate from the Crayhay era, such as Max Crayhay and a Crayhay son's friend, and the unfortunate Rose. A ghost antedating the Crayhays is the lady who was murdered. There is another old lady who just seems to have wandered in. Finally, there's the cat, whose identity has not been established.

Personalities of ghosts: Not hostile, unless you count the old lady who hit Mrs. Woodlock on the nose.

Witnesses: Seemingly much of the state of New Jersey. Mrs. Woodlock often conducted tours of her house.

Best time to witness: The house's other-dimensional occupants seem active day and night.

Still haunted? The cat is still there; that seems fairly certain. At least something is creating those warm spots. Mrs. Woodlock feels all of the human actors in this psychic drama are still onstage, except for Rose, the Juliet of Midland Park, New Jersey. Mrs. Woodlock had a particular attachment to this ghost, with whom she felt she had often communicated by Ouija board. She wanted to release Rose from her astral prison into "heaven." Three priests—Catholic, Episcopal, and Zen Buddhist—had a go at it, but Mrs. Woodlock says the ghost still walked. Finally, a psychic suggested that she paint Rose to heaven. So she painted a picture of Rose with two children and the putative father. Once Rose had seen herself as a family, Mrs. Woodlock is convinced, her spirit was released to higher realms.

Investigations: Dozens of psychics have visited the house, and many have sensed spirits. Many are well known in the field, such as Karlis Osis, Keith ("Blue") Harary, and Ingo Swann. The place has been written up in many newspapers, and a number of TV shows have been done on it.

Data submitted by: Ethelyn Woodlock, David Anderton, James and Anita Ford. Various newspaper articles, as well as material from Mrs. Woodlock's book, *Dreams Have Wings* (Fidelity Printing, 1985).

**41
Is This
Restaurant
Haunted?**

The Society Hill
Restaurant
Morristown, New
Jersey

Location: The Society Hill Restaurant is at 217 South St., Morristown.

Description of place: The structure was built as a private house in 1749 by a well-to-do resident of Morristown. It became a restaurant in 1946. After a disastrous fire in 1957, a great deal of renovation was done, and additions made. The restaurant, in the center of Morristown, an affluent community twenty-five miles west of New York City, now has some twenty-five rooms.

Ghostly manifestations: They purportedly spring from a triple murder that took place in the house in 1833. Stories are rife, and the restaurant uses them in promotional material; the back page of the menu is devoted to the history of the place and the supposed ghostly happenings. These include the usual menu of parapsychological appetizers and entrees, including chairs that rock mysteriously, lights that go on and off when no waiter or even busboy is nearby, cold spots, touchings by unseen hands. However, no dinner check has ever been known to dematerialize.

One of the current owners is David DeGraff. "I'm not a believer in ghosts myself," he says. "You hear of lights going on and off. Supposedly candles are relit that had been blown out. But these things are stories; I don't know, maybe somebody forgot to blow the candles out in the first place." However, he did witness one discomforting and fairly mysterious occurrence. "On our grand opening party, four years ago," he says, "a punch bowl for no apparent reason just cracked and exploded. It was sitting on a table, and punch was being put into it, and all of a sudden it just broke, and the punch went all over the place."

The previous owner for twenty years was William McCausland, who also is a qualified skeptic. "It had a reputation for having ghosts," he says. "It was good conversation for the kind of business we're in. I never tried to dissuade anyone." However, as he got warmed up in the interview, he did think of a couple of things. "We had incidents," he says, "when people would claim they felt someone's hands on their shoulders. We had a young lady who was cleaning up after a private party. We had several private dining rooms. There was a room that was always supposed to be cold. [It was a room where the body of a murdered servant girl was found in 1833.] She [the waitress] came down the stairs terrified, saying someone had put hands on her shoulders."

After some hesitation, McCausland told one on himself. "One day I lost my keys. I had put the keys on the desk. It was a Saturday morning, and I was there by myself. I put the keys on the desk, and I sat down at the desk. I reached for the keys to unlock a cabinet, and they were gone. I looked and looked and looked. I looked everywhere for those damned keys. I left that office and walked into the one next to it, which is my private office, and then I walked back again. I looked for the keys again and couldn't find them, and I went over to the cabinet. My back was turned to the desk, and then I heard some keys drop. I turned around, and there they were, right on the desk."

History: The house was built in 1749 by John Sayre, and his family lived there for several generations. Other people later lived in the house until 1946, when it was turned into a restaurant. It has had various owners since then.

The key incident for enthusiasts of ghostly happenings occurred in 1833. At this time, the owner of the place was Samuel Sayre, who lived there with his wife Elizabeth and a servant girl, Phoebe. Sayre hired a sailor from the West Indies, who was unemployed in New York City, by the name of Antoine LeBlanc. There was an immediate misunderstanding. LeBlanc thought he was coming to Morristown as superintendent of a sizable operation, whereas Sayre wanted him as a farmhand. He stayed on but became more and more frustrated and isolated. He couldn't speak English and became very much a loner. Finally, he decided to go back to New York, if possible in style. He thought the Sayres had a great deal of money secreted in the house, so one day he killed man, wife, and servant girl. He found some money and took off for New York, but a posse caught up with him. He was tried, found guilty, and hanged on Morristown Green. To pay for the trial and to celebrate the festive occasion, the skin was stripped from his body and made into purses and wallets. Some Morristown residents still have them.

Identity of ghost: According to the Society Hill

menu, it's pretty little Phoebe, the servant girl, who is haunting the place. However, after the punch bowl exploded, the new owners decided they could use a little expert advice. They brought in a team of psychics, Ed and Lorraine Warren of Monroe, Connecticut. In an interview, Lorraine said, "The spirit was that of a man. It was the man who murdered the girl whom I communicated with, and I believe it is the man who had made his presence known in different ways throughout the building. I think the owners felt it added more to the romantic element to say it was the beautiful young woman who was murdered than to say it was the man who had been the murderer. And certainly what contributes to it all is the way his life ended, what had been done to his body, the selling of his skin."

Personality of ghost: Whoever the ghost is, nothing truly malevolent seems to have happened, at least in living memory—just the usual pranks and mischief.

Witnesses: David DeGraff, William McCausland, and employees and customers of the restaurant.

Best time to witness: The happenings seemed to take place at various times of the day and night.

Still haunted? Lorraine Warren says it isn't. She and her husband recommended that a Roman Catholic priest be brought in to perform an exorcism. This was done, and Lorraine says it was successful. A contributing factor to the supposed cessation of happenings might be that the Warrens recommended to the owners that they eliminate a custom, Ouija Board Night. Says DeGraff: "Before the Warrens came in, one of the promotions in our lounge was a Ouija Board Night. Once a week we'd give out Ouija boards. We were playing up the fact that the house was haunted. The Warrens said that stirs up problems, and they recommended that we discontinue it, which we did immediately. We don't do that anymore."

Investigations: An investigation by Ed and Lorraine Warren and an exorcism by a priest.

Data submitted by: David DeGraff, William McCausland, Lorraine Warren, and Lauren Kirkwood, Morristown historian.

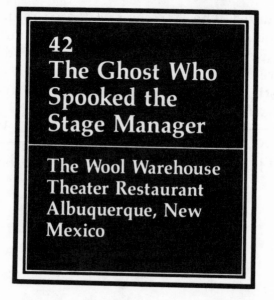

**42
The Ghost Who
Spooked the
Stage Manager**

**The Wool Warehouse
Theater Restaurant
Albuquerque, New
Mexico**

Location: The Wool Warehouse Theater Restaurant is located at 502 First Street NW, Albuquerque.

Description of place: Originally a wool warehouse, the building was converted in 1984 into a theater-restaurant. It is a two-story brick structure that stands near a railroad line. The present owners are George and Betty Luce. The theater and restaurant occupy the second floor; the first floor is not currently being used.

Ghostly manifestations: When the theater opened, the first production was *Blithe Spirit*, a comedy by Noel Coward. Possibly by coincidence, the play is about ghosts. The stage manager was a professional theater person by the name of Victoria Bradshaw. She is the only person who seems to have seen the ghost.

"It was very strange," Vicki says, "because I am not necessarily given to seeing ghosts. But there was this wonderful man, and I was absolutely terrified of him. I would see him just go past. The first few times I didn't actually see him; it was like a cream-colored thing going past me. Then one night, during an intermission, I went around to stage left, and there he was, very nice-looking, standing there looking at me. He was wearing a double-breasted cream-colored suit. He was very clean. It was like he was pleased about the fact that the space was being used. He was strictly watching, like an interested bystander. He seemed perfectly happy with what was going on."

Al Jones, an assistant to the producer, says he did not see the ghost, but he did see Vicki right after she had seen it. "Her hands were cold," he says, "and she was very white, a little shaky. She was quite upset for several days afterward."

Vicki says Al's evaluation of her state of mind is correct. She says she wonders if her reaction might have had something to do with her professional role. "When you're a stage manager," she says, "you have the power. You have control of that stage. You're responsible; you're part of creating that hour and a half of magic. When a stage manager sees a ghost on stage, it's like, 'Wait a minute, you don't fit in here. Excuse me, you're something I can't control; you shouldn't be back here.' Part of my concern was, what if one of the actors walks up and he's standing there? What's that going to do to the actors, to their performance? To have this man standing over there by the prop table was not really what I needed."

(The author of a book on hauntings such as this sometimes wonders if he is being manipulated, used for hype, by public institutions such as restaurants, inns, and theaters and tends to weigh his interviews and interviewees carefully. So it was a bit reassuring that both Vicki Bradshaw and Al Jones had somewhat bitterly fallen out with the owners, the Luces, and were no longer associated with the theater. "It's very interesting," Vicki said, "that my experience can somehow be recounted to help the Wool Warehouse, which I don't really care to have happen at all.")

History: The building was put up in 1929 by Frank Bond, originally from Quebec, who had extensive ranching interests in New Mexico and was a big man in the wool industry. He built the warehouse as a sort of headquarters. The architect was a native Hollander by the name of T. Charles Gaastra, a young man on his way up. This was one of his first big projects. He had just returned from a sojourn in Egypt, and the building shows a vaguely Egyptian influence. The Bond family eventually lost the building, and for about ten years it was used by the city as a records warehouse. The Luces bought it in 1984 to turn into a theater-restaurant.

Identity of ghost: No one seems to have any firm opinion, but Vicki Bradshaw says that local people she talked to seemed to think it was one of the Bonds. Others speculate it is a descendant of Gaastra.

Personality of ghost: Vicki Bradshaw says: "I saw him clearly only once, but he seemed very pleasant."

Witnesses: The only actual witness seems to be Vicki Bradshaw. Al Jones saw her immediately after her experience. "I don't think anyone else saw him," Vicki says. "The only person who might be able to shed some light on it might be Nicola Kaplan. She was playing the medium, Madame Arcati." Reached in New York, Ms. Kaplan said Vicki might have somehow confused her role in the play with her real personality. "I played a medium," Ms. Kaplan said, "but I'm such a skeptic that ghosts don't want to mess with me. I think you have to be receptive to them in order to see them, and I don't think I give them much room. I may have played a medium, but theater is illusion and magic, after all. All the magic I can muster is my craft and sullen art."

Best time to witness: This ghost took the stage not long after 8:30 P.M.

Still haunted? So far, it appears to have been a one-night stand.

Investigations: A psychic has told the Luces there is a good feeling about the theater-restaurant building, but she was not referring specifically to the ghost.

Data submitted by: (In order of appearance) Betty and George Luce, Al Jones, Victoria Bradshaw, Nicola Kaplan. Article by Bart Ripp in the October 29, 1985, issue of *The Albuquerque Tribune*. Original tip by Mark and Marianne Newton of Rio Rancho, New Mexico.

43
The Ghost Who Makes Phone Calls

The Lodge
Cloudcroft, New Mexico

Location: The Lodge overlooks the settlement of Cloudcroft, NM, about 90 miles north of El Paso, Texas.

Description of place: The Lodge is a strikingly attractive mountain inn, three stories high, with an imposing tower. The construction is of wood, painted light gray with burgundy trim. There are forty-seven rooms and suites, a restaurant—named after the supposed ghost, Rebecca—and a saloon in the basement called the Red Dog. Portraits of Rebecca and even a stained-glass window portraying her decorate the inn.

Cloudcroft is a village of about seventy people, most of whom work at The Lodge. The altitude is nine thousand feet; the area is traditionally a summer refuge from the heat of El Paso, Texas, ninety miles to the south. For entertainment, in addition to Rebecca, The Lodge offers a golf course and a ski area.

The Lodge, at Cloudcroft

Ghostly manifestations: The ghost—who provides the gamut of parapsychological incidents, ranging from an apparition to footsteps to doors opening and closing—is believed to be the spirit of a chambermaid-waitress-hostess who came to grief in the early 1930s when her lumberjack lover found her in the arms of an effete Easterner and opened fire. Other versions of the story say it was the owner of the lodge in whose arms she was surprised. Much of the history of the ghost is anecdotal—even the name Rebecca. Nobody seems to have done much historical research on the unfortunate lady. But she—or somebody—certainly seems to be hanging around the place.

Her most individualistic trick is phone calls. For some reason, she seems to be attracted to Suite 101, the Governor's Suite. It's the best suite in the house, so maybe she's just got class. For generations of

switchboard operators, 101 has kept lighting up. The
current assistant manager, Glynda Bonnell, who has
been associated with The Lodge for many years,
says, "Years ago we had the old plug-in type of
switchboard, the kind where you pull out a peg and
plug it into where a light comes on. Periodically the
light to that room would come on. It would happen
many, many times, when no one was in the room. It
would interfere so much sometimes that we would
just plug in a plug and leave it so we wouldn't have to
be bothered." Jerry Sanders and his wife, Carole, are
the present owners of the place. Sanders says that
this is still going on, even with a modern, electronic
switchboard. Not only do calls from the room light
up the switchboard, but often the phones in the
room will ring. "Sometimes guests will be in the
room," Sanders says, "and will call the switchboard
and ask why somebody is ringing their room."

A number of employees of the hotel claim to have
seen apparitions of Rebecca. One is Pancha Madred,

An artist's conception of Rebecca.

who was doing washing in the laundry room in the basement. Others have been bartenders and desk clerks. Rebecca is described as red-haired, attractive, and wearing a long gown. In the Red Dog saloon, one bartender testifies that flames sprang up in the fireplace even though there was no wood or paper in it. Ashtrays slide across tables unassisted. One guest reported that his watch floated from his bed stand and came to rest on his chest. Other guests see doors open and close.

Glynda Bonnell says: "My most vivid experience was when I was redoing some drapes in the Governor's Suite. I was up on a step ladder and had the drapes over my arm. I heard the door open, and I heard footsteps, and I thought it was my husband, Ted. I called his name, but there was no answer. I was startled, and I dropped the drapes and came down off the ladder. Then I heard the door shut again. I checked the hall and the rooms nearby, and there was nobody there."

Jerry Sanders says he and his wife didn't believe in ghosts when they bought The Lodge. When they arrived, they lived for a short time in the basement, which at one time was maids' quarters. Part of the place's folklore was that after Rebecca's abrupt termination, she was buried by her lover in the basement. Sanders says it was as though Rebecca wanted to make her presence known to the new owners. The Sanders moved in and bought their own locks. They constantly found lights on that shouldn't be on, furniture moved, abrupt sounds like that of a pipe breaking when none had. Sometimes faucets had been turned on, obviously just before the Sanders had entered.

History: The Lodge was put up in 1899 by the El Paso and Northeastern Railway, which provided transportation to logging country. It burned down in 1909 and was rebuilt in its present form by 1911. It had been operated by many people, perhaps the most notable being Conrad Hilton, who leased it from 1932 to 1935. It was Hilton's third hotel, according to Jerry Sanders. Ted and Glynda Bonnell owned the place for two years before they sold it to the Sanders in 1983. Ted and Glynda are now manager and assistant manager, respectively.

Identity of ghost: If it isn't Rebecca, they'll have to remove a number of portraits and take out a stained-glass window.

A stained glass window of Rebecca.

Personality of ghost: "We've had a good relationship with her," Sanders says. "The staff likes her. Whenever a dish is broken, the waiter or waitress says Rebecca did it."

Witnesses: Dozens of the staff and guests of the hotel.

Best time to witness: Mostly at night, but often during the day.

Still haunted? Doors are still opening and closing; the switchboard is still lighting up. Recently, Sanders says, a guest told him he had gotten up in the middle of the night to get a drink at a soda machine and had seen Rebecca rearranging flowers in the hall. Sanders says he sometimes wonders if people are just getting into the spirit of the thing.

Investigations: Various psychics have checked the place out. A reporter for the Gannett newspaper chain, which includes the *El Paso Times,* recently did a series on haunted places in the Southwest. She took a psychic along on her investigations, who supposedly declared The Lodge as the most definitely haunted of all the places they had visited. Rebecca has been the subject of a segment of the TV show "That's Incredible."

Data submitted by: Jerry and Carole Sanders, Glynda Bonnell, Marilyn Haddrill of the *El Paso Times;* articles in a variety of southwestern newspapers and magazines. This case was suggested by a mention in Curtis Fuller's column in the April 1985 issue of *Fate* magazine.

**44
Ghosts of the
Pioneers**

Reed Canyon,
The Back Country of
New Mexico

Location: The haunted area, now known as Trail
Creek, can be reached by going to Cuba, NM, which
is about 80 miles northwest of Albuquerque. Go east
out of Cuba on Route 126 for about 30 miles. Signs
will identify Trail Creek and adjacent Calavaries
Canyon.

Description of place: The area is now owned by
the U.S. Forest Service, but at one time it was
divided into holdings by settlers. Now almost deserted, it once was what is considered thickly settled
in those parts, about one family every five miles.
There was a small village there, and an old cemetery
remains. A pioneer trail ran through the area. The
spot in question, once called Reed Canyon, is now
known as Trail Creek. It is about eighty miles northwest of Albuquerque. The nearest town, Cuba, is
about thirty miles away.

Ghostly manifestations: The area has long had the
reputation of being haunted. Mark Newton of Rio

Rancho, New Mexico, wrote this account of an experience he had there about thirty years ago:

"Since my lifetime occupation has been that of a forester and timberman, it was not unusual to find myself alone in the rugged back country of New Mexico, on a crisp November evening in 1956. Reed Canyon was new to me, however; early in the morning I would start cutting Christmas trees. But first I was looking forward to a good night's sleep on my bedroll in the back of my pickup. I had just fallen off to sleep about nine o'clock when suddenly I was awakened by the sound of someone coming with wagons and teams. My first thought was that I had parked on a road and I must move my vehicle to let them by. Upon looking about, I could see no one, however, on this bright moonlit night.

"Meanwhile, the sounds were getting louder and coming closer. Wagon wheels were now scraping against rocks, whips cracked like gunshots amid men's shouts of 'Gee' and 'Haw,' while the horses labored for breath. I found myself engulfed in a sea of sounds. Dogs barked, a baby was crying, and people were talking above the din of dishes and utensils clattering and banging inside wagons. At one point a woman's voice seemed to pass right by my ear as she said, 'I must stop and milk Bossie when we get to the bottom of the hill.'

"For several hours the sounds continued as they laboriously climbed the steep hill, diminishing only after they had reached the top and started down the other side. Then once again it was still. What were my reactions to this strange phenomena? First, I was curious, then came apprehension, followed by disbelief, and finally fear after the final impact hit me. I was in an isolated wilderness ten miles from the nearest ranch and thirty-three miles from the nearest town. Upon my return to town, I told several people about my experience, and they stated they had heard almost identical sounds while tending sheep in this region on numerous occasions. It is generally believed that this was part of an old pioneer wagon trail, and the local inhabitants in this part of the country try to avoid Ojitos Mesa as much as possible, for it has the reputation of being haunted. Since I still had many more trees to cut and had only begun, business took precedence over ghosts, and I returned to the area for an extended period of time. I encountered the same phenomena several times more, always during the nighttime hours, with the exception of one afternoon right before a heavy snowstorm. Also of interest is that no form of wildlife will inhabit the mesa, skirting the area completely."

History: The area was settled after the Civil War by people moving west. The immediate vicinity was called Reed Canyon, for a man whose first name seems lost in the mists of time. He is referred to simply as "Old Man Reed."

"It was an outlaw hangout for a long time in the old days," says Mark Newton. "It was very well protected by the terrain. One man could stand up there with a Winchester and hold off an army. Reed died around 1900. He wasn't a rancher; he had a hole-in-the-wall place. The ruins of his house are still there. He protected outlaws, and he charged them for it."

Mark Newton on the trail.

In the 1930s, Newton says, "They tried to log that country for timber. Everything in the world would happen to them. Nobody got killed, but they just couldn't handle it. The trucks would just buckle in two, the axles would snap for no reason. The trucks wouldn't start when they should start. I had that same thing happen to me. I had a Dodge Power Wagon. I had that thing up there, and it was running perfectly. I stopped it, went on about my work, came back, and I could not get that thing started. The ignition points were perfect, it was getting gasoline, but it would not start. It was parked on a hill, and I thought I'd get it started by letting it roll and putting it in gear and letting out the clutch. And as soon as I got out of that little area it kicked right over, and I never had a problem with it after that."

Identity of ghosts: Outlaws? "No," says Newton, "I don't think this is part of it. I think the people I heard were just people coming west looking for a better life."

Personalities of ghosts: "They haven't hurt anybody," says Newton, "but they sure put running chills up and down your backbone."

Witnesses: Newton and many people in the area.

Best time to witness: Newton found that the phenomena usually began in the early evening and continued through the night, although one time he was aware of it in the middle of the day, just before a storm.

Still haunted? Probably.

Investigations: Testimony by Newton: "Nearest thing is I had a Mexican fella working for me. He was a stranger. He'd migrated to Colorado from Old Mexico, and he was working his way back home, and I hired him. He went out there and refused to go in. He said, 'Muy malo.' It's bad, very bad. That's all he would say.

"I hired an Indian by the name of Sam Comanche. He was kind of a medicine man. He quit right during the middle of the first day and walked out. He didn't say a word, just put down his tools and left. About a week later I saw a trader who knew him, and I asked him why Sam had quit all of a sudden, because Sam was a good worker. He said that Sam said 'Chinde,' which is Navaho for 'ghost.' "

Data submitted by: Mark Newton.

**45
The Night
Watchman Who
Kept on Watching**

The New York State
Capitol
Albany, New York

Location: The New York State Capitol overlooks the main business district of Albany.

Description of place: The New York State Capitol, on a hill overlooking the business district of Albany, is perhaps the chief architectural landmark of the city. It was built in French Renaissance style. Construction was begun in 1868 and completed in 1904 at a cost of $25,000,000. The Senate chamber is often cited as one of the most beautiful legislative chambers in the world. However, this account is chiefly about the Assembly chamber.

Ghostly manifestations: For many years, employees at the Capitol who worked at night spoke of a ghost that haunted the place, often on the fifth floor, but particularly in and around the Assembly chamber. The ghost was referred to as George, although no one seems to know how he got that name. Some employees asked to be transferred to other state buildings. For example, elevator operator

John Williams told of hearing jingling keys, a turning doorknob, and the door flying open—with nobody there! He got a transfer to another floor. John Ross, a custodian, told of rattling doorknobs, mumbling voices, footsteps, and moving shadows. "After a while," he says, "I just didn't let these things bother me anymore. I just went about my business." Lena Thomas, a custodian, told of feeling someone rush by so fast that it whipped her skirt around. This was in the Speaker's room, and from then on she stayed out of that room. Custodian Michelle Farrington,

The New York State Capitol

while vacuuming in a small room on the fifth floor, tells of seeing a grayish blur rush toward her and go right through her body. She felt an icy chill as it went through her. She got a transfer to another part of the building. The testimony could be multiplied. There seems no doubt that something, or someone, was hanging out in the Empire State's Capitol.

In 1981, an Albany TV station, WNYT, was doing a series on hauntings. Bryan Jackson was the newsman and Frank Cirillo the photographer. They decided that an ideal Halloween program would be Albany's best-known ghost story, the Capitol ghost. They got together with Ann Fisher, a professional psychic who lives in Albany, and decided to have a séance with Fisher in the Assembly chamber. After going to the chamber and feeling a presence, interviewing employees, and doing research in the *Albany Times-Union*, Fisher felt that the ghost was a nightwatchman who had died in a fire at the Capitol in 1911.

Fisher, who teaches courses in parapsychology at the State University of New York in Albany, brought along some of her students. Late one night, she says, "We marched in with Channel 13 cameras, and nobody said a word. There was nobody in the Assembly chamber." Jackson and Cirillo started out as skeptics, but their minds were rapidly opened. Cold air surged through the chamber. Camera lights went out for no apparent reason. But the most puzzling manifestations were two loud bangs that resounded through the chamber, bangs that did not register when the sound track was played back in the studio. "It wasn't on the tape," Jackson, who now works in the Capitol himself on the press staff of the governor, says, "although everyone heard it."

Fisher says she contacted the spirit, who was puzzled, she says, as to why all these people were in the chamber at night, and told him that he was dead and they only wanted to send him on his way to the spirit world. "He seemed to understand and then vanished," she says. Sharon Rigby, one of Fisher's students, said she felt someone touching her head, and Peter Sokol, who sat next to her, says he saw the hair on the young woman's head move as though someone were running fingers through it. Fisher suspects it may have been an expression of gratitude by the ghost before he departed.

Sam Abbott, the watchman

PHOTO COURTESY OF LAWRENCE CORTESI

History: From the start, Fisher suspected the ghost might be someone who had suffered a violent death in the building. In the newspaper files, her attention was drawn to accounts of a $5,000,000 fire that raged through the capitol in 1911. The only person to die in the blaze was a nightwatchman, Samuel J. Abbott. Two days after the fire, his charred remains were found in the rubble.

Identity of ghost: Fisher believes it was Abbott.

Personality of ghost: Apparently nothing hostile,

merely confused and tied to his last earthly sur-
roundings—for seventy years.

Witnesses: Many employees of the building, as
well as those who took part in the exorcism.

Best time to witness: The manifestations always
seemed to happen at night.

Still haunted? According to Fisher, Sam Abbott
has shaken the dust of Albany.

Investigations: The séance conducted by Fisher.

Data submitted by: Lawrence Cortesi, who wrote
an article on the case in the February 1985 issue of
Fate magazine; Ann Fisher; and Bryan Jackson.

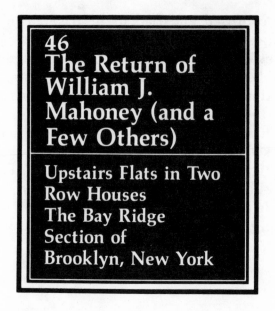

46
The Return of William J. Mahoney (and a Few Others)

Upstairs Flats in Two Row Houses
The Bay Ridge Section of
Brooklyn, New York

Location: The Makutas' apartment is at 544 Bay Ridge Parkway, Brooklyn. Contact the Makutas before visiting.

Description of place: The disturbances began when Kevin and Linda Makuta lived in the upstairs apartment in a two-story row house in Brooklyn. Later, they moved a few blocks away to another upstairs apartment in a row house.

Ghostly manifestations: "We have a whole bunch of spooks," says Linda Makuta, around whom they seem to cluster. Linda is a legal secretary who is currently staying at home caring for her children, Justin, four, and Lauren, two. Her husband, Kevin, works, as she puts it, as a "computer jock." Both of them are very psychic, and thereon, possibly, hang several of these tales. As psychic people, they seem to be able to tune in to what is going on around them in a world that is invisible to most of us; perhaps they even attract ghosts.

The manifestations began in the first apartment, shortly after Linda's grandfather, William J. Mahoney, died on March 30, 1980. Linda reports: "Grandfather has been with us—this sounds so silly—five

William J. Mahoney

years. He's been with us since he died." And she chuckles heartily. Linda has quite a bouncy natural humor. "He was an old man when he died. We were extremely close; I was his first grandchild. He was a mounted policeman in the New York Police Department." Linda says her own parents are quite uneasy about the ghostly manifestations. "They won't baby-sit in my house," she says. "My sisters won't baby-sit in my house, either.

"It started in the other apartment. Lights flashed on and off, and doors slammed; you'd hear heavy footsteps. It got to a point where I was scared to go home. I would wait on the stoop for Kevin to come home. One time I came home and heard music. But it wasn't rock music; it was music from the thirties. When I opened the door, it stopped. When I'd be home alone before my husband came home, someone else would come in. You'd hear the downstairs door open and shut and somebody come down the hall, an invisible person. That happened many times. Sometimes there'd be a knocking on the door; you'd go to the door, and there'd be nobody there. You'd hear heavy walking on the roof, running on the roof. The first night we slept there there were these three loud, boomy knocks on the bedroom wall. It scared the hell out of us. We'd hear a man walking down the hall, the shuffle of his feet. One time my little son Justin asked who was the old man in the hall. He insisted there was one and told what he looked like."

By this time the Makutas felt they could use a little expert advice. They had read of the American Society for Psychical Research, a long-established and highly respected organization, in an article in *OMNI* magazine. Its headquarters are in New York City at 5 West 73rd Street, and it was only a local call to Dr. Karlis Osis, now retired but then its chief investigator. After a number of phone conversations, Osis came to the Makutas's first apartment, accompanied by a colleague, Donna McCormick, and a well-known psychic, Alex Tanous. The ASPR people visited the Makutas three times, in both apartments, each time bringing a different psychic. In accordance with professional parapsychological procedures, the psychics were kept "blind"; that is, they were told nothing of the circumstances until they had formed and stated their impressions.

Linda says: "Alex described the main spirit in particular. He said, 'It's a man who is attached to you, but more than to you he's attached to your son.' He said my son sees the ghost and speaks to him. When Justin was a baby, I used to hear a man talking. So when Alex said all this, I thought, I guess I'm not crazy after all; I wasn't imagining I was hearing this stuff. It was my grandfather, and I eventually did see

Mahoney and Linda on her fifth birthday.

him. The first time I saw him I was coming out of the bathroom. I had hand wash in my arms, and there was this man standing right in front of me, smiling. I just kept going. It was like a delayed reaction. I said, 'My God, that was my grandfather!' I kind of like went *through* him. When I got into the bedroom, I put the clothes on the radiator and stood there for a moment, and then I said, 'Holy shit!'

"It was eleven o'clock on a Saturday morning. And you think you see spooks in the dark, with thunder and lightning! We've had things disappear. There'd be a book on the table. You'd walk away from it, and you'd come back and it would be gone. It might be gone for a week, it might be gone for a month. We just got a pencil sharpener back that had been missing for a year. We played cards last night. I put my cigarette down—this is chronic—I put my cigarette in the ashtray to throw a card out, and when I went to pick it up it was gone. So my girlfriend Cathy is now crawling on the floor under the dining room table looking for it, and I told her, 'Don't bother; it's gone.' My grandfather is the one who takes my cigarettes. He's taken cigarettes at least fifty times. Once he made a whole pack disappear, but most of the time they just disappear out of the ashtray. Occasionally he puts them out. He never wanted me to smoke. When he was alive, he used to take the cigarette out of my hand and put it out. He said nicotine was bad for you.

"In the other apartment I lost my wedding ring. We moved into this apartment, about two years ago, and we were here about three months, and I was putting coffee mugs away in the closet. As I went to put the second mug in, there was my wedding ring, on the shelf! I was afraid to touch it, but I picked it up, and it was my wedding ring that I'd lost four years before.

"Another ghost is a man named Otto, who belongs to the other house, but he came with us when we moved. I think he lived there. He has a cigar smell that goes with him. They each have their individual sound or odor that goes with them. I have a lot of glass, and my grandfather clinks on it. Kind of like saying, 'I'm here; hi, Jack.' He raps too, on the china closet or a desk."

The Makutas did not move from their first apartment because of the ghosts, but for the mundane reason that the people who lived downstairs, who owned the house, needed the upstairs apartment for some of their relatives. When the Makutas moved into their present apartment, it was quiet for six weeks before the familiar noises began. They called the ASPR again, and Osis and McCormick came, bringing with them a woman psychic who prefers to be anonymous. This psychic told Linda the ghost of a woman whose name was Eileen had come with them from the other house and that she was trying to get in touch with Linda. According to the psychic, Eileen was very upset and wanted Linda to call the police.

"The last couple of weeks we were in the other apartment," Linda says, "I heard a woman very loudly and distinctly call my name. I would say,

Linda Makuta

'What is it?' but never heard anything but my name being called. The psychic said Eileen wanted me to call the police and tell them that 'they' had knocked her on the head on the stairs. She had an Italian last name; I forget what it was. She never said who knocked her on the head. The psychic says that the woman has no idea she's dead. This woman comes and goes, but she hasn't been back for a long time."

Linda said the woman psychic also told her that her grandfather wanted her to stop reading so much. "I read incessantly," says Linda. "He also wanted me to stop doing that theater stuff, the psychic told me. I was really heavy-duty into community theater. He wanted me to get a job. 'Did he say what kind of job?' I asked the psychic. She said yes, he did, that he said taking in wash would be good for a start. That had been a running joke between us. The psychic said that he knew he was dead but was here to watch out for everybody."

In the first apartment, a local New York TV show was done. In the current one, an Italian film crew did a TV show. They came with Osis and McCormick of the ASPR, who also brought with them a Brooklyn psychic, Ann Rychlenski. Ann recalls the occasion thus: "Only one person in the film crew spoke English; it was like being in a Fellini film." At the beginning of the session, Ann, who was "blind," sat with Linda in the kitchen, having a cup of coffee. "She said someone had just rubbed her cheek," Linda recalls. "She described a man. It was my grandfather. She also said there was a woman at the top of the stairs. I wasn't surprised, because a friend of mine, Richie, had seen her. He still sees her. If she's around when he's here, he sees her. My husband has seen her, and I've had a glimpse of her. She is attached to this house. Her name is Clarisse. According to Ann, she knows she is dead, but she waits at the top of stairs, waiting for a letter to come in the mail. I cannot figure this out, but this is what the lady is doing. When she is here, you see lights, like flash-bulbs going off—different colors. And she comes with a very strong flowery scent. She's a petite blonde, dressed in a gown, with a lot of jewelry. She looks young, but that doesn't necessarily mean she was young when she died; that's the way she's manifesting herself. Ann said this woman was very reluctant to let go of her youth; that's why she's always in a gown with the jewelry. She always looks like she's waiting for somebody to pick her up and take her out to a dance. Sometimes I hear her walking in the hallway. Ann said there's also a child at the top of the stairs with the woman. They're there together, but they're not connected to each other. It's not a mother-and-daughter act or anything like that. The girl—she's no more than six—has been seen by my husband and friends of mine."

The Makutas also had a one-evening visitor, a lady ghost who followed Kevin home after seeing Linda in the musical *Godspell*. The show was done in a historic church in Brooklyn; Washington had attended services there, according to legend, and there was a cemetery next to the church. Linda was president of the theater group and also the producer of this particular show. "I was playing Mary Magdalene," she says. " 'Turn Back, O Man,' that was my big number. I came out on the stage and looked to see how the house was, and I noticed that the front row stage right only had one person in it. I remember thinking to myself, Why didn't they sell those tickets? Why is that whole row empty? There's only one person sitting there. Then I noticed there were two women sitting there. Then after the show we went out, and the stage manager starts telling me about this lady who just glided in from the patio and sat herself down in the front row. And I said,

'Nobody can come in that way; there's a fence there. They'd have to climb the fence.' And then I looked at the stage manager's face. I said, 'Wait a minute, she glided in?' I said, 'Well, the church is very old and there are people buried in the courtyard like from the 1700s and 1800s. Why wouldn't they have spirits here?' She had on a bluish print dress. She was maybe in her sixties. She was an old lady with blonde hair, you know, dyed.' "

Kevin was in the audience and also saw the woman, as did another member of the cast. Linda relates, "I don't think it was me she followed home; I think it was Kevin. I went out to the cast party, and when I went home he said, "You know that lady in the first row? I was here watering the plants, and when I turned around there was the woman watching me. The more I watered the plants, the more she smiled. She was there for about ten minutes, and then she faded out." Linda says the lady hasn't been back, to her knowledge.

"I'm psychic, and my husband is psychic," Linda says, "so this makes it great for any spooks who are floating around here. Dr. Osis says, 'Linda, you are very, very psychic. Why don't you open up a little more?' I said I'd have to think about that. A *New York Times* writer called me up today and wants to do a story. All these people floating in and out of my house—I ought to charge admission."

History: There are no known reports of psychic events before the Makutas moved into the two places.

Identity of ghosts: The chief ghost, from the Makutas's point of view, is Linda's grandfather, William J. Mahoney. It's not clear who the other ghosts were in life.

Personalities of ghosts: Most seem pathetic, wandering spirits. Some know they are dead; some do not. All are glued to this plane for reasons of their own. When psychic Ann Rychlenski came to the house, Linda gave her a fedora hat that had been worn by her grandfather. Ann specializes in psychometry—deducing from physical objects. Sitting in the kitchen over a cup of coffee with Linda, Ann recalls: "I picked up an elderly man and a woman, but they were not related. They seemed like overlaps of two different times. I banged my fist on the table and said to Linda, 'With this man you want to say, "Law and order, law and order." And I got a tap on the back of the head—twice. I felt this was someone who could not show affection easily. The taps were a sign of affection. Instead of saying 'I love you' to some-

Ann Rychlenski

one, he'd rap you on the side of the head and say, 'Get out of here, knucklehead.' I felt he was estranged from his children during his lifetime, and Linda said that was right. I felt she was the one close person to him out of the grandchildren. My feeling was that he was around because of her children. I felt there was a very protective feeling. I think he felt he had been deprived of his own children during his lifetime and now there was this. He seemed extremely protective."

Concerning the woman, Ann relates: "The dress she was wearing was flowing chiffon, with a lot of jewelry. The feeling was of someone who did not want to get old, a woman who was probably well into her sixties and still trying to look as though she were thirty-five. There was a sad feeling to that person. I think she had something to do with the house. I felt that the woman was somehow attached to the child, but I couldn't figure out how."

Witnesses: The Makutas, including their little boy; Karlis Osis and Donna McCormick of the ASPR; three psychics, including Alex Tanous and Ann Rychlenski; and many friends of the Makutas. Linda tells many stories about their friends. Here is an example: "Once we did *Babes in Arms*, and we had a cast party in my house. One of my friends came over, and he didn't know which door was ours, so he got his lighter out so he could see the names on the bells. And the door opened for him. It's a four-hundred pound oak door. He's kind of flaky, so he said, 'Thank you very much' and walked up the stairs. Incidentally, at that party the stereo went on all by itself."

Best time to witness: Seems like just about anytime.

Still haunted? At the time of the interview, Linda said the resident ghosts seem to have settled down to four—Mahoney, Otto, Clarisse, and the child.

Investigations: People connected with the American Society for Psychical Research visited the Makutas' apartment on three occasions. They are Karlis Osis and Donna McCormick, parapsychologists; Alex Tanous and Ann Rychlenski, psychics; and another psychic who prefers to remain anonymous.

Data submitted by: Primary interview with Linda Makuta; other interviews with the three psychics, including Alex Tanous and Ann Rychlenski; case suggested by Donna McCormick of the ASPR.

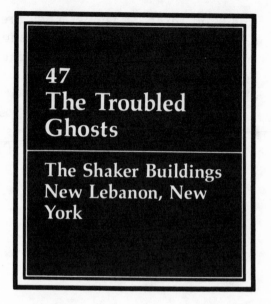

47

The Troubled Ghosts

The Shaker Buildings
New Lebanon, New
York

Location: The Shaker buildings are on an old dirt road off U.S. Route 20, about 30 miles east of Albany, N.Y., and six miles west of Pittsfield, MA. The old road runs about four miles parallel to Route 20; both ends of the old road come out on Route 20. The easier entry is adjacent to the Massachusetts-New York State line marker on Route 20. Go down the dirt road and you will reach Darrow School in about a mile and the Sufi settlement in another mile.

Description of place: A group of about twenty large, sturdily built, wooden buildings, constructed in the early part of the nineteenth century by the Shakers, a religious sect that espoused a communist life. The buildings line a narrow dirt road that was originally the main road between Boston and Albany. For three or four miles, this old road runs parallel to the modern Route 20, branching off from the modern highway and then rejoining it about thirty miles east of Albany. The westernmost build-

264

ings are used by Darrow School, a private secondary school. The easternmost buildings house the Abode of Message, headquarters of a spiritual group known as Sufis.

Ghostly manifestations: Generations of students at Darrow School have talked about Shaker ghosts and sometimes have claimed to have seen them. The most often spotted apparition is described as a woman who wears a bonnet and an apron. She is traditionally seen looking out the empty windows of the Carriage House, a dilapidated, unused old building. She is always seen at night, and girls' screams have many times resounded through a dormitory building about two hundred feet away. Understandably, ghosts are a common topic of conversation at Darrow School. Ed Noggle, formerly an English teacher at Darrow who also taught a class in mysticism there, found the school's preoccupation with ghosts intriguing and suspects there is something behind it all. He contrasts the Shakers, with their nonmaterialism, their supposed visions, and the abstinence from sex that was one of the tenets of their religion, with the modern, affluent young people who now inhabit these buildings. "These young people," Noggle says, "are very much of this world, very sensual, sexual beings. It has always been a matter of 'Ha, ha, what would the Shakers do if they could see all this? They'd roll over in their graves.' It's something on people's minds—'Maybe they *can* see all this. Maybe they're going to get back at us some day.' "

When the Sufis moved into the other part of the Shaker group of buildings in 1975, they say they immediately were aware of scores of spirits hanging around the place. They did not see ghosts so much as sense them. Puran Khan Bair—a name assumed on joining the Sufi order—is at first blush a typical youngish American professional. He is an engineer, now director of engineering for a company that manufactures robots. When the Sufis came to New Lebanon, he became vice president of the order and was in charge of their financial system. "What makes a ghost," says Puran, "is a person who dies especially in a tragic or traumatic way, unprepared for death, and who resists the natural progression of things that leads to evolution on the other side. Instead, they hang around, which is unnatural. You get a lot of ghosts then with accidents and with people who were unhappy with their lives. The Shakers were in that category of unhappy people. They came to the community because they were seeking a spiritual ideal, and what they found was a very difficult path—celibacy, poverty, and submission to the will of the elder. As a result, a lot of them felt very unfulfilled as human beings, cut off from the opposite sex. So because of the great number of unhappy souls there, when we got to the abode it was just full of beings. I can't say that we ever saw anything move, or saw anybody's face, but we're fairly tuned in, and we got it in other ways. What we got were feelings, images, trains of thought. We have a meditation for feeling the presence of these spirits. The other thing was that they would show up in people's dreams. We felt that we had quite a lot of effect on them. At this point you'll find very few ghosts there, because, we feel, our form of spiritual life showed these beings that it is possible to lead a spiritual life and not be celibate, to have families. The fact that the place was overrunning with children, I think, was a tremendous revelation to these ghosts. That's our contribution; that's what we did for the Shakers. Anyway, the ghosts have gone."

History: The Shakers were a Christian sect that conducted one of the most successful experiments in religious communal living in nineteenth-century America. They originated in England in the eighteenth century, an offshoot of the Quakers. The Shakers acquired their nickname from their practice of whirling, trembling, or shaking during religious services. They believed that people could rid themselves of sin or wicked habits by engaging in such ecstatic religious exercises.

Their leader was Ann Lee, who was persecuted for her beliefs in England and came to America in 1774. She was called Mother Lee, and she set up the first

Shakers at a meeting.

American Shaker settlement at Watervliet, New York. Many other Shaker settlements were subsequently established in New England, the Midwest, and Florida. At one time, Mother Lee lived at the New Lebanon settlement.

The Shakers became expert craftsmen and are remembered today largely for the beautifully simple pieces of furniture they created, which are now prized antiques. Largely because of their stricture of celibacy, the sect did not expand. It began to dwindle after the Civil War. The last Shakers, a handful, left the New Lebanon settlement in the early 1940s. A man and wife bought the property and for about thirty years ran a summer camp there, at which children were taught Shaker craftsmanship. When the man died, the woman sold the property to the Sufis. The leader of the Sufis, Pir Vilayat Inayat Kahn, says that he received a message through intuition that the Shakers wanted a spiritual group such as the Sufis to take over the property and rebuild it.

Identity of ghosts: Presumably members of the former Shaker community.

Personalities of ghosts: According to Puran, "troubled, curious, fascinated with the way that we approached our spiritual life. Jealous, a bit. We had found a way to do it with families. I felt like they were involved with us."

Witnesses: The Sufis, who say they sensed the Shakers, and Darrow School people, some of whom have said they saw ghosts dressed like the Shakers.

Best time to witness: According to Puran, "They seemed to bother people mostly at night, probably because people get into a more reflective state then."

Still haunted? The Sufis say there are very few ghosts on the premises now.

Investigations: Puran says, "No investigations were done. It was so clear to us that there were ghosts there. Our focus was how to get them to give us a little space so we would not be so burdened by their emotions, how to help them so they would move on. That's what we focused on, and I'd say it worked."

Data submitted by: Puran Bair and Taj Inayat of the Sufis, Ed Noggle of Darrow School.

48
The Inadvisability of Puttering with Black Magic

An Elemental, a
Thought Form, and
Just Plain Ghosts
A House in
Utica, New York

Location: The people involved in this case did not wish their identities, nor the location of the house, revealed.

Description of place: A tall, three-story, wooden frame house, typical of the 1920s, in a working-class neighborhood in a small, upstate New York city. Bill and Ruth A., the owners, lived with their two young daughters in an apartment on the first floor. Bill's nephew, Randy, and his wife, Ginny, lived in a second-floor apartment. The third floor was an attic. The period covered in this account includes the late 1970s and early 1980s. (All names, except those of the Piles and Joy McDonald, have been disguised.)

Ghostly manifestations: Strange, frightening manifestations had been occurring intermittently in the house for three or four years. In 1982, Ruth asked Clare, a young woman who lived in the neighborhood and had had some psychic experiences, to check out the house. Clare found the vibrations there very frightening. At this point, a more experienced parapsychologist was brought in. He is Roger Pile, currently of Ivoryton, Connecticut, who has investigated many hauntings. He brought with him his wife, Nancy, and a student-associate, Joy McDonald, as mediums. To begin, Pile interviewed Ruth, who seemed to have had the most unusual and distressing experiences. Excerpts from her testimony are as follows:

"My sister was visiting from Georgia three years ago this Christmas, and she brought with her a year-old daughter. The second week she was here she woke up and found this woman standing over her daughter's crib, leaning over the child. She described her as wearing a dark green skirt with a long-sleeved, white blouse, and that she had long hair and no face. But she didn't tell me because up till then I had always said no to this sort of thing. I didn't believe in it; I wouldn't listen; it always freaked me out. She told my mother and father the next day.

"A few months later my dad was here with us, and he saw this woman on more than one occasion, but he still didn't tell me. But in May, our daughter, Debbie, who was eight, woke up screaming that there was a lady standing in her room, staring at her. She described her as wearing long green pants, a white turtleneck, with long hair and no face. I told this to my mother, and she looked at me and said, 'Talk to your father.' I did talk to the Catholic Church, but they didn't give us any satisfaction. One night not long after, Debbie was sleeping on the couch because she wouldn't sleep in her room, and I saw a handprint press down on her pillow.

She woke up and said something had touched her. Once before it had touched Debbie when I was sleeping with her in her bed because she was afraid to sleep alone. She couldn't wake me up, but she said this lady came in and was pulling on the covers and touching her.

"I have an Aunt Margaret in California who is a minister, and I called her, and she spoke in tongues. While we were on the phone, I heard a rumble underneath the house. Aunt Margaret said, 'Now your home is safe.' And things were quiet for a while, but then they started up again. This time it was a man. It called to Debbie, called her by name two times. One of her friends heard it. Also, something damaged my violin. [Ruth is a music teacher.] The pegs had been pulled out and the strings ripped.

"One time I was alone in the house. I was washing my hands at the kitchen sink, and something grabbed me by the back of the neck and pounded my head on the kitchen sink. I left the house to talk with friends. The car felt fine on the way up there, but on the way back something took the car over. It went faster and faster and sped through intersections at fifty, sixty, seventy miles an hour. I could work the gas pedal and the brake pedal, but I had no control over the car until we hit a street near here; then I had complete control. All I could think of was, Why am I not hitting another car? I just went straight as could be, right through the intersections, red lights and all.

"I called Aunt Margaret again, and she said it was because I didn't believe strongly enough. I had seen a big black form at the foot of my bed, and she said that was the spirit of fear, that I had brought it on myself and that I should read the New Testament every night. Again she spoke in tongues, and this time the rumble was worse than the first time. So I assumed it was gone again, and all was quiet until this year.

"I don't know how to describe this year [1982]. Our personalities changed. We got irritable, short-tempered, and cried very easily. I started seeing things in the house, hearing noises. I would see black forms scoot past the doorway. I'd see black and white dots that I would see only in this house. There would be footsteps; doors would rattle; there would be pounding noises overhead all day long, especially when I was alone. About a month ago I was practicing piano, and this voice came up from behind me, a man's voice, a tenor. He said, 'Ruth.' I was alone in the house. He said, 'Ruth, what are you doing!' But it wasn't like a question; it was more like he was being sarcastic. I got scared, and I played really loud till Bill came home.

"A few days later I was in the bathroom, putting my makeup on, and this tenor voice came again, behind me, but I couldn't understand what he was saying this time. I came downstairs, and I could hear a child calling out to me. It kept calling me Mommy. This went on for a week. During the night I'd hear a child's voice come out of the center of the house, calling, 'Help, help, Mommy, help!'

"Nothing is missing; nothing has been moved, but we now have two dead hamsters here. At night you'd hear a noise as though someone were pounding on the sides of their cage. I'd think it was the hamsters playing; they're

nocturnal. But every morning the top of the
cage would be off. Both are now dead. We had
two cages, a metal cage and a plaster cage. The
plaster cage was ripped apart.

"Election Day I went down the street to vote,
and as I went down the street this voice, which I
had not heard before or since, cackled in my ear.
It was just a mean, old voice, right in my ear.
Almost like another language. I looked around to
make sure nobody was on the street. The only
person I saw was a lady across the street, raking
her leaves. And it did this all the way down the
street till I voted, and then when I came back I
didn't hear it anymore.

"Something uses my voice to lure Randy, and
Randy's voice to lure me. We have an intercom
system going in case we need each other. I heard
over the intercom what I thought was Ginny's
voice, to come upstairs. I did, and when I got to
their door and knocked, I heard this hissing
sound. I flew down the stairs. Then I heard
Randy call again, and I thought I'd better go up.
This time I went out the back door and up the
back stairs. When I got to the top of the stairs, I
heard a rustling sound across the floor on the
other side of the back door. It stopped when I
got to the door. I left; I wasn't staying up there.

"Twice something has touched my other
daughter—Margot's—head. Something touched
my foot once under the table, and I think I
kicked it. My foot hit something like a pillow.
One thing that has helped me a lot is that my
students also hear these noises. It's helped me a
lot that other people hear these things, too."

Pile then interviewed Randy, who told of feeling

Roger S. Pile

chills as he worked around the house. This was before he had moved in. "One night," he relates, "I called Ruth's aunt, and she went through her tongues or whatever it is she goes through. That night I left late to go home, and Bill lent me his car. I got in, and I knew that thing was in the car with me. I tried to ignore it, and I turned the radio on. I pushed every button, and I couldn't get anything except one station, and that was church music. As soon as that music came on, the thing was gone."

Randy told of moving in and beginning to see "quick things out of the corner of my eye. There'd be black forms, gray forms, white lights straight on. One time I decided to try to meditate in my living room, and I heard, 'Help me.' It sounded like a child's voice. One time I heard a man's voice say, 'Hey,' out of the blue."

One experience that particularly interested Pile was this: "I could hear footsteps in the attic upstairs," Randy said. "I heard a chant, a bell ring, wooden sticks being hit together." Pile asked if it sounded like a ritual, and Randy replied, "That was my first impression."

Pile then interviewed Clare, the young local psychic who had gone through the house. She said that on her visit she could also hear chanting. She suspected that there had once been a witches' coven in the building. "I also," Clare said, "felt there were children here who had been mistreated. I felt little tuggings on my clothes, very low down. I also felt there was a nanny who didn't like them. I felt they met their deaths at the hands of this woman. The mother was not at home a lot. I often felt several good people in spirit here. There was a little room off the attic, like a closet room, where I felt the children had been put. I got the idea that they were not allowed to use the bathroom, that they were banging on the door to get out. I was terribly frightened in the attic. It was very evil."

Both Ruth and Randy said they had several times been aware of a stench around the house, as though an animal had had severe diarrhea. And once a squirrel was found on the front lawn, its head gone, legs severed, body gutted.

History: Ruth and Bill knew little about previous owners and/or residents of the house. However, a séance conducted by the Piles and Joy McDonald indicated that about thirty years before a group of people had been playing with Satanism and black magic, probably using the attic for such rituals.

Identity of ghosts: Pile reports that his group contacted three ghosts—deceased human beings—as well as an elemental and a thought form. The elemental was the most difficult to deal with, Pile said, and the thought form the second most difficult.

"We found two energy columns that went straight up through the house from the ground," Pile says. "If you walked through them, they would make you feel nauseated, they were so powerful." Pile explained the nature of an elemental as follows:

"Elementals are very negative. They belong to the earth. They come forth only when evoked by certain rituals. They have complete disdain for the human race."

A thought form, Pile said, is much easier to get rid of because its energy field can be reversed. A large percentage of paranormal happenings are caused by thought forms, according to Pile and other parapsychologists. They are caused by the way people think. Sometimes they can be brought forth by, as Pile put it, "people fooling around or playing with Satanism and black magic and things like that in which they try to create an energy and control it. Unfortunately, it usually ends up controlling them."

Pile says that in a séance, with Nancy Pile and Joy McDonald acting as mediums, he was able—with the help of higher spiritual forces—to reverse the negative energy of the thought form and to force the elemental back down into the earth. The Piles and Joy McDonald then, through visualizing white light, "capped" or "sealed" the columns they had felt earlier. Supposedly the protective and salutory effect of their meditation would ensure that the elemental and thought form would not come back up out of the earth and into the house.

After these encounters, the dealings with the human ghosts were quite mild, according to Pile. One of them was the nanny, who had been overly strict, even brutal, with the children. A child had died as a result of this, although the nanny had not meant for this to happen and was appalled and guilt-ridden. It was her guilt that was tying her to the earth plane, in this house. She was literally afraid to go on to higher spiritual planes because she expected severe punishment, according to Pile. He persuaded her not to be so hard on herself and to go on to higher spheres, which she did. The little girl whose voice was heard in the house had been under the care of the nanny. She had died and was still looking for her mother. Pile persuaded her to go on, too. The last ghost said his name was Myron. He mentioned he came from Ohio and had taught violin, as Ruth did. How he came to be in the house was not clear, but he too was "rescued," as Pile calls sending earthbound spirits on to higher planes.

Personalities of ghosts: The elemental was dreadful and arrogant until overcome by higher spiritual forces, according to Pile; the thought form was arrogant at first, but quickly folded when its energy was reversed; the nanny was filled with self-recrimination; the little girl was frightened and lonely; Myron seemed friendly.

Witnesses: Bill and Ruth and their two young daughters; Randy and Ginny, who lived upstairs; Clare, the young Utica psychic; Ruth's father and sister; a number of Ruth's music students.

Best time to witness: Things seemed to happen all around the clock.

Still haunted? Pile says the house appeared to be quiet when his group left. Bill and Ruth have since sold the house and moved south, but not, Pile says, because of ghostly happenings.

Investigations: A session conducted by Roger and Nancy Pile and Joy McDonald and visits by the young psychic from the neighborhood.

Data submitted by: Roger Pile, Nancy Pile, and Joy McDonald.

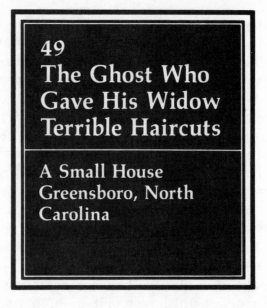

**49
The Ghost Who
Gave His Widow
Terrible Haircuts**

A Small House
Greensboro, North
Carolina

Location: The people in this case did not wish their identities, or the location of the house, revealed.

Description of place: A one-story, cement block and stone bungalow, in a subdivision dating from the 1940s.

Ghostly manifestations: Mary and Jennifer Johnson (not their real names) were mother and daughter, living in this small house. The mother was about sixty, the daughter about thirty. Mary did not go out to work, but Jennifer had a job as an interviewer for a housing project. The father, Roger, had died of a heart attack about twenty years before. Mary and Jennifer told Jeannie Stewart, the source for this report, that immediately after his death they had begun to be aware of sounds in the house, especially at night. They heard knocking, footsteps, voices whispering, although they couldn't understand what was being said. They saw vague apparitions. The sounds were also heard by relatives and other visitors.

But the most terrifying aspect of the women's twenty-year ordeal was that Mary would constantly wake up in the morning and find her hair cut, in a random, haphazard, disfiguring manner. Parts of her head looked as though it had been shaved.

In 1985, Mary and Jennifer began seeing Jeannie Stewart, a psychologist and medium who uses her psychic abilities in her therapy practice. She is currently partner with Dr. William G. Roll, a nationally known, highly regarded parapsychologist, in Parapsychological Services Institute, the intent of which is largely to help people who are being attacked and frightened by discarnate entities of one sort or another. Mrs. Stewart saw Mary and Jennifer several times in her office and made a number of visits to their home. Roll also visited the house and saw them in the offices of PSI.

Jeannie Stewart,
psychologist and medium

"When this hair cutting happened," Jeannie Stewart says, "Mary would look terrible. Her hair would look awful. I don't know how anything could take that much hair without awakening somebody. She would get so disturbed when it happened."

The daughter would also get very upset when this happened. She would sometimes wonder if she had been possessed and had sawed at her mother's hair without either of them knowing it. They were certain it was the spirit of the dead father who was doing this, but Jennifer sometimes suspected her father had entered her psyche and was somehow controlling her.

Both mother and daughter were usually aware when an episode was coming. They would begin to drift irresistibly off into sleep, or what might better be described as a trance. They had a phrase for this; they called it "going into a spell." But according to Stewart, even if Jennifer had conceivably sometimes cut her mother's hair, she could hardly have done it all the time, for her mother often locked her bedroom door and sometimes had been known to nail it shut, and still the hair cutting occurred. As for the possibility that the mother had cut her own hair, they said they would never allow scissors or razors in their house.

History: The family had originally come from North Carolina but had lived for a time in Columbus, Ohio, when Jennifer was small. They lived near Marcie, Mary's sister. Marcie and Roger formed a close tie, which Mary sometimes felt was a union against her. Both Marcie and Roger were involved in the practice of black magic. Mary eventually became so alarmed about this formidable duo that she left Roger and brought Jennifer back to North Carolina. However, Roger followed them and lived with them in the Greensboro house until he died suddenly.

Identity of ghost: "They felt it was pretty much the father," Stewart says. "But they also felt there was this man in the community who handles roots, and they suspect he is also involved in doing this."

The Johnsons are black, and Stewart says: "There is a whole belief system among many black people in black magic. There is a labyrinth of community involvement with occult things, even with people who are quite ordinary. A lot is attributed to demons. They use roots to put these hexes and curses on people. It's a very powerful suggestion, at the least. It gets a lot of results."

Stewart said that during the times she was in the house, she was aware psychically only of Roger, not the man in the community whom Mary and Jennifer also suspected. She worked with the mother and daughter in meditations to release the spirit of Roger from the earthly plane.

Personality of ghost: Seemingly hostile and vindictive.

Witnesses: The mother and daughter, relatives, and other visitors to the house. These people have spent the night with Mary and Jennifer, heard noises, and found Mary with her hair wildly shorn in the morning. An episode also happened during the time Jeannie Stewart was seeing them.

Best time to witness: Most of these things happen at night, but sometimes during the day.

Still haunted? At the time of this interview, in late 1985, Jeannie Stewart said there had been no manifestations for about five months, since the sending away of Roger's spirit.

Investigations: Those conducted by Jeannie Stewart and William Roll.

Data submitted by: Jeannie Stewart.

50
The Ghost Who Canceled the Second Shift

A Furniture Factory Thomasville, North Carolina

Location: The address of the San-Mor Company factory is 20 Peace St., Thomasville.

Description of place: A one-story cinder block, flat-roofed building, containing about twenty thousand square feet of floor space, built in the 1940s. It houses the San-Mor Co., which produces furniture. Thomasville is a town of about fifteen thousand, a furniture and hosiery manufacturing center.

Ghostly manifestations: This ghost may be the most frequently seen apparition in this book, with the largest number of witnesses. It appears to be a man of about fifty, about six feet tall, wearing a long-sleeved, tan and blue checkered shirt and khaki work pants. The most frequent apparent viewer is Victor Couch, president and part owner of the company, who has by now supposedly seen the apparition between fifty and a hundred times. Newspaper stories usually describe Mr. Couch as very much a solid citizen, a Civitan and a Republican. (Are

Republicans less likely to see ghosts than Democrats?)

When Couch first began seeing the apparition, he went to a psychiatrist, who told him, "I can't find anything wrong with you, but I appreciate your money." He went to an optometrist, who found his eyes OK. And when the well-known parapsychologist William Roll of the Psychical Research Foundation gave him a test called Inventory of Childhood Memories and Imaginings, he produced, according to Roll, "a low score of eight, indicating a fairly modest imaginative life."

In any case, Couch is far from the sole viewer of the apparition, which has been nicknamed "Lucas," short for Lucifer. More than a dozen employees on the evening shift—Lucas seems to appear mostly in the evenings, and possibly at night if anyone were there to see him—have seen the apparition. So many, in fact that people refused to work the evening shift, and San-Mor had to cut back to a single

The San-Mor Company's haunted factory

day shift several years ago. Many people have quit. "Lucas makes them a little bit nervous," Couch says.

Half a dozen people at a time have seen the apparition. The usual parapsychological tricks are played: tools and other objects are moved; loud sounds are heard as though lumber is falling over, but none has; women say they can feel something breathing on the back of their necks. One of Couch's brothers, Allen, says he has felt a hand on his shoulder; another, Chip, says he has seen the apparition's feet under the door to a back room.

Although the apparition usually appears in the evening, he has been known to be abroad during the day. Couch's daughter, Beverly, works at the factory but had never seen the ghost until recently in 1985. "It was about 9:30 in the morning," Couch relates. "I was in the machine room, and I heard Beverly let out a blood-curdling scream. I ran back there thinking she had hurt herself." But she had just seen Lucas.

An example of Lucas's tricks is contained in an article Roll wrote for *Theta* magazine, of which he is the editor, as follows:

> [This occurrence] took place during a night shift when a man and his wife were the only ones working. The man was cutting 6½" squares of wood into circles, using the bandsaw. He picked up 15 squares at a time. When he had done the 15th, Couch said that:
> . . . 14 of them would somehow be back on the stack behind him where the balance of his work was. And this happened two nights in succession. . . . He said, "Something's the matter here. I'm not on drugs. I don't smoke pot. Something is wrong." He blamed his wife; he asked her, "Are you picking up my work and stacking it behind me?" and she said, "No. . . ." He subsequently quit.

History: The building was put up in the 1940s by Tom and Clyde Alexander, brothers, who established a company there called the Glenda Table Co., named after Tom's daughter. The company eventually went out of business, and in the early 1970s Couch and his brothers took over the building to house San-Mor.

Identity of ghost: Here the plot thickens. For many years, it was thought by Victor Couch that the ghost might be Clyde Alexander, one of the owners of Glenda Table Co. Clyde had had a stroke, and Couch befriended him and spent time with him. Many psychics visited the place, often with Dr. Roll, and some tended to agree with Couch's suspicion that Clyde Alexander was returning to his earthly milieu, perhaps hoping to somehow help his old

William G. Roll

friend. However, Couch was a bit puzzled by the apparition's rough working attire, since Clyde Alexander had been an executive and a natty dresser.

During one psi session, one psychic, Elizabeth Anderson of Atlanta, Georgia, had an interesting intuition. The word *peace* kept coming to her. "It was so strange," she says. "I thought it was a word. I didn't realize it could be a name."

Around this time, Lucas was beginning to get a lot of publicity. Cindie Stephens, a reporter for the *High Point* (North Carolina) *Enterprise,* wrote a story about the haunting that was picked up by the Associated Press and published in many parts of the world. Couch got letters from England, Canada, the Philippines. Radio stations, TV networks, tabloids clamored for interviews. And many longtime residents of Thomasville, who knew something that Couch, a Virginian comparatively new to the town, didn't know, began to buttonhole him. He found that the reports of a haunting antedated San-Mor's taking over the building. "I found out that the apparition was here long before we came on the scene," Couch says.

Friends and neighbors began to fill Couch in on a bit of local history. Before the factory building was put up, there was a farm on the site, with a house and a barn, which were razed when the factory building was erected in the 1940s. The family that had owned the farm had a retarded son, who at the age of fifty hung himself in the barn and was not discovered for twenty-four hours. "The barn was where our building is now," Couch says. The family's name was Peace.

Couch says that recently a Thomasville man took him aside and told him a story that dated from the man's youth. The man said he had been a friend of Glenda Alexander and had often visited her house. One time Glenda's father, Tom, offered to show him something interesting. He took the young man to the factory on three successive nights. On the third night, the man told Couch, they saw an apparition. Clyde Alexander was still alive at that time.

Personality of ghost: The apparition never speaks

or interacts with people, although he occasionally plays tricks.

Witnesses: Apparently scores of people, employees, and managers of the two companies that have operated in the building, as well as some visitors.

Best time to witness: Almost always in the evening or at night, rarely during the daylight hours.

Still haunted? There have been recent sightings.

Investigations: Many psychics have checked out the place. William Roll and his associates visited several times.

Data submitted by: Victor Couch; Dr. William Roll; Elizabeth Anderson, Kelly Powers, and Elaine Gibbs, psychics who visited the place; Cindie Stevens in articles in *The High Point Enterprise* (Oct. 31, 1982; Nov. 2, 1982; Dec. 15, 1982; April 22, 1984); Sue Ann Pressley in the Nov. 7, 1982 issue of the *Charlotte Observer*; article by Roll in the Spring 1985 issue of *Theta: The Journal of the Psychical Research Foundation*.

51
Some Researchers Don't Know When to Quit

The Historical Wing of the Public Library Wilmington, North Carolina

Location: The address of the New Hanover County Public Library is 201 Chestnut St., Wilmington, NC

Description of place: The New Hanover County Public Library moved into its present quarters in 1981. The building was converted from a department store, which was put up in the early 1950s. A librarian described the building as "typical 1950s architecture, a big, square, brick building, with a basement and three floors." The top floor is not being used. Wilmington is a pleasant resort city on the ocean, with a permanent population of about fifty-five thousand.

Ghostly manifestations: Most of the happenings seem to take place in the historical wing on the second floor of the library; the chief source for this account is Beverly Tetterton, the state and local history librarian. She has had a number of experiences herself, many of them auditory.

"Some of them are noises that maybe only a

The New Hanover County Public Library

librarian would be familiar with," Ms. Tetterton says, "the noises of people putting books on a shelf or flipping through a book looking at an index and going back and forth to a page. The rustle of pages, the sound of people knocking against metal book shelves, putting their elbows on them to read. Some nights I work, and there is so much activity back there in the shelves, and I'd know I'd just talked to the last person to leave. You hear footsteps and the thumping of books.

"Sometimes we'll lock up night, and when we come in in the morning the pamphlet file cases will be unlocked. Sometimes a drawer will be slightly opened, but all of them will be unlocked, every one."

There have been three known sightings of apparitions during the past two or three years, Ms. Tetterton says. She preferred not to identify the people, all library patrons, who did the sighting. On separate occasions, she says two men saw a short woman who, Ms. Tetterton says, "looked very much like a woman we all knew and loved very much. She was a local historian who died about three years ago."

The other person who reported an apparition was a woman who was coming around a corner in the stacks. She saw a human figure that was fading. She went closer and tried to touch it, but it had disappeared. She could not tell if it was male or female.

History: Two other buildings are involved in this account. One is a building two blocks away that previously housed the New Hanover County Public Library. The other is a house on the current site that was razed when the department store was built.

The earlier library building is described by Ms.

The John Taylor house

Tetterton as "a very strange building." It was originally built as a house and was known as the John Taylor House. Later it was converted into an armory for the Wilmington Light Infantry, a local military group, now disbanded, that fought in several wars. It became a library in 1954. Ms. Tetterton says, "It looks like it was never meant to be a house, but when it became an armory they put little cannons on the roof, and it looked even stranger. They heard noises mainly. People say they saw shadows and heard footsteps. I worked there only a year before we moved to the new building. I saw a shadow one night when I was at the checkout desk. I had just started. I told the girl I was working with that I thought there was somebody in the building, and she said, 'Get your hat and pocketbook and let's get out of here.' "

The house that was razed when the department store was put up also had the reputation of being haunted. It was a large, three-story Italianate house, built in the 1860s. A well-to-do family by the name of Wood lived there. The family donated many books to the library, many of which are now housed in the historical wing. Ms. Tetterton says, "Father and son were both doctors. The story goes that footsteps could be heard on the second floor. At one time a locally famous duel was fought, and one of the duelists spent the night before the duel in the house. He was killed, and everyone thought those were his footsteps."

Identity of ghosts: Former patrons of the library? The lady historian? The unfortunate duelist? The odd ghost who moved over from the John Taylor House? Take your pick, gentle reader.

Personalities of ghosts: Quiet and orderly. None have been known to spirit away books or documents.

Witnesses: Ms. Tetterton and various employees and patrons of the library.

Best Time to Witness: "Mostly during the day," says Ms. Tetterton. "I don't know what happens around here at night. The janitorial staff stays till about ten or eleven. They don't usually hang around this area of the library at all. They like to be on the first floor of the library after it's closed, and I can't blame them."

Still Haunted? The sightings of the apparition that faded away was quite recent, in the summer of 1985.

Investigation: Ms. Tetterton says no psychics have checked the place out personally, to her knowledge.

Data Submitted By: Beverly Tetterton; information from an article by Diana Lynn in the *Raleigh News and Observer;* tip from Rusty Spears of Rocky Mount, North Carolina.

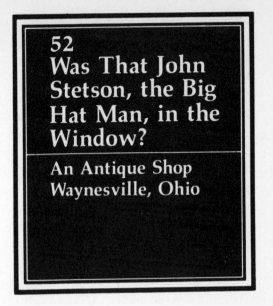

52
Was That John Stetson, the Big Hat Man, in the Window?

An Antique Shop
Waynesville, Ohio

Location: The address of the Stetson House is 234 South Main St., Waynesville, Ohio.

Description of place: "It's a neat little early building," says Dennis Dalton, the town historian, who works out of the local library. A two-story house with six rooms, it is called the Stetson House. It was used as a private home during most of its history, although the last two occupants have, since the mid-1970s, used it as an antique shop. "It's a cottage on Main Street at the edge of the village's original public square," Dalton says. "It's probably the earliest frame building on the street. It looks very Victorian. It has a gingerbread front porch and dormers, but the basic shell of the house probably dates from before 1820."

Waynesville is a town of about eighteen hundred living souls—and apparently a lot of dead ones—in southwestern Ohio, about fifteen miles from Dayton. It would be hard for a strong man to throw a stone in town without hitting a supposedly haunted house. Historian Dalton is possibly the town's most enthusiastic spook buff. Every Halloween he conducts a tour called "Toast Your Ghost." "I dress in late-eighteenth-century costume," he says, "and take people on a ghost walk. We visit some of the haunted spots and houses in town after dark. Then we come back and toast our ghosts with cider. A lot of us could probably use something stronger at that point, but the town is dry." As a final note on the sociology of Waynesville, it might be interesting to observe that there are some forty antique shops in town.

Ghostly manifestations: The primary "hauntee" of record of the Stetson House is Marjorie Dodd, who ran an antique shop in the building for seven years up through the early 1980s. The present owner of the shop, Arthur Wood, says he has not been aware of anything unusual during his tenure. But Mrs. Dodd seems to have had one wild experi-

The Stetson Place

PHOTO BY ARTHUR WOOD

ence after another. Her first awareness that there might be something strange going on came soon after she moved in, and it was an expensive experience. "My main problem was with antique mirrors," she says. "I'd come in in the morning, and they'd be broken on the floor, with the chain intact and the pin still on the wall. It happened twice downstairs and once upstairs. Those mirrors are fairly expensive; you can't replace the old beveled glass. After that I didn't bring them to the shop anymore."

Another item in the folklore of Mrs. Dodd's occupancy involved a sighting of what might have been an apparition, by a man who lived across the street. Dalton says, "A neighbor stepped out to check the weather about 11:00 P.M. and saw a small, dark-haired woman standing at the front door. He thought it was Marge Dodd, but she didn't work at night. Then as he watched she walked away from the door and dissolved into the wall."

Who do the ghost fanciers of Waynesville think this woman might have been? Two possibilities are suggested. The Stetson House is so called after John Stetson, the famed hat maker of the nineteenth century, who often visited—sometimes for extended periods—his sister, Louisa Stetson Larrick. Louisa came to Ohio in the mid-1800s from Connecticut after marrying a local farmer and apparently cordially hated the place. She left Larrick's bed and board early in the marriage and moved into this little house in the middle of town, living there for the rest of her life.

Another candidate for the apparition's identity is Lila Benham, a schoolteacher who lived there in the first part of the twentieth century. A psychic who visited the place once said she could see a woman standing near the chimney in the room that was originally the kitchen, very unhappy, weeping. Her name, the psychic said, started with *L*, which might make her either Lila Benham or Louisa Larrick.

Dennis Dalton and Marge Dodd are pretty sure Lila Benham's spirit inhabits the place, whoever the apparition at the front door might have been, and they cite the following incident. Dalton was having tea with Dodd one December afternoon when two elderly sisters came calling. They were from Dayton but had been brought up in Waynesville and were returning for a visit. Lila Benham had been one of their teachers; they had heard that her ghost was haunting Stetson House, and they wanted to have a look for themselves. While Marge Dodd and Dennis Dalton continued their afternoon tea, the sisters wandered around the house, upstairs and down. Dalton relates: "I was sitting talking with Marge, and on a bench was a little glass dish with a little glass hen on its cover. The two sisters walked out of the back room, which had been the original kitchen, and one said, 'I don't think this place is haunted.' The other replied in a similar vein. With that, it was as though somebody had made a swipe and knocked the glass hen dish off the bench. It came apart and broke and slid on the floor right up to their feet. That made believers out of them."

Throughout Marge Dodd's occupancy, she says, there were the usual paranormal occurrences—things moving about, things falling off the wall, things disappearing. One such incident stands out in her memory. "At work one day I got ready to go home and went to get my keys. I looked where I always put them, and they simply weren't there. I called my husband at home, and he came and helped me look, and we looked and looked and looked. Well, there was no way to lock the shop, so we spent the night there. My post office key was on that ring, my car keys, the key to home— everything. I had to get new keys made. We had to have all the locks changed. About three months later, the keys just appeared one day. They were lying on a shelf, not even above eye level. I'd moved things on that shelf at various times, and I never saw any keys there."

The media has paid quite a bit of attention to Marge Dodd's ghostly adventures. One day a TV crew from station WHIO in Dayton was producing a show at the place. A young woman camera person had just finished shooting in one of the rooms. As she was leaving, a piece of crockery fell off a shelf and broke. To paranormal fans such as Dalton and Dodd, who were nearby, this was definitely a paranormal occurrence. The camerawoman, however, was skeptical. "Who knows why it fell?" she said to this investigator. "It just fell off the shelf." She requested that her name not be used.

Another bit player in the saga of Stetson House who requested anonymity is a young policeman who in the early 1980s, after Arthur Wood had opened up the place, says that one night while making his rounds he was passing and looked up to see the face of a man looking out an upstairs window. He said it was the face of a man of about forty, with a pronounced nose. According to historian Dalton, that sounds like John Stetson. "I looked back," the policeman told this reporter, "after just a quick glance. I did a double take, and it was gone."

As a final note, let us cite an olfactory item. Dalton says that one summer afternoon he went over to visit his friend Marge, and as he entered the place he seemed to smell fresh, ripe cantaloupe. He went into the other downstairs room, the one-time kitchen, where Marge was, and suddenly he could smell gingerbread. He must have sniffed, because as he relates the incident, "Marge smiled at me for a moment and then said, 'Can you smell it?' I said, 'Yes it smells like gingerbread baking,' and she nodded. It hung in the air for several moments, and then all of a sudden it was gone. That was a one-time experience."

History: Dalton says the house was probably built by a builder named John Satterthwaite, who put up several houses in the area between 1810 and 1825. It has usually been used as a dwelling, although at one time it housed a wagon shop. Louisa Stetson Larrick is known to have been living there in 1861. "John Stetson first came to visit her around that time," Dalton says. "He'd been turned down for a partnership in his father's hat-making business in Philadelphia. The Stetsons were all hat makers. John was asthmatic and consumptive, and they thought he'd never amount to anything. So he went West. There was a gold rush in the late 1850s. He stayed with Louisa a few days, then hooked up with some other gold seekers and walked seven hundred miles to Colorado. He panned some gold and got enough to open a brickyard in St. Joseph, Missouri. He got flooded out by the Missouri River and came back penniless and stayed with his sister. He had regained his health, but he left his consumption with Louisa, and that's what killed her eventually. She died in 1879 and is buried in a local cemetery. It was here in 1865 that he developed his plans for a one-man factory. Louisa grubstaked him to sixty dollars to go back to Philadelphia." The rest is hat history.

A strange aspect of this case is that there seem to have been no observances of paranormal activities before or after the occupancy of Marge Dodd—

except for the report of the young cop. Yet she says she was never aware of things happening around her before she purchased the Stetson House and hasn't been since she left the place.

Identity of ghosts: Obvious nominees would be John Stetson, Louisa Stetson Larrick, and Lila Benham. In addition, some psychics have said they could feel the presence of children about the place. Whether or not she was influenced by this, the last two years Marge Dodd had the place she replaced her antique furnishings with antique dolls and toys, and after that there were no further events, she says.

Personalities of ghosts: "Friends of Denny's were psychics," Marge Dodd says, "and their readings coincided that there was sadness there but nothing vicious. I'm not the bravest person in the world, but I had absolutely no fear of that house. I'd go there at night and work alone."

Witnesses: Marge Dodd; Dennis Dalton; the two elderly sisters from Dayton; the TV camerawoman; the young policeman; the neighbor; many others.

Best time to witness: Most reported events took place during the day; the place was rarely occupied at night.

Still haunted? Things seem pretty quiet these days.

Data submitted by: Marjorie Dodd, Dennis Dalton, the young camerawoman, the young policeman, Arthur Wood. An Associated Press article by Joe McKnight in the October 30, 1983, issue of the *Dayton Daily News*; an article in the September 11, 1976, issue of the *Dayton Journal-Herald*. A discussion by Curtis Fuller in his column in the June 1984 issue of *Fate* magazine.

53
A Musical Spirit

Pacific University
Forest Grove, Oregon

Location: The address of Pacific University is 2043 College Way, Forest Grove, Oregon.

Description of place: The building believed to be haunted, Knight Hall, houses the Music Department of the university. It was converted from a Victorian family home, three stories high, of wood painted white with black and red trim. Pacific University is a private, coeducational institution of eleven hundred students. Forest Grove is a town of twelve thousand, some twenty-five miles west of Portland.

Ghostly manifestations: The ghost is one of the traditions of the university. It gets constant media attention, and reaction from students and faculty ranges from disbelief through skepticism to true belief. There are a respectable number of professed witnesses, however, and it is unlikely that rumors of Vera—the name given to the ghost—are likely to fade away.

Vera, it would seem, sings and plays the piano,

walks around making footsteps, opens and shuts doors, sometimes emits a blue light, and occasionally frightens faculty, students, and dogs.

A sample witness is Dr. Donald Schwejda, a retired music professor. His office door, Schwejda says, had a tendency to close by itself without human assistance. Further, he says, a cleaning man once told him the door had slammed shut. But Schwejda's outstanding experience occurred on a Christmas Day in the early 1980s. He had been trying to record some music at his home, but the holiday festivities were hampering his efforts, so he decided to do it at Knight Hall. The place was

Knight Hall at Pacific University

deserted during the holiday season. He was in the midst of his recording when he heard footsteps coming down the hall. He hoped whoever it was wouldn't come in, speak, and ruin the tape. He tiptoed to the door to warn the person, but there was no one there. Further, he says, if someone had come into the building, he would have heard the front door close.

Schwejda said nothing about the incident at the time, but a couple of days later a professor from another department was working in the same building and experienced the same thing. This professor, Schwejda says, would not go back into the building again during the holiday recess.

Another witness is a Pacific University graduate with a responsible position in what he terms "a conservative community," who was willing to be interviewed but not identified. When he was a student at the university in the late 1960s he had a part-time job as a watchman. One of the buildings he was assigned to watch was Knight Hall. One night he went in to give the place its good-night check when he heard a female voice singing. He went through the entire building but could find no one, although the singing continued. At one point, he says, he felt as though he were in the center of the music. As he closed the front door, he says, he suddenly saw a blue light, vaguely resembling a female form, materialize down the hall.

This man also figures in the German shepherd story. This dog was a habitué of the campus and often used to follow him on his rounds. One night as he approached Knight Hall it ran ahead of him, leaping against the door and barking furiously. But its mood changed suddenly; it cringed, turned tail, and took off across the campus as though it had seen a ghost.

Another aspect of the Knight Hall folklore is a mysterious piano playing. A number of people say they have heard this. In 1979, two reporters on the student newspaper, *Pacific Index*, decided to stay in the building overnight. They just about made it, quitting the place at 5:30 A.M. after a night of intermittent fright. They reported hearing footsteps, having lights go on, hearing the singing of an alto voice, hearing the rustling of what could have been a long skirt. At one point one of the reporters began to play the piano and says that he twice heard a female voice whisper in his ear, "Oh, please stop!" According to their story, the next night they returned to the building with some friends to describe what had happened. In the room where the ghostly voice had been heard one of the friends began to play the piano, and they heard a heavy sigh. A ghostly critic!

History: The building, put up in the late 1800s, was later converted from a private home to an apartment house. In 1947, it became a girls' dormitory for the university. Some years afterward, it became the home of the Music Department.

Identity of ghost: Tradition has it that the ghost is a music student who either committed suicide or died by accident in the building, although no one in the administration of the university seems to be certain whether this is fact or fiction. Some years ago an English professor and some students held Ouija board séance in the building and supposedly contacted the spirit. The university's director of planning, Kenneth Combs, once a music professor, says, "The board spelled 'Vera.' She said she had been a student here. Research was done, and it was discovered there had once been a music student named Vera who fit the pattern and then died. I'm not sure she committed suicide. It's said she died in the building, but that could just be a story."

Personality of ghost: Seemingly the classic pattern of a spirit who wants to make its presence known.

Witnesses: Quite a number of faculty and students.

Best time to witness: Things seem to occur when the building is almost unoccupied, such as at night or during a holiday season.

Still haunted? "I haven't heard of anything lately," says Charlotte Filer, Director of Public Information of Pacific University.

Investigations: Several psychics have checked out the place, and almost all have said they were aware of a spirit.

Data submitted by: Charlotte Filer; Dr. Donald Schwejda; Kenneth Combs; Dr. Elliot Weiner, former professor of psychology at the university; various other members of the administrative staff of the university; the one-time student watchman who prefers to remain anonymous; articles from campus publications such as *Pacific Index* and *Pacific Today*.

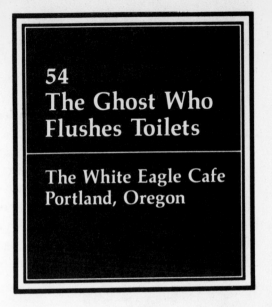

**54
The Ghost Who
Flushes Toilets**

The White Eagle Cafe
Portland, Oregon

Location: The White Eagle Cafe is located at 836
North Russell St., Portland, Oregon.

Description of place: "Sort of a popular place in
Old Town Portland," is the way Suzanne Jauchius, a
psychic in Portland, describes the tavern. "It's real
clean inside; lots of good jazz and bluegrass music."
The present proprietor, Chuck Hughes, gives the
building's statistics as follows: Built in 1889; about
thirty feet wide, seventy feet long, forty feet high.
Two stories and a basement. Brick. Two windows in
the back on the second floor; two windows in front
on the ground level; four windows in front on the
second floor. "This used to be a hard-core neighborhood," Chuck says. "It's not far from the docks. It's
one of the oldest sections in the city, actually the
oldest. Now a lot of the old buildings have been
knocked down, and the area is mostly industrial."

Ghostly manifestations: The place has been in its
time a whorehouse, a beat-up hotel and rooming

house, and always a bar, except during Prohibition. A tough joint during much of its history, it seems to have some tough ghosts.

Item: A waitress known as Yvonne was going down to the basement one night after closing. The basement was once the domain of the black whores. The white whores were stationed on the second floor. This was before integration. To get to the basement stairs, one must go through huge metal double doors, like those of a bank vault. Yvonne was going to "do her money," as Chuck Hughes puts it—tally the money with the meal checks—and was going to use the adding machine that he keeps in a basement office. Suddenly an unseen hand seemed to push her,

Suzanne Jauchius, a Portland psychic

and she went elbow over teacup down the stairs, screaming. The bartender and the doorman rushed down to pick her up, and as they got to the bottom of the stairs a mop bucket at the top of the stairs came flying down after them, unassisted by corporeal hand or foot. Yvonne quit the next day.

Item: The second floor is not used now, and a few

years ago Chuck Hughes went up there to take a lock off a door to use downstairs. As he was working on a door, he heard a woman crying. It seemed to come from the end of the hallway, and he walked down that way to investigate. As he got toward the sound, it disappeared. He checked all the rooms, found nothing, and went back to removing the door bolt. The crying started again. He walked toward it, and it stopped. Suddenly he felt a chill, as though ice water were being poured down his back. He turned and went downstairs in a hurry. He went outside and across the street, where he stood and looked at the building. Then, he says, he saw an image in an upstairs window. "I couldn't identify it," he says. "It was like a human form, but more like a teardrop." He walked around to the back of the building and saw the same image in an upstairs window. "I didn't go back up those stairs for almost a year," he says.

Item: One of the rooms on the second floor once housed a man called Sam, who has been nominated in recent years as one of the ghosts, since he died there in the 1930s. Sam, an orphan, was adopted when he was about ten by one of the tavern's early owners, William Hryszlo. Tom Mish, who at eighty-five has been a regular at the White Tavern for most of this century, remembers Sam as a "roustabout." Mish says, "He cleaned up the joint. He had a harelip." Sam died when he was about thirty, presumably of natural causes, and his longtime protector and employer had the body removed and locked up the room, leaving Sam's clothing and meager belongings in it. It remained locked for many years. Nowadays, Sam's door won't stay open. Chuck Hughes first became aware of this aspect of his newly purchased building when one of his bartenders, name of Skip, told him he had opened Sam's door, gone back in a couple of days, and found it locked again. "He said this had happened more than once," Hughes says. "I didn't believe it, so I went up and unlocked the door myself. I checked two days later, and it was closed and locked. I wondered if Skip was playing a joke on me. Then he left, and I had the only key. I tried it again, and the same thing happened. I know nobody had been up there."

Item: Hughes has a bed in the cellar that he uses when he works late. "One night," he says, "I woke up and I was rocking. Not the bed, *me—I* was rocking. No one was touching me, but I was rocking, and I didn't want to rock. I got up and went home."

Item: Hughes says that sometimes when he is downstairs in the basement he can hear voices and people walking around upstairs in the bar after the place is closed. He goes up and checks, but nobody is there. Sometimes he hears voices saying his name. Nowadays, if he is working on his books downstairs and hears voices, he just turns up the TV.

Item: Hughes says that he occasionally finds coins on the floor of the basement, where he knows there weren't coins last time he looked. They are old coins, relatively speaking. The oldest is a 1934 buffalo-head nickel. Others date from the 1940s and 1950s.

Special item: Perhaps the most intriguing aspect of the cafe's ghostly manifestations is the flushing of the toilet in the men's room. Many people, staff and customers, have heard this, according to Chuck Hughes and others. The rest rooms are off the barroom. There is a door that leads to a very short corridor, off which there is a men's room on one side and a women's room on the other. Hughes says that on the men's side, usually after closing, since it is quiet then, one can sometimes hear footsteps in the corridor, the men's room door open and close, and then the toilet flush. On checking, no one will be found there. It's not a faulty toilet, say Hughes and his chief cook, Paul Stone, because it has happened with two toilets. A few years ago a motorcycle gang wrecked the first toilet, but its replacement flushes on. The first toilet was put in relatively recently, in 1974. Before that, there was an open trough in the same area.

History: Much of this historical information comes from Paul Stone, who was brought up in the area. "This area was thick with bars," Stone says. "It was a melting pot—Chinese, Polish, Russian. The original structure was made of wood. It was built by Polish people and was a bar from the start." In 1905, the building was redone with bricks, laid around the outside of the wooden siding. "In those days," Stone says, "there were tunnels, and they'd shanghai sailors through the tunnels down to the docks and put them on a ship." Traditionally, there is said to be a tunnel that leads out of the basement of the White Eagle. "The one from this building was sealed up a long time ago," Stone says. "I'm not sure where it is."

The place was probably a whorehouse from its earliest days till it burned in 1912 and was closed for about a year. "I think that was when the tunnel was sealed," Stone says. "When they stopped the shanghaiing, they stopped the prostitution as well."

The bar itself could be one of the historical sights of Portland. Hand-carved in Boston, about forty feet long, it was transported around the Horn in 1900 and took first prize at the Seattle World's Fair. It was installed in the White Eagle a couple of years later. The floor around the bar is also noteworthy. Constructed of tile, probably around 1914, it is designed in the pattern of a Navaho blanket. "There are deliberate mistakes in it," Stone says, "since the

Navahos believe that only God can or should make anything perfect."

During Prohibition, the place was known as Risko Brothers Soft Drink Emporium. When a son of the family came back from the Navy after World War II, the name was changed from Risko's Cafe to the Blue Eagle Cafe, and around 1950 that was changed to the White Eagle Cafe. The building, which had been empty for some years, was bought and renovated in the 1970s. Chuck Hughes, a tool and die maker who had always wanted to own a bar, bought the place in 1978.

Identity of ghosts: Most of the bar's staff and habitués feel that it's Sam who is flushing the toilet in the men's room, although why he is elected is not clear. Some of the dire doings in the basement are attributed to the ghost of a Chinese bouncer who ran a tight ship on the lower level in his time. One night he turned up missing and was never seen again—nor was he missed, from all accounts. Who is scattering the outdated small change on the basement floor is anybody's guess. The crying that Chuck Hughes heard on the second floor might be attributed to one of the ladies of the evening.

Personalities of ghosts: "My feeling has been that they are trying to get me out," Hughes says. One day, he relates, two women came in for lunch. One said she was a psychic and asked if she could go downstairs. When she came up, she said she could sense violent beatings. "She said that place has bad feelings," Hughes relates, "vibrations of violence and death." Suzanne Jauchius says she could feel a lot of sadness on the second floor. She says that Sam is mobile, that she could feel him in various parts of the tavern.

Witnesses: Many people who work and drink at the White Eagle.

Best time to witness: Things have happened all around the clock. Hughes says that the most active times are when the place is quiet, which usually means the late night and early morning hours.

Still haunted? The White Eagle's top feature, the toilet in the men's room, hasn't flushed for about three years, Hughes says. However, more routine manifestations, such as cold spots, mysterious touchings, things falling off shelves, still occur.

Investigations: Many psychics drop by to see what they can sense. The place has been written up many times in local publications.

Data submitted by: Chuck Hughes, Paul Stone, Suzanne Jauchius.

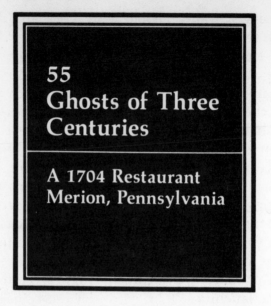

**55
Ghosts of Three
Centuries**

A 1704 Restaurant
Merion, Pennsylvania

Location: The General Wayne Inn is located at 625 Montgomery Ave., Merion, PA.

Description of place: The General Wayne Inn, which opened its doors in 1704, is reputed to be the oldest operating restaurant in the United States. It was twenty-eight years old when George Washington was born. The building has three floors and a particularly significant basement. The original architecture is Colonial, and that part of the building is still used. Additions have been put on over the years, and the restaurant now seats four hundred diners. Situated in the Philadelphia Main Line suburb of Merion, it is a mile from the city limits and seven miles from downtown Philadelphia.

Ghostly manifestations: The ghosts of the General Wayne are no secret in the Philadelphia area. Says Barton Johnson, who bought the inn in 1970, "I've lived in Merion since 1937, and we all knew there were ghosts here. It's been in all the newspapers, on television." Manifestations are manifold and appear to have been happening well prior to the memories of people currently inhabiting this mortal coil.

"Things don't continue forever," Johnson says. "They change." For a while, he recalls, most afternoons would find the glasses hung over the bar shaking. For several months, one of the crystal chandeliers at the top of a flight of stairs swung constantly. Table settings are rearranged by unseen hands; other things are moved; locked doors are found unlocked—the whole gamut of the usual parapsychological phenomena, and then some.

"The ghosts played with our electrical systems," Johnson says, "both the lighting and the sound systems." One time, he says, there was a ten-minute segment on TV about the Wayne's ghosts. A set in the inn's barroom, which had never given any trouble before, went haywire while the segment about the inn was on. "The picture kept going around," Johnson says. "As soon as the segment was over, it was OK."

Some ghosts seem to like to flirt with the female customers. Women will be sitting at the bar, Johnson

The General Wayne Inn

says, ten or twelve in a row, and they will feel someone blowing on their necks. "We get arguments that way," Johnson says. "They blame the men standing behind them."

"Something happened just last Friday," Johnson says. "In one of the private dining rooms there is a portrait of Benjamin Franklin. There was a girl from the Midwest eating there with a private party. She had a roll in her hand. She was talking about Ben Franklin and what a rogue he was. Without any warning, the roll flew out of her hand and hit the wall."

Over the years, many people have seen apparitions of Hessian soldiers, one of whom they called Max. One witness is a man who worked at the inn for some forty years, as waiter, bartender, maître d', and assistant manager. He is now retired. Asked for an interview, this man declined. "I don't want to get involved," he said and urged this reporter to talk with a man who had once been bar manager at the Wayne and who now works at another restaurant in the area. "He'll talk to you," the former maître d' said. "His story is about the same as mine, anyway." They had both seen Hessian soldiers in the basement. Owner Johnson said, "We had a maître d' here who refused to go to our wine room in the basement. And a former bartender, he was down there, too, and had an experience with them. He didn't like going down there at all."

The bartender said, "One thing happened, but I really don't want to go into it." However, after a moment he did continue. "There's a room down in the bowels of the General Wayne Inn where we have a lot of liquor. I went in there one night five years ago. There are three lights in the room. They started to flicker." He hesitated, then said, "I still get bad vibrations from it." And he said he didn't want to talk about it anymore.

History: Originally, the place was called Streepers Tavern, but in 1795 a three-day party was held for General "Mad Anthony" Wayne, who had conquered land from the Indians between Ohio and Mississippi, and the name of the building was changed in his honor. The inn was almost a hundred years old at that time and already had a rich history. One of its rooms housed a post office for 134 years, from 1704 until 1775 under three King Georges of England, and from 1830 to 1897 under nineteen American presidents. In 1763, Benjamin Franklin, as Postmaster General for England's American colonies, came here and supervised the business of the post office. The room is now called the Franklin Post Office and is used as a dining room. It is, in fact, the room where the disrespectful young woman from the Midwest had the roll torn from her hand. In September of 1777, Anthony Wayne ate a meal of "pot pies, beet greens, corn, and beans" there with his officers. The following night, legend has it, George Washington and the Marquis de Lafayette supped there. Many signers of the Declaration of Independence and members of the Second Continental Congress and their families dined at the inn during the flight to York in 1777. For three months during the Revolution, the British––and the Hessians—occupied the inn, and on at least one occasion Lord Cornwallis dined there.

Parts of the basement were sometimes used as a military prison, and some Hessian soldiers were imprisoned there.

Starting in 1839, Edgar Allen Poe dined frequently at the inn. In 1843, he is reputed to have scratched his initials on one of the window sills. It is said that some of his work on "The Raven" was done in the Franklin room.

Identity of ghosts: A few years ago, a psychic who lived in the area, Jean Quinn of Haddonfield, New Jersey, became intrigued with the inn and asked Johnson if she could investigate the place. She visited a number of times without charging any fees. When she first arrived at the restaurant, Johnson says, she headed immediately for the basement. "She came up," Johnson says, "and said, 'You don't have one ghost; you have several.'"

According to Jean Quinn, there are some seventeen ghosts inhabiting the place, among whom eight are Hessians, two are women, one is a black man, one is an Indian, and one is a little boy. They span three centuries.

One particular entity, she says, was definitely a spirit, rather than a sort of place memory. "I was aware of the spirit of this young man," she said, "aware of the distress, the need to communicate, and also the fact that he was just wandering, very much wandering. He wasn't at peace." She told of hearing about a man who lived in a different part of Pennsylvania who was drawn to the inn because of an apparition that repeatedly appeared to him at night.

Johnson identified this man as Michael Benio, a building contractor who lives about a hundred miles away, in Olyphant, a suburb of Scranton. Benio was a psychic. He showed up at the inn when Johnson was on vacation, and the manager asked him to come back in a couple of weeks, which he did. In fact, he returned several times. Benio told Johnson that recently an apparition of a Hessian soldier had constantly appeared to him in his bedroom. In an interview, Benio said this is what had happened long ago:

During the time the Hessians were occupying the inn, the Colonists secreted a spy in the cellar to report on their activities. One of the Hessians, whose name was Ludwig, went down to get some wine, and he surprised the spy, who killed him in order to escape. The other Hessians buried Ludwig behind a wall. The reason the entity was still roaming was that he craved a ritual Roman Catholic burial, according to Benio.

Benio, Johnson relates, wanted to look for the remains of Ludwig, feeling that would put his spirit at rest. He wanted to dig into the walls, but Johnson was reluctant, fearing this might cause a collapse. However, Benio convinced Johnson that as a building expert he would know how to dig, and Johnson let him and a helper dig for two days. When they got out under the parking lot, Johnson lost his nerve and called a halt. Johnson seemed a bit contrite, feeling that, if he'd let them go on digging, they might have found some remains and put the ghost to rest. But he takes comfort in the fact that Benio has said the ghost no longer appears to him at night, apparently feeling he'd done his best.

In addition to the Hessian soldiers, Jean Quinn was aware of a woman named Mary, probably a barmaid. She says she could see Mary giving out drinks and tea. She also saw a black man, whom she called "a very gentle soul." Johnson feels this is a man who was working in the kitchen at the time he bought the place. In a séance conducted by Jean, Johnson thought he recognized this man.

"When I first bought this place," he said, "there

was an old colored man in our kitchen. When I went to the séance I felt he was from this century, and I think it was that man, who died a few weeks after I bought the place. I think it was him, the way he was talking about the former owners."

Jean Quinn also says she saw an apparition of Edgar Allan Poe at the inn. She thinks it was a place memory rather than the actual spirit of the writer. "He was sitting, writing by one of the windows," she says. "I saw him quite clearly for a brief moment."

Personalities of ghosts: Many, Jean Quinn says, are not real spirits but place memories, with about as much actual life as the images on a TV screen. Others are real spirits, she thinks. Johnson says the manifestations have done a little damage, but not much.

"The place is so full of energy," Jean Quinn says. "I was so aware of so many different energies there, so many personalities."

Witnesses: Over the years, countless employees and customers of the restaurant.

Best time to witness: Things happen at various times of the day and night.

Still haunted? The intensity of the manifestations waxes and wanes, Johnson says. "Right now I think we're in a lapsed period." (Apparently he's not counting the wild roll in the Ben Franklin room.)

Investigations: Several visits by Jean Quinn and Michael Benio.

Data submitted by: Barton Johnson, Jean Quinn, Michael Benio, the former maître d', and the former bar manager. Also Sister Gregory of the Sisters of Mercy Rectory next door to the inn, who was a witness at Benio's excavations.

56
The Ghost Who
Took Baths

A White Elephant House
Merion Station, Pennsylvania

Location: The address of this house is 511 Winding Way, Merion Station. The present owners would prefer no visitors.

Description of Place: Now a private home in an affluent suburb of Philadelphia, the building was once half of the clubhouse of the now defunct Belmont Race Track, which operated several blocks away. In the words of a one-time owner, Meredith Smith—Meredith Stevenson when she lived in the house from 1964 to 1968—"It shot up in the air, with a red tile roof, four stories high in the back as the land sloped away, and was rather huge compared to the neighboring houses as it had nine or eleven bedrooms. It was clearly a white elephant, and we purchased it for a song." She describes the architecture as Italianate.

Ghostly manifestations: Mrs. Smith writes:

> "Many, many nights I would get up and check
> on my little children due to the piercing screams

that would wake me up. Nothing was ever amiss, and eventually I realized that the screams came from a *woman*, not a child. I never found her.

"Early on in our life there, we had a few people in for drinks one Sunday afternoon. After they were all there I locked the front door. I was standing in the living room, with several friends, and saw this woman come in the front door, totally clothed in black or dark gray, and I couldn't see her face. She went up the stairs. I thought that I was seeing things but pretended to have the air of a perfect hostess. Much to my surprise, the man next to me said, 'Who was that woman who just went up your front stairs? I saw you lock the front door.' I was so relieved that someone else had seen her that I confessed that I really didn't know and we had better search the house. We did and found nothing. But the man, in searching through the house, felt the very strong presence of the woman, especially on the third floor.

"On several occasions we went to Maine for a couple of weeks, leaving the house empty of people and locked. Two times we came home to find that the hot water in the third-floor bathroom had been turned on and let run. Nobody used the third floor, so it wasn't an oversight before we left the house, and it never happened when we were in residence."

(The current owners of the house, who prefer to remain anonymous, say that nothing unusual has happened during their occupancy, except that once they went away for the summer and had a friend house-sit for them. When they returned, the friend told them that someone seemed to have used the third-floor bathtub.)

Mrs. Smith continues: "The noises of breaking glass during the night were frequent occurrences. Usually it sounded as if a storm window had come off a top floor window onto the driveway. We never found any broken windows. However, once there was a huge crash during the night, which seemed to come from inside the house, on the first floor. The next morning we found a painting on the floor of the living room. The odd thing about it was that the hook in the wall was still there and the wire on the painting was still very much intact."

History: The original building was part of the clubhouse of the Belmont Race Track, dating from the late nineteenth century. Mrs. Smith relates, "After the racetrack became defunct, the house apparently turned into one of 'ill repute,' as they say. At some point in time, the clubhouse was sliced in half." The two halves were moved several blocks to their present locations, serving as private homes only a few doors apart. (The owners of the other half, who have lived in their house more than thirty years, say they are unaware of any unusual occurrences.)

Identity of ghost: Who is the party-crashing woman in gray? Who is taking all those baths on the third floor? Who is screaming her head off? Who is breaking glass and knocking pictures off the wall? Mrs. Smith suggests: "My very own theory was that there was a young girl, turned whore for needs, who was left in the house. She had to get out."

Personality of ghost: She sounds distraught, and there is a definite suggestion of the Lady MacBeth syndrome.

Witnesses: Meredith Smith, a male guest at her

party, the house-sitter of the present owners.

Best time to witness: Occurrences seem to have happened both day and night.

Still haunted? The present owners are apparently unaware of anything unusual at this time.

Investigations: No formal psychic inquiries.

Data submitted by: Meredith Smith and present owners of both parts of the original building.

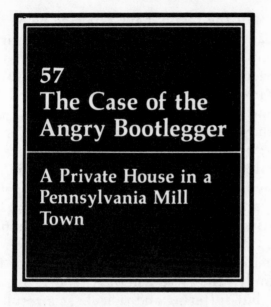

**57
The Case of the
Angry Bootlegger**

A Private House in a
Pennsylvania Mill
Town

Location: The American Society for Psychical Research has not revealed the whereabouts of this house.

Description of place: The house is located in an industrial town, built by a Yugoslavian immigrant in the mid-1920s, when a farm was divided up for urban development. The current occupants have done extensive renovation, and thereon, it is suspected, hangs this tale.

Ghostly manifestations: In 1958, a couple of years after the present owners moved in, the family, composed of a man and wife and seven children, began to notice parapsychological phenomena. Every member of the family has reported apparitions, varying from shadowy forms to lifelike human figures; tapping and banging, footsteps, sounds that resemble the movement of furniture and the opening and closing of doors; cold spots; occasional movement of objects in the presence of witnesses. Four members of the family have reported being victims of "a real hard grab." After twenty years, in 1978, the family had had enough and contacted the American Society for Psychical Research. Karlis Osis, well known in the parapsychological field, and Donna McCormick did an investigation and wrote a paper in which they mentioned, "As a rule, all proper ghosts keep out of sight when the investigators are about, but not this one from the unsophisticated milieu of a mill town." All ASPR investigators experienced sounds, and Osis and another investigator experienced visual phenomena, Osis a shadowy apparition and the other investigator a wisp of smoke. To the investigators, there seemed no question of fakery. "The family," they wrote in their report, "has gained nothing but suffering and ridicule as a result of the phenomena in their home; there was no motivation for collusion that we could discover." Phenomena have been observed by many witnesses, often collectively. For example:

1. The two oldest girls went upstairs to fetch a dress and saw a tall, skinny man with dark eyes. They took him to be a burglar and ran screaming downstairs.

2. The father, a factory foreman, has reported seeing a well-structured apparition on six occasions. He believes it to be a man, although the head is always turned away from him so he is not sure.

3. Others most frequently report seeing a man, but occasionally a female figure. It can be seen standing, zooming by, or sitting in a chair. The duration of the image varies from a second to a minute.

4. The father has heard a voice telling him to get out of the house.

5. One night a younger sister awoke to see a man and a woman in her bedroom, watching her and her brother. She ran to the room of her oldest sister, who gave the ghosts a tongue lashing, and for a short time sounds of footsteps were heard on the stairway, and the brother awoke to see a tall man bending over his bed. The phenomena then stopped, but the family feels the ghosts were responding to the oldest sister's "arrogance."

6. The oldest sister felt a presence in the basement, started up the stairs, and says she was grabbed by the back of her sweater, which was pulled and stretched before she escaped. The mother and son have reported walking through the apparition.

7. From the ASPR report: "Generally, in human relationships, people begin to take each other for granted as time progresses. This may hold true for one's relationship with a ghost: Jack and his youngest daughter, Irene, were in the basement fixing a screen door that was resting on a work table when they suddenly looked up and found that 'he' was standing there—five feet away from Jack, eight feet away from Irene. Both individuals said they looked up simultaneously, then looked at each other, determined they were both seeing 'him,' then continued their work."

History: The Yugoslavian immigrant who built the house in the 1920s began distilling moonshine on the premises, then got to drinking it. In 1927 he deserted his family. His wife took over the still and raised the children on its proceeds. The husband returned and secretly tried to sell the house. He was not only unsuccessful; he was imprisoned and through a legal twist was forced to sign the house over to his wife, who converted it into a boarding house during the Depression. In 1943, she sold the house, resulting in uneventful occupancies by two different owners. In 1956, it was acquired by the present owners, and the trouble began when they started to remodel the interior of the house.

Identity of ghosts: The ASPR brought in two psychics. One described a young couple, lovers, who had both died an at early age—the woman in the house, the man on a World War II battlefield. No historical facts supported this story. However, another psychic, unapprised of the history or the phenomena, identified the apparition as the man who built the house and said that he had made and bootlegged moonshine and that he bitterly complained that his wife had swindled him out of ownership of the house. The psychic said that the deceased was very much attached to the house he had built, believing it his rightful possession; that he hated the remodeling of the house, which he considered the destruction of his handiwork; and that he wanted to scare the present owners out.

Personalities of ghosts: The most frequently seen figure, presumably a man, seemed unfriendly but not particularly malevolent.

Witnesses: The ASPR interviewed some sixteen witnesses. There seem to have been many other casual witnesses. In its report, the ASPR said: "The family soon learned not to talk about the haunting in a mill town. They were rudely ridiculed when they did so. When the girls began to date and marry, every one of their boyfriends was either kept ignorant or else ridiculed the women about it; that is, until they experienced it for themselves. Then a sudden conversion occurred. For example, one skeptical suitor 'came out of the bathroom white as chalk, he couldn't speak, his hands trembled,' after having seen a hairbrush floating in midair. The usual quips then ceased."

Best time to witness: During the time of the phenomena, they seemed to occur both during the day and at night.

Still haunted? The second psychic, who had identified the ghost as the original builder of the house, said she tried to intervene in a way that would release the energies of the old alcoholic. When the ASPR followed up several months later, it was found that the phenomena had indeed faded. Only one incident, sounds heard by a single observer, had occurred. A possible explanation is that the psychic's intervention was successful.

Investigations: An extensive investigation by the American Society of Psychical Research, involving visits by three parapsychologists and two psychics.

Data submitted by: Karlis Osis and Donna McCormick of the ASPR.

**58
Was That a
Dragon That Just
Went By?**

A Small Informal
Commune
Denton, Texas

Location: The community is located off Mills Road
on the eastern edge of Denton. Susie Mills says call
her if you get lost.

Description of Place: A loose-knit community of
fourteen houses and forty-seven residents, all of
whom are tenants of Susie Mills. Except for one
two-story house, all of the houses are one-story
structures. Susie rents to people she finds congenial,
and she calls the place The Writers' and Artists'
Retreat, although the majority of the residents don't
seem to belong to either of those categories. They go
out to work in Denton, a university town that
surrounds Susie's land but has never annexed it. On
the approximately ten-acre property is a natural
stone circle atop a cliff, with a spring beneath it, that
was, according to tradition, long a sacred Indian
place.

Ghostly manifestations: The main fun began in
1984 when the people began seeing a "dragon,"

sometimes in the sky as though it were formed by clouds, sometimes on the ground only a few feet away. One evening a group of the boys and girls were gathered in Susie Mills's backyard, chatting and having a beer or two, and Susie decided to take a picture of them. No one was smoking, Susie says. When the photo was processed, there was a smoky excrescence hovering just above and behind the gathering. All concerned insist it is the dragon. The picture is reproduced here, and readers can make up their own minds.

Susie feels the dragon is a friendly presence, which manifests to guard the colony from harm. "It's something that comes near us in time of trouble," she says. Nancy Guesman, a young woman who belongs to the community, says she has seen the dragon three or four times. "The dragon was in the sky last night," she said during an interview, "a big monstrous dragon—looking like a cloud—going from north to south." The dragon seems visible only

See that wispy form over the heads of the frolickers?

to members of the community. Nancy says, "I've never heard anyone else talk about it."

History: The area was originally farmland owned by the family of Susie's former husband. With its Indian background, the area has long had a mystical reputation. "Legend has it that the area we live on is an old Indian burial ground," Nancy says. Susie says: "There is enough manifestation in the area to communicate peace and a deep need for the place in Indian-blood people or any troubled person. Horses born here often have blue eyes. They are invariably paint or Appaloosa, despite the breeding. My dogs generally have at least one blue eye."

The community wisdom has it that people who never had psychic proclivities prior to moving in soon develop them once they are there. Nancy says in recent years her dead grandmother has taken to visiting her at night, especially when Nancy is having a crisis in her life. She says she can smell her grandmother's perfume. Nancy says both she and others in the community often see sort of astral projection images of their friends. They'll be talking with a person, look away momentarily, and see the person go out the door. When they look back, the person is still sitting where he had been.

"People will swear they hear people talking," Nancy says. "I have. And the animals act funny. I've seen my dogs chase things in my house when there seems to be nothing there. They'll be running full tilt and then suddenly stop, dumbfounded, as though they're saying, 'I *know* I saw that.' There'll be the darnedest expression on their faces. Sometimes hunters come around here, but they never come back. They feel a presence that makes them uncomfortable."

Identity of dragon: Nancy showed the photo to a

Chinese friend who said it was a Ming dragon, a bearer of good fortune. *Ming,* he said, means "light." It is a white dragon, he says, but looks blue when it is seen at night. Susie leans toward its being a Welsh-type dragon, as depicted on the Welsh flag. She calls it Argynr; and sometimes Argynr/Ming. Questioned about the matter, a Connecticut parapsychologist, Boyce Batey, had this to offer: "I knew a woman who was very psychic and kept seeing a chameleon. Finally she realized it was something she was seeing in another dimension of reality, and she was seeing it psychically, that other people did not see it." But several people claim to see this Texas dragon.

Personality of dragon: Definitely a good dragon, there to help, everybody concerned seems to agree.

Witnesses: Susie Mills, Nancy Guesman, and a number of other people in the colony.

Best time to witness: Argynr/Ming seems to show up at various times of the day and night.

Still haunted? At this writing, in late 1985, Argynr/Ming was still being sighted off and on.

Investigations: No formal parapsychological or psychic studies have been done.

Data submitted by: Susie Mills and Nancy Guesman.

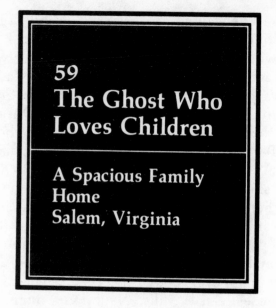

59
The Ghost Who Loves Children

A Spacious Family Home
Salem, Virginia

Location: Address of the house is 229 Union St., Salem, VA. It would be advisable to call the Crocketts before visiting.

Description of Place: A three-story, brick house, dating from the early 1800s, of Georgian design with casement windows. It is a spacious house, with three bedrooms upstairs and a dormitory arrangement in the attic. Salem is a town of about twenty-five thousand.

Ghostly manifestations: Nedra Crockett was pregnant with her first child when she and her husband, Robert, a college English professor, moved into the house in 1960. The baby was about two months old when Nedra had her first ghostly experience—the first, she says, in her life. The Crocketts' system was that she would nurse the baby at 2:00 A.M., but since Nedra was a very sound sleeper, Robert would wake up and bring the baby to her. One night he had a cold, took some medication, and failed to wake up at the appointed hour. Nedra relates:

"All of a sudden, I felt someone shaking me. I opened my eyes and there was a little, old lady standing over me, shaking me. I bolted upright to a sitting position, right into her, and she disappeared."

Nedra never actually saw the apparition again, but the lady seemed far from finished with the Crocketts. She became so much a part of the place, in fact, that Nedra felt she should have a name. She dubbed the ghost "Mrs. Anderson," after a name on the original 1838 deed to the property.

The Crockett family grew to six children, and two of those children had experiences with apparitions. When son Edgar was about 2½, the family went Christmas shopping. They piled into the car, but Edgar slipped out unobtrusively to go back and get a different pair of boots and was left behind. They had gone about ten miles before noticing his absence. They realized the little boy was alone in the house and felt he must be scared out of his wits, so they hastened back home.

"When we got back, I rushed into the house," Nedra recalls. "I called to Edgar. I thought surely he'd be crying, but there was no noise. I found him in the library, drawing. 'Weren't you afraid?' I asked. He said no, that a little, old lady came and took care of him, telling him that he didn't have to be afraid, because his family would be back soon. He said she disappeared when we opened the door."

It appears that Mrs. Anderson has a companion ghost, although Nedra hasn't gotten around to naming him. She was told about this spirit, an elderly man, by her daughter Luella, when Luella was about five. Robert Crockett had a comfortable, black leather chair in the living room that the children loved to sit in when he wasn't there. But Nedra noticed that there were times when Luella wouldn't sit in it. One day she asked Luella why, and Luella replied, "Mama, the old man's in that chair. Don't you know that he comes and sits in Daddy's chair when Daddy's not here?"

Someone—Nedra is certain it's Mrs. Anderson—makes her presence felt in various ways. For example, potato peelers keep disappearing from the kitchen. Nedra says about a dozen have vanished over the years, and she feels Mrs. Anderson is a potato peeler fancier. She feels Mrs. Anderson hangs around the kitchen, which is in the old part of the house. Christmas seems to bring on manifestations. Nedra says that one year at that time she was making candles in the kitchen, and she heard the sound of an elderly woman laughing. Often in the kitchen people will feel a movement of air near the old hearth. There is an area on the wooden floor in front of the hearth where worn tracks indicate that people once did a lot of rocking in rocking chairs. Nedra suspects they're still doing it.

And there is the case of the small silver bell. At one time the Crocketts dug up a wooden walkway leading from the house and found a variety of artifacts—thimbles, broken dolls, bottles, and a little bell—underneath. They were tossed into a jar and put on top of the refrigerator. One night the family had been decorating the house for Christmas. The next day they found the silver bell perched high on the sill of the kitchen door. Nedra says it was too high for the children to reach, and her husband denies implication. She's sure it was Mrs. Anderson, getting into the act.

Many people have felt the traditional cold spots in the house and sometimes at night while in bed the live people of the house hear what sounds like others moving around downstairs.

And then there's the Halloween incident. Some years ago, Nedra came home from her job as an accounting clerk to find all the pictures in the house tilted at an angle. She is certain the children were all in school and her husband was at work. The door was locked. "I don't think it was a joke," she says. "I think it was Mrs. Anderson or the old man."

History: The house was built in the 1830s, consisting originally of one room and an outdoor kitchen. Since then it has been expanded into a spacious home. The Crocketts have done a certain amount of renovation, and Nedra says she's noticed an increase in ghostly action during those times. For years the house has had a reputation of being haunted. People moved in and out a great deal, but Nedra says she decided the day after her first—and only—sighting of Mrs. Anderson that this was the Crocketts' house and they were going to stay there. Many people in the past complained of draftiness, Nedra says, possibly not realizing this might be psychic cold. One neighbor told the Crocketts of a woman who lived in the house who periodically would be seen sprinting out of the house at full speed—almost as if she'd seen a ghost. And one elderly man in the neighborhood refuses to walk by the place at night—he crosses over to the other side of the street.

Identity of ghosts: Mrs. Anderson? The old man—could he be Mr. Anderson? And possibly a few of their friends and neighbors?

Personalities of ghosts: "Benign," says Nedra Crockett.

Witnesses: The Crockett family—particularly Nedra, Luella, and Edgar.

Best time to witness: Just about any time, it would seem.

Still haunted? "Things happened primarily when the children were small," Nedra says. "I feel very, very little activity now."

Investigations: No professional psychics have checked the place out. Nedra Crockett says, "I am to some degree psychic, and I would probably be more so if I would allow myself." Concerning the two children who saw apparitions, she says, "Luella is an artist, and Edgar is majoring in music at college. These two are artistic. I think maybe people who have more creativity may be more aware."

Data Submitted By: Nedra Crockett; article by Agnis Chakravorty in the *Salem Times-Register;* case suggested by Barbara Guthrie of Salem, Virginia.

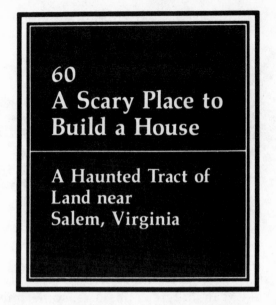

**60
A Scary Place to
Build a House**

**A Haunted Tract of
Land near
Salem, Virginia**

Location: The Guthries' land is located on Route 11460, three miles west of the city limits of Salem. Barbara Guthrie says visitors are welcome. The place may be identified by a sign, Fruit of the Bloom Winery. The Guthries operate a winery on the property.

Description of place: The primary haunted place is a three-bedroom, brick, ranch-style house, built in 1971. However, two other structures on this acreage also seem haunted, one a house, the other a trailer home.

Ghostly manifestations: When Jim and Barbara Guthrie built the house on land that had been in Barbara's family for many generations, they got a few surprises along with a home. Their first night in the house, Barbara says, she heard music on being awakened around 3:00 A.M. A man was singing a song that seemed from some past time. Within a few nights, Jim Guthrie also heard the singing. Often

The Guthries' house, haunted from the first day.

when they were downstairs in their family room, they would hear footsteps upstairs, sometimes quite heavy steps. And when they were upstairs, they would hear the footsteps downstairs. Sometimes doors would slam and chairs would move although there was no one in that area of the house at the time. These noises were heard by many friends and relatives. Within a few months, the Guthries and their three children began hearing distinct moaning in the house. Strange lights began to flash in various parts of the house, small circles that would appear briefly and then disappear.

Four years after they had moved into the house, Michelle Guthrie, then ten, and the Guthries' niece, Angela Clark, then eight, were sitting in the kitchen and saw through a glass door a dark-skinned boy standing in the garden. The lower portion of the boy seemed solid, but the upper part seemed transparent, and he soon disappeared. He had short, dark hair and was wearing blue jeans, according to the girls. He was seen twice in the summer of 1976 by another daughter, Carmen, and each time he vanished. One time Barbara awakened to a tapping sound in her bedroom and an offensive odor. In October of 1978 she woke to hear a male voice say, "I could kill you, you bitch!" She was aware of a stench at that time, too. Several relatives have seen apparitions of a man in various parts of the house.

"I think it's the land more than the house," Barbara Guthrie says. "We've sold a parcel to a couple

Jim and Barbara Guthrie

and they've had things happen. They've seen lights flash periodically and heard some noise, but nothing like us. My sister lives in a trailer on another parcel of the land. Sometimes there is so much noise at night that she has to get up and turn on the lights, which stops it. We lived in a trailer here for a while before we built the house and the same thing happened to us."

History: The land, now owned by Barbara Guthrie, has been in her family, the Rettinger family, for some hundred years. It has long had a certain reputation. "When I was a child," Barbara says, "this land was very secluded and kind of a lovers' lane. People would come up here and park. But it got such a reputation that people were afraid to park up here. My cousin and his girl used to park up here, and he said that on several occasions the car would start vibrating. The car would just rock. Other people who would park cars here said they had the same experience. One group was camping here, and one of their cars started vibrating so much it went over a hill and they had to get a wrecker to pull it out."

Identity of ghosts: Mrs. Guthrie notes that battles were fought in this area during the Civil War, probably on this land. Also, there seems to have been

Michelle and Carmen Guthrie standing in area where Carmen saw a small brown boy playing.

an Indian settlement there at one time; many arrowheads are found on the land. And the acreage contains many caves, some big enough to walk into. The Guthries suspect that this background has something to do with the haunting of the property.

Personalities of ghosts: Some seem detached, although the male voice that offered to kill Mrs. Guthrie, calling her a bitch, certainly didn't seem very friendly. No one has ever been hurt, only scared.

Witnesses: The Guthries and many friends and relatives.

Best time to witness: The manifestations occur at various times of the day and night.

Still haunted? There are still occurrences, Mrs. Guthrie says, although she adds, "Things seem to have calmed down a little lately."

Investigations: None have been carried out by psychics or parapsychologists up to this time.

Data submitted by: Barbara Guthrie, in an interview and also through an article she wrote for *Fate* magazine, which appeared in the May 1981 issue.

61
The Haunted Museum

The Adam
Thoroughgood House
Virginia Beach,
Virginia

Location: The Adam Thoroughgood House is located at 1636 Parish Rd., Virginia Beach.

Description of Place: Reputedly the oldest brick building in America, built in 1636, it is a small house, with two rooms and a hall upstairs and two rooms downstairs.

Ghostly manifestations: The first curator of the museum, Mrs. Martha Lindemann Bradley, says even before the place became a museum, when it was uninhabited, people thought of it as a haunted house, and they told of seeing a woman standing in the windows with a lighted candle. When Mrs. Bradley became the first curator, she and her staff quickly became aware of various manifestations. Things would be moved, and the staff denied having moved them. Mrs. Bradley says, "One day a party with the wife of the ambassador of Denmark was being taken through the house. I was conducting the tour. All of us saw a candlestick actually move. Later

342

on, the ladies who worked for me in the house began to see the same thing." The idea that the place might be haunted was carefully kept from the media, but children on tours would often see things, particularly a small man dressed in a brown suit, whom Mrs. Bradley suspects is Adam Thoroughgood or

Martha Lindemann Bradley, curator, observes the haunted museum.

possibly his wife, Sara's, second husband, John Gookin. Early on, a tourist, a lawyer from Texas, told Mrs. Bradley he had seen an oddly dressed little man, but at that time she put scant stock in what he said. "Now I know I should have listened to him a little closer," she says.

In a bedroom, a chair would constantly be moved, and an indentation would appear, as though someone had lain down in the bed. Once the chair moved and the indentation appeared in front of a group of children and their adult escorts. How did the people react? "Screamed," laughs Mrs. Bradley. "The children became very restless." There has been much poltergeist activity. Windows open and shut when no one is nearby. Tapes recorded in the house turn out blank. Once, in front of about thirty tourists, four glass domes protecting Christmas candles suddenly levitated and crashed to the floor.

History: Adam Thoroughgood came from England as an indentured servant. He acquired land and built the house, a small house by modern standards but quite imposing in its day. The Thoroughgood family lived in the house up through the middle of the eighteenth century. After that the house changed hands many times. Then it stood empty for decades, often used to shelter livestock. In the late 1950s, a group of people bought the old place and gave it to the city of Norfolk, and the house became an adjunct to that city's museum. It was restored and refurnished, and Mrs. Bradley, who had an interest in the empty house since her childhood, became the first curator. By now, the haunted aspect of the house has been written about extensively in the Norfolk newspapers, the *Virginia-Pilot* and the *Ledger-Star*.

Identity of ghosts: Possibly Adam Thoroughgood

or John Gookin. Mahalia Munden of Mrs. Bradley's staff once reported seeing a man and woman dressed in old-time clothing, who smiled and disappeared. The woman, it is thought, might have been Thoroughgood's wife, Sara Offley Thoroughgood.

Personalities of ghosts: The ghosts seem harmless, sometimes rather friendly, although sometimes distinctly mischievous.

Witnesses: Mrs. Bradley and many tourists and members of the museum staff. Reba Karp, a feature writer for the *Norfolk Ledger-Star,* reported in her March 27, 1971 article that she had encountered phenomena.

Best time to witness: The Thoroughgood House is open to the public on Tuesdays through Saturdays from 10:00 A.M. to 5:00 P.M.

Still haunted? When Mrs. Bradley resigned from her position in 1972 to marry, she was succeeded by one of her hostesses, Mrs. Alice Pfinst, who told Reba Karp of hearing the rustle of "tuffet" skirts in the upstairs hallway. However, a hostess recently contacted denied abruptly that there were ghosts in the house.

Investigations: Local journalists have written extensively about the house, but no formal psychic investigations have been conducted.

Data submitted by: Principally Martha Bradley, who currently lives in Denver, Colorado.

62
The Apparition of the Dead Sales Manager

A Radio Station in Virginia

Location: The Psychical Research Foundation has not revealed the whereabouts of this radio station.

Description of place: The building, constructed in the 1940s, is in a grove of trees away from the street. Over the years, new walls have constantly been added to provide more office space. The building's interior is therefore like a maze and has been described as "spooky" by some of the employees because it is so easy to get lost in it.

Ghostly manifestations: In 1981, the station manager phoned the Psychical Research Foundation in Chapel Hill, North Carolina. He said that five current employees had reported independent viewings of an apparition, and he asked for an investigation. He wanted to avoid publicity but wished to rid the station of the disturbances. After correspondence and phone conversations with the witnesses by William G. Roll, Pauline Philips, and Teresa Cameron of the Psychical Research Foundation, Cameron visited the station and interviewed the percipients. Apparently the first present employee to see the apparition was an engineer, who had looked across a hall into the sales office and had seen a figure near a window about fifty feet away. At first he thought it was headlights reflecting off the windows, but then he said it moved. A short time later, he saw it again, this time about twenty feet away. He went toward it, and it disappeared. The figure seemed to take a couple of steps each time he saw it, but he did not remember seeing any legs or feet; nor did he see a head. But he judged it to be a male figure dressed in a brown and tan suit jacket, of middle height and stocky. He said nothing to other members of the station staff, but a few days later he heard a young woman employee, a writer of commercials, say she had recently seen a similar apparition. They compared notes and felt the apparition reminded them of a former friend and fellow employee who had died two years earlier. The woman witness said she thought it was this person because of his "slump and the way he held his hands," although she did not remember having seen a face nor legs and feet.

Another young woman, a receptionist, a few months later thought she saw an apparition floating down a hall. She ran into a room where others were having lunch and screamed, "Oh, my God, I saw a ghost!" She had joined the station after the earlier sightings and said she had not heard anything about apparitions prior to seeing one herself. Two young male employees—one an announcer, the other an engineer—also reported having seen the apparition. Both said they had heard nothing about ghosts prior to their own sightings. A former employee reportedly saw apparitions many times inside the building as well as outside. She declined to be interviewed.

History: Charles Michaux, the presumable apparition, had formerly been sales manager of the station. An office he had used was where the engineer's sighting took place. He was fired in 1977 under stressful conditions, a few days before Christmas. Many at the station were bitter about his leaving. Emotions had run high, and a violent fight broke out at the station's Christmas party. The sales manager died of a heart attack a few months later, but not before he bounced back professionally after leaving this station, becoming part owner of another radio station.

Identity of ghost: Only two of the five interviewed witnesses had known the sales manager, but both thought the apparition looked like him.

Personality of ghost: Not known, since the apparition did not interact with any of the witnesses.

Witnesses: The five station employees and one former employee.

Best time to witness: The apparition was sighted at various times during the station's working hours, the earliest sighting about noon and the latest in the evening.

Still haunted? No recent reports have been received from the station.

Investigations: The Psychical Research Foundation is involved in investigations of parapsychological occurrences. Following her investigation, Cameron presented a paper, *An Investigation of Apparitional Experiences,* at the Convention of the Southeastern Regional Parapsychological Association, at the University of North Carolina. The five witnesses were questioned about previous apparitional experiences they may have had and were also given a test called the Inventory of Childhood Memories and Imaginings. At least one witness, the engineer who first saw the apparition, seems to be very a down-to-earth type, free of emotional problems. Others seemed to be predisposed to apparitional experiences and/or moodiness. In her paper, Cameron drew no definite conclusions. "It seems likely," she wrote, "from the accounts of [the sales manager] that he may have been depressed at the time of his firing. If some of the percipients were depressed at the time they saw the apparitions, this emotional state may have played a role in their experience. Perhaps the percipient of an apparition is not a neutral observer but evokes an image of a particular person or event that matches the percipient's own emotional state." However, she carefully hedges her bets, adding, "This does not mean the apparition is not 'real.' It could still represent a conscious surviving personality, an unconscious psychic trace, or something between these extremes."

Data submitted by: Teresa Cameron and William G. Roll of the Psychical Research Foundation.

63

The Stage Manager Who Won't Retire

The Grand Opera House
Oshkosh, Wisconsin

Location: The address of the Grand Opera House is 100 High Avenue, Oshkosh.

Description of place: The Grand Opera House was opened in 1883 and served as the main theatrical outlet in Oshkosh through the turn of the century, the vaudeville era, and the onset of movies. It was a movie house for many years.

Ghostly manifestations: The building has long had the reputation of being haunted. Members of a local theater group, The Drama Lab, that often used the building, tell of fire doors opening and slamming shut, apparitions, and other such happenings. One of the choicest tales is that of an actor who tells of rushing from a dressing room to the stage, rounding a corner, and seeing a man wearing turn-of-the-century clothing. The apparition, says the actor, was carrying a playbill, which he held up. It was for *The Bohemian Girl*, which played there in 1895.

Bob Jacobs is an experienced Hollywood producer

who now is a professor of radio-TV-film at the University of Wisconsin at Oshkosh. In 1977 he, assisted by students and local residents, made a fictional TV film about a haunted movie theater. They used the Grand Opera House as their set, and they couldn't have operated in a more appropriate

The Grand Opera House in Oshkosh

place, says Jacobs. Making the movie turned out to be more exciting than the movie itself. Recent legends have centered on Percy R. Keene, who was stage manager of the Grand from 1895 till he died in 1965. Actors are sure he is still watching benevolently over them. Jacobs is convinced that some benign force saved one of his young assistants, Larry Schroeder, from serious injury or death. Schroeder had been hoisted high above the stage and hung there for about an hour while a shot was being made. When he was lowered down, as soon as his feet touched the stage the rope that had supported him broke. On inspection it was found to be a very old rope, but Jacobs points out that it did not break until the young man's weight was taken *off* it and he was safe.

Various people connected with the production saw apparitions. They include Jan Turner, an assistant producer, and two grips (handymen), John Jansen and Dennis Payne. Turner not only saw an apparition in an underground passage; she also says at another time something grabbed her right ankle. Jansen and Payne say they saw a man walk out of the orchestra pit and go through the door of a small room that had no other exit. The man didn't come out, and they didn't recognize him, so they investigated and found no one in the room.

Bill Seaton, who owned the theater at the time, tells of being alone in the balcony one night, taking rubbings of old wallpaper, when he heard footsteps come up the stairs. No one appeared at the top of the stairs, but the footsteps came across the balcony and stopped in front of him. At that point, Seaton says, he made steps himself.

Jacobs's favorite story involves himself. When the film was finished, two days before it was to have its premiere, he and six other people who had worked on the picture gathered in the theater for a preliminary, private showing. When it was over, Jacobs says, he looked up at the balcony and saw smiling down a man in a white shirt and no tie, with a round, friendly face. He wore glasses, and his gray hair was close-cut, with a receding hairline. Jacobs says he is certain it was an apparition of Percy R. Keene.

History: In the days of live entertainment, Oshkosh was a major way station between Chicago and Minneapolis, and most of the greats of show business appeared there. These included Houdini, Enrico Caruso, Anna Pavlova, the Marx Brothers, Paul

The old building on a snowy night.

Robeson. Percy R. Keene knew them all. Bill Seaton
bought the building in the early 1970s and did a great
deal of renovation. The city of Oshkosh now owns
the building and is continuing with renovation.

Identity of ghosts: Percy R. Keene is a popular
choice. But who was the actor who held up the
playbill of *The Bohemian Girl*? The ghosts of flops and
hits are probably still wandering through the premises, looking for extra bows. In the early 1980s, the
ghost-hunting team of Ed and Lorraine Warren
psyched out the place. Lorraine says she sensed a
male presence and also a dog. After checking with
Keene's family, it was found that he at one time kept
a dog in the theater.

Personality of ghosts: According to tradition, the
forces there are beneficent. Like ghosts in most
places, they just seem to want to get into the act.

Witnesses: Bob Jacobs, Bill Seaton, Jan Turner,
John Jansen, Dennis Payne, and presumably dozens

of thespians and backstage people who have worked and played in the old theater.

Best time to witness: Most of the phenomena were observed at night, if only because little theater groups usually rehearse and perform in the evening and because the film was shot in the hours after midnight, when the regular movie showings were over.

Still haunted? Presumably it is. In an interview in late 1985, Jacobs said that only two days before he had had an indication that spirits still roam the old building. "An associate of mine, a cinematographer, just arrived here from California," Jacobs said, "told me he had passed the theater last night and saw the night-watchman looking out of a window. First, he had heard nothing about the place being haunted; second, there is no night-watchman."

Investigations: One, by Ed and Lorraine Warren.

Data submitted by: Bob Jacobs, in interviews and in an article in the March 1984 issue of *Fate* magazine; and Ed Warren.

**64
A Haunted
Hunting Cabin**

A Small Frame House
near
Hancock, Wisconsin

Location: The house is situated on Country Road GG, about 3½ miles east of Hancock. Bob Stahl requests that anyone wishing to visit contact him first. He may be reached at 8609 West Crossfield Ave., Milwaukee, WI 53225.

Description of place: The house, a small wooden frame house on a stone foundation, was built in farm country near Hancock, Wisconsin, in 1904. It is a two-story house, and in the mid-1970s the present owner, Bob Stahl, built an addition onto it.

Ghostly manifestations: Stahl, an engineer who lives in Milwaukee and uses the house as a hunting cabin, said that three strange things happened within a year and a half of his putting on the addition about ten years ago. The first incident involved his wife. "One morning," Stahl says, "I went out bow hunting. My wife was sleeping in the attic, and she felt someone grab her. She didn't tell anyone until some time later." About a year later,

Stahl says, he was sleeping in the house's addition. "All of a sudden," he says, "I felt something grab me on the shoulder. I tried rolling over to see what it was, but the thing put more pressure on me, and I couldn't turn to see what it was. I couldn't even say anything; I couldn't get words out of my mouth. I was alone in the place; some friends were coming to hunt, but they hadn't arrived yet. I could see the moon outside the window, and I was certain I wasn't

The haunted hunting cabin

dreaming; I was awake. After a while the pressure released, and I started to turn, and all I saw was just possibly a black image, for just a second."

A month later, Stahl says, four couples came up. Three of them slept in the new addition. The Stahls were sleeping upstairs. Stahl got up in the middle of the night and then went outside for a breath of air. One of the men sleeping in the addition was wakeful and came out to join him. The next morning the man asked Stahl if he had come downstairs twice. No, just once, Stahl said. The man then said he had seen someone come down the stairs. "It looked like he had a sheet wrapped around him," the man told Stahl. One of the women in the addition was also awake and said she, too, saw the figure. Nothing has happened since, Stahl says, but he's still fascinated by his strange hunting cabin.

History: Stahl has tried to check out reports of any unusual events in the place before he owned it, but nothing has turned up. The house was built in 1904 and was used as a farmhouse until about 1918. Then a couple bought it and used it as a summer cabin until they sold it to Stahl about twenty-two years ago. Stahl says he asked the former owner, who is now in his eighties, if anything unusual had happened during his ownership, and the man said nothing had, to his knowledge.

Identity of ghost: Unknown, at least at this point.

Personality of ghost: Rather disquieting. Few people like to be grabbed by unseen entities.

Witnesses: Stahl; his wife, Patricia Anne; and two of their guests.

Best time to witness: All three of the occurrences took place at night.

Still haunted? The occurrences took place within a year and a half of the construction of the addition, ten years ago, and nothing has been noted since.

Investigations: None so far, but Stahl would like to have a psychic check the place out and has made some efforts to contact one.

Data submitted by: Bob Stahl.

Need Help with Your Ghost?

While researching this book, sometimes I interviewed people who were aware of paranormal phenomena on their own premises and would like to know more about what was going on, but who were at a loss as to where to turn for help.

It occurred to me that a helpful appendix to this book would be some signposts to informed, reputable parapsychologists and psychics. A psychic is an individual who is able to tap into the dimension from which these phenomena seem to spring. A parapsychologist is essentially a researcher; he may or may not be psychic. Most parapsychologists work with psychics.

It is easy in this field to run into phonies, but the people listed here are reputable, honest, and know what they are about.

Charges are variable. They can range from a few hundred dollars to nothing at all.

Other resources are:

The American Society for Psychical Research, 5 W. 73rd St., New York, NY 10023; (212) 799-5050.

John F. Kennedy University, Parapsychology Dept.,
12 Altarinda Rd., Orinda, CA 94563; (415) 254-
0105.
Spiritual Frontiers Fellowship, 10819 Winner Rd.
Independence, MO 64052; (816) 264-8585. Ask to
be put in touch with the SFF chairperson in your
area, who is likely to know of psychics nearby.

Ann Rychlenski is a New York City psychic often
used by the prestigious American Society for Psychical Research. In this book, she figures in the case
of the young Brooklyn couple with a houseful of
ghosts (Chapter 46). Educated at New York University, she has worked in advertising and public relations. Ann says that although she was intuitive as a
child, she became "psychic" quite suddenly when she
was twenty. She had been practicing yoga, doing
breathing exercises and meditation, with the mundane aim of increasing her attention span. One day
she suddenly had an out-of-body experience, which
terrified her at the time. Soon after, she began
seeing and hearing spirits. She may be reached at
132-23 114th St., Ozone Park, NY 11420; (516) 868-
8277.

William G. Roll is one of the best-known parapsychologists in the country, author of more than a
hundred professional papers and writer or editor of
some thirteen books. He is editor of the scholarly
journal on parapsychology, *Theta.* He holds a degree
from Oxford University and has been initiated as a
Zen monk. He was involved in a number of the cases
in this book, including the haunted furniture factory
in North Carolina and John Wayne's yacht (chapters
50 and 6). He holds a faculty appointment at West
Georgia College, the first professorship in the

United States designated for teaching and research in parapsychology. He may be reached at West Georgia College, Carrollton, GA 30118; (404) 834-1423.

Suzanne Jauchius is active as a psychic in the Portland, Oregon, area. She often lectures on hauntings at schools and colleges in the Northwest. She says, "I have lived with the various kinds of 'phenomena' all my life. As a child I knew when certain things were going to happen to family members and friends. I had precognitive dreams. I frequently had out-of-body experiences. I saw light-beings or apparitions. It wasn't until I was in my teens that I realized that this wasn't normal." Concerning her work today, she says, "Occasionally I am able to see an apparition, but more often it is a 'sensing' of spirits or events that may be haunting the homes or buildings I am asked to investigate." She may be reached at PO Box 256, Gresham, OR 97030; (503) 771-4874.

Ruth Berger is unusual among psychics in that she usually does her investigations of hauntings by long-distance. She tells of sitting in her office with clients and "exorcising" spirits in their homes, miles away. "You don't really have to go to their homes," she says. "I also help people on the phone." Ruth is proprietor of a large bookstore dealing with books on the metaphysical. She publishes a newsletter on the psychic, called *Rainbow Search*. Aside from her psychic activities, she has been an electronics buyer and a piano teacher and has managed a retail store. She has five grandchildren. She can be reached at Rainbow Search, 7925 N. Lincoln Ave., Skokie, IL 60077; (312) 679-4900.

Kerry Gaynor is a researcher who has investigated more than six hundred cases of hauntings and poltergeists. He has been associated with the well-known parapsychologist, Thelma Moss, for some fourteen years. There is no charge for their services. They concentrate on cases in southern California. He may be reached at 3536 Centinela Ave. #12, Los Angeles, CA 90066; (213) 397-6622.

Petey Stevens calls herself "a practicing professional psychic," and as such she has been involved with a wide range of aspects of the field of metaphysics, including hauntings. She and her husband, Rick, were founders of Heartsong, a training school for the psychic in the San Francisco Bay area, which has been attended by more than ten thousand people. She may be reached at Heartsong, 900 Santa Fe, Albany, CA 94706; (415) 527-4833.

Nancy Osborn is a researcher, an investigator of

the paranormal, who has checked out many haunted places. She is the author of a number of books on hauntings. She has had training in the psychic and in metaphysics, although she often works with a psychic. She is an excellent resource for information. She may be reached at 2216 Cypress Bend Dr. N., Apt. 109, Bldg. 14, Pompano Beach, FL 33060; (305) 972-4826.

Elaine Gibbs has been a formally practicing psychic for only a few years, but she has been psychic all her life. She is a graduate of Texas Christian University and a partner, with her husband, in a manufacturers' representative business. "In my childhood," she says, "if you thought things like I'm doing now, the men in the white coats would take you away." Her daughter, Sandi, is a talented psychic, and to develop her gifts Elaine sent her to Patricia Hayes's school in Atlanta. Afterward, Sandi persuaded her mother to take the training. Elaine has investigated many hauntings and done several "soul rescues," as she calls them, referring to the release of earthbound entities to send them on to higher planes. She may be reached at PO Box 36190, Fort Worth, TX 76136; (817) 430-1861.

Ron Mangravite is a psychic and has been active as a teacher and lecturer on metaphysical phenomena. Among his other activities, he has investigated many hauntings. His "mundane" field is chemistry, and he has been a manager and owner of industrial companies and inventor of a number of scientific analytical techniques. He may be reached at 218 Columbia Ave., Fort Lee, NJ 07024; (201) 224-3158.

Patricia Hayes is a psychic well known throughout the country. She began her training in parapsychology with the late, famed psychic Arthur Ford. In 1974, she founded The School of Inner Sense Development, in Georgia, where she worked with thousands of students in various aspects of the metaphysical. She is the mother of five children. She was helpful to the author of this book in providing information in two cases, John Wayne's yacht (Chapter 6), and the return of the suicide in Atlanta (Chapter 16). She may be reached at PO Box 767121, Roswell (Atlanta), GA 30076; (404) 887-5824.

Jeannie Stewart has a master's degree in clinical psychology and has a private psychotherapy practice in Lexington, Kentucky. However, she is a psychic and is very much involved in metaphysics. Her involvement often emphasizes therapy; she works with people who are confused and frightened by parapsychological events that have been thrust upon them. An example of her work is the case of the woman in North Carolina whose dead husband seemed to be giving her unwanted haircuts (Chapter 49). In this sort of work, she often collaborates with William Roll, in Georgia. She may be reached at Route #1, Irvine, KY 40336; (606) 723-7103.

Alex Tanous is an extraordinarily versatile psychic, perhaps best known for his "fly-ins," out-of-body trips that have been tested by the American Society for Psychical Research, in which he projects his astral body from his home in Maine to rooms at the ASPR's headquarters in New York City and describes the contents of the rooms accurately. It is said that he began to display psychic powers at the age of eighteen months. He often investigates haunted places. He is a graduate of Boston College and has advanced degrees from Fordham and the University of Maine. He was involved in three cases described in this book, two in Maine (Chapters 24 and 25), and one in Brooklyn, NY (Chapter 46). He currently teaches at the University of Southern Maine in Portland. He may be reached at Box 3818, Portland, ME 04104; (207) 773-8328.

Mike Doney is an experienced dowser, well known in the Northwest. Some time ago, he says, he discovered that dowsing rods and pendulums can be used in contacting spirits. Once found, Doney says, the ghosts can be urged to leave the premises, to seek help from the other side, and they usually do. Doney, now retired, lived in a log house as a child. "Dad was an old-time cougar hunter," he says. Mike was a logger in his youth, then "by pure accident" a policeman, then an investigator for the Oregon Liquor Control Commission. He can be reached at 10122 S.E. Hollywood, Milwaukie, OR 97222; (503) 659-0165.

Boyce Batey has been involved in parapsychology since he was an undergraduate at Princeton University. Later, he studied at Dr. J. B. Rhine's Parapsychology Laboratory at Duke University. An executive with an insurance company in Hartford, Connecticut, he has been very active in parapsychology in his own state and beyond. He often lectures and gives workshops on metaphysics. He is executive secretary of The Academy of Religion and Psychical

Research. He has investigated many hauntings and poltergeist cases, including the moving dolls case in Connecticut described in this book (Chapter 12). He may be reached at PO Box 614, Bloomfield, CT 06002; (203) 242-4593.

Roger S. Pile has been a trainer of psychics, mediums, and healers and a lecturer on metaphysical subjects. In addition to his extensive experience in otherworldly matters, he has participated actively in things of this world. He holds an M.B.A. and has more than thirty years of experience in management. For sixteen years he ran his own management consulting firm. He contributed information on three cases in this book: the strange creatures in Utica, New York (Chapter 48); the lighthouse in Connecticut (Chapter 10); and the farm in New Hampshire (Chapter 38). He may be reached at PO Box 606, Ivoryton, CT 06442; (203) 767-8911.

Lynn Gardner is a psychic and medium who is engaged in a wide variety of activities relating to parapsychology, from leading tours to training executives to become more intuitive to working with people who wish to become more informed about metaphysics. She has investigated many hauntings. As a child, she was an actress in Hollywood films. She has lived in Indiana for many years. She has eight children. She may be reached at 4146 N. Illinois St., Indianapolis, IN 46208; (317) 283-7638.

Index

Mabry, Dr. Bob, 99–101
MacTavish, Allison, 89–90
"Mad Duchess," 95
Madison, Dolley, 89
Madison, James, 89
Madred, Pancha, 238–39
Mahoney, William J., 252–63
Maine
  sightings in, 140–56
Makuta, Justin, 252, 255
Makuta, Kevin, 252–60, 262–63
Makuta, Linda, 252–60, 262–63
Makuta, Lauren, 252
Malin, Connie, 83–84
Mangravite, Ron, 364
Mangy Moose Saloon, 15–20
Marietta, Georgia
  sightings in, 103–106
Martin, Earl, 105, 106
"Mary," 317
Maryland
  sightings in, 157–62
Massachusetts
  sightings in, 163–208
"Max," 314
May, Antoinette, 47, 53
McCausland, William, 228–29,
  230–31
McClain, Debbie, 165–66, 170
McCormick, Donna, 254, 257,
  262–63, 324, 327
McDonald, Joy, 269, 270, 275–
  77
McDonald, Kyle, 164, 170
McDonnell, Ann, 133
McKinney, Debbie, 14, 16, 20
McKnight, Joe, 299
McNeil, W. K., 212
Merion, Pennsylvania
  sightings in, 312–18
Merion Station, Pennsylvania
  sightings in, 319–22
Michaux, Charles, 348
Milam, Francis, 99–102
Mills, Susie, 328–31
Minot, Capt. James, 177

Minot, Dr. Joseph, 178
Minshall, Bert, 37
Mish, Tom, 307
Mississippi
  sightings in, 209–212
Monroe, James, 90, 132
Montanelli, Richard, 122, 123–
  24, 125
Monticello, Arkansas
  sightings in, 24–29
Morristown, New Jersey
  sightings in, 227–31
Morrow, Taryn, 83
Moss, Thelma, 361
Mount, The, 180–90
Munden, Mahalia, 345
Murphy, Beth, 56
Murphy, John, 53, 56
"Myron," 277

National Society of Colonial
  Dames of America, 130
New England's Ghostly Haunts, 152
New Hampshire
  sightings in, 213–19
New Hanover County Public
  Library, 288–92
New Jersey
  sightings in, 220–31
New Lebanon, New York
  sightings in, 264–68
New London, Connecticut
  sightings in, 63–68
New Mexico
  sightings in, 232–46
Newton, Marianne, 235
Newton, Mark, 235, 242–46
New York
  sightings in, 247–77
New York State Capitol, 247–
  51
Nogales, Arizona
  sightings in, 21–23
Noggle, Ed, 265, 268
North Carolina
  sightings in, 278–92